DATE DUE

NOV 17 1994	
APR - 4 1997.	
APR 13 1998	

BRODART   Cat. No. 23-221

THE STUDY OF HUMAN VALUES

Richard W. Kilby

San Jose State University

**UNIVERSITY
PRESS OF
AMERICA**

Lanham • New York • London

Copyright © 1993 by
University Press of America®, Inc.
4720 Boston Way
Lanham, Maryland 20706

3 Henrietta Street
London WC2E 8LU England

Acknowledgements appear on page ix.

Library of Congress Cataloging-in-Publication Data

Kilby, Richard W., 1919–
The study of human values / Richard W. Kilby.
p.   cm.
Includes bibliographical references and indexes.
1. Social values.   2. Social psychology.   I. Title.
HM73.K54   1993   303.3'72—dc20   92–34729 CIP

ISBN 0–8191–8944–8 (cloth : alk. paper)

Table of Contents

PREFACE

This book grows out of a long-felt need for a readable source that explores all aspects of people's values. Good information on the subject exists scattered about in various sources, spanning disciplines and decades, but it is not easily located nor readily assimilated and organized in mind. The book attempts to remedy the situation.

More specifically, it is intended as a general comprehensive work on human values and is composed of five chapters: types of human values, their nature, their role in lives, their origins, and methods of their study or assessment. Each chapter is included for a specific need or purpose and together provide a treatment of the major aspects of the subject. It was written on the assumption that most of its readers would know little of the subject, rather than be specialists, but the main consideration was to include everything that was pertinent and to do full justice to each topic. One portion or another should be useful to someone, be it student, instructor, researcher, or general reader.

The first chapter lists all of the types of values that could be identified. Though we often speak of values, most persons will know of only one or two types, the moral values being best know by far and usually the only ones known, so all readers should benefit from a rather full survey. Twenty-eight types are identified and described, though not all are distinct forms of valuing and there is considerable overlap. Such a listing of specific types also helps bring an otherwise vague entity down to earth and sets the stage for its further study.

The second chapter is on the nature of values and attempts to define and clarify their nature. It seemed necessary because the term "value(s)," in its popularity, has acquired a number of popular meanings, thus turning it into a vague entity of limited usefulness. Too, scholars have used it with different meanings, further adding uncertainty as to the nature of values and reducing usefulness. So I have surveyed usages, proposed an integrative definition, and then tried to place values relative to the closely-related dispositions of attitudes, interests, and motives.

The third chapter is on the role of values in lives. It is the one most obviously needed, dealing as it does with the function or role of values in our lives. Some of these functions will be fairly obvious, for by definition most values are judgmental, evaluative, choice-determining dispositions. But not all are evaluative and they have a variety of interesting additional functions when seen both in terms of individual experiencing and of group functioning.

The fourth chapter is on origins of values and is another that obviously is needed. It lists and elaborates all the numerous value-forming sources -- parents, peers, school, college, religion, mates and other adult associates, models, community or society, personal experiencing, and other. Most of these are well known sources, some having an extensive research literature in support. Because of their number our treatment necessarily had to be brief for each, and the greatest value of the chapter may be simply that of providing in one place a panorama of the whole.

The final chapter is on assessment of values and attempts to survey all the methods of studying people's values, as by interview, questionnaire, or behavioral observation. It is included for benefit of persons wishing to do research on values or learn the values of given individuals. Since the reader might easily assume that research on values can be done only by specially trained persons it is pointed out that the most sensitive study method, the interview, is one of the simplest to use, and anyone who wishes to study values certainly may do so without extensive training. This chapter may prove useful even to the experienced researcher because it includes certain methods used by earlier investigators that may not be known to younger ones (the familiar case of things getting lost in the literature).

I had thought to include a sixth chapter which would review efforts at deliberately shaping or changing values, as by psychological experiment, reform programs in prisons and reformatories, and indoctrination programs in the military. A very important topic considering the profound role of values in lives. There is a considerable literature on the changing of attitudes, but only two studies on value change were found, both by Rokeach and associates. Books on corrections-penology cite no applied studies and one gets an impression from them that there are no systematic programs to change values. In light of this general dearth of information, no attempt was made to investigate the single topic of military indoctrination. The Rokeach studies are reviewed in the chapter on origins of values.

There is an extensive literature on the subject of values (and the related or identical topics of ethics, morals, and conscience), most of it written by scholars with philosophy backgrounds, which is to be expected since ethics or values is one of philosophy's traditional concerns, dating from the Greeks. But these scholars are concerned with matters other than the specific values lived by ordinary people -- our concern; rather, usually with value questions in the abstract, and there is no duplication between those writings and this.

Also, there is a considerable literature on the subject by behavioral scientists -- anthropologist, sociologist, and psychologist. Anthropologists have always been most concerned since a major part of the culture of a people is its values and many specific examples are to be found in anthropological reports on whole societies. Sociologists have been especially interested in the values of the social classes and other segments and groupings of our society. Psychologists are late comers to the subject because of their early employment of the related and sometimes identical concept of attitudes. Their work on the moral development of children is especially impressive. Of course I have taken advantage of all of this material -- the book would not have been possible without it -- and have the pleasure here of expressing my indebtedness to a long list of fine scholars: the Kluckhohns, von Mering, G. Allport, J. Piaget, Ch. Morris, H. Cantril, K. Horney, A. Maslow, R. W. White, N. Haan, L. Kohlberg, M. Rokeach, R. Williams, C. Osgood, E. Maccoby, and M. B. Smith.

There is also a fairly extensive literature of research studies on values. Almost all of these are on narrow topics, as such specificity is dictated by the requirements of empirical research; an example would be learning the correlation between values as assessed with a questionnaire and some other characteristic of a group (age, sex, type of experience, etc.). Since this book is intended to be general in nature few such studies have been included. All specific studies on a given general topic need to be reviewed and published together; I had thought to include a chapter here on the specific topic of cross-national or cross-cultural studies of values, as I have done several such studies, but soon found that it would take considerable space and simply didn't belong in a general presentation.

Though the five chapters cover the essentials of values study, much more could be said if the perspective were broadened. It would be useful, for example, to supply perspective by drawing upon the work of historian or anthropologist and compare the values of earlier generations with those of the present, or our values with those of peoples of smaller, more traditional societies, for our value concerns may be largely unique to a modern complex, individualistic, democratically-governed society, where traditional sources of value direction have largely disappeared, leaving the individual essentially on his own to discover his own values, and where the issues and problems demanding judgement are numerous.

Another topic that might be pursued is the role of values in the political process. We do have a section on the appeal to values in modern warfare (p. 73-76), but values are there throughout the political process -- in the wording of party manifestos and platforms, in the candidate's appeal to the voter (the new candidate is always advised to begin an address by identifying himself with cherished values), in the voter's choice of party and candidate, in statements of national ideology, and in the "hidden agendas" of nations in their interactions.

A topic that we do treat but which deserves much more exploration and empirical study is that of the extent of practice of professed values, or, put in another way, what people actually do in the value-challenging situation. As is pointed out in chapter 3, it is unreasonable to expect perfect correspondence between the professed and actual since all our behaviors have additional determinants besides values, but still instances of inconsistency occur with some frequency and challenge our understanding of the actual role of values in our lives. It has been a very difficult subject to study but we are able to describe one thorough study, that of Haan and her associates, and it gives us an idea of what value interaction is really like, how different it can be from our preconceptions.

Another topic that appears to deserve more exploration is the functioning of conscience in ordinary persons (not the maladjusted). When writing on the subject I found myself having to draw upon my own experience for want of reports of others, yet wondering all the while how typical my experience is. There may be reports that I missed; in any case, it is a fascinating subject, for conscience is a remarkable thing.

I have the pleasure of expressing grateful appreciation to Emi Nobuhiro who functioned both as typist and editorial advisor in preparing camera-ready copy of the manuscript. Always the patient, good-natured helper as she worked through my numerous reformulations and corrections, the book would be the poorer without her contribution. Indebtedness of another sort is due my wife Tai Y. Kilby, who kept me well-fed and healthy through long months of writing. Had the body faltered, so too the mind. Body stayed in excellent condition; mind muddled through.

The author would like to thank the following for permission to reproduce material in this book:

New York University Press, for the excerpts from *On Moral Grounds*, by Norma Haan, E. Aerts, and B. A. B. Cooper. Copyright 1985 by New York University.

Alfred A. Knopf, Inc., for Table 19.1, p. 459 from *Elements of Psychology*, by David Krech, R. Crutchfield, and N. Livson. Copyright 1969, 1974 by Alfred A. Knopf, Inc..

Virago Press, London, and Paul Berry, Literary Executor of Vera Brittain, for the excerpts from *Testament of Youth*, by Vera Brittain, 1933, 1980, 1989. Copyright Paul Berry and Virago Press, London.

Abigail J. Stewart, Department of Psychology, University of Michigan, for the excerpts from A. J. Stewart and J. M. Healy, Jr.. The role of personality development and experience in shaping political commitment: An illustrative case. *Journal of Social Issues*, 1986, 42, #2, pp. 11-31.

The Society for the Psychological study of Social Issues for excerpts from the above Stewart and Healy report. Copyright The Society for the Psychological Study of Social Issues, 1986.

William Ready Division of Archives and Research Collections, Mills Memorial Library, McMaster University, Hamilton, Ontario, for quotations from unpublished letters and diaries from the Estate of Vera Brittain.

*I believe that we have to content ourselves with our
imperfect knowledge and understanding and treat
values and moral obligations as a purely human
problem -- the most important of all human
problems.*

Albert Einstein

CHAPTER 1

TYPES OF VALUES

The number of types of values that we list depends upon the definition of human values that we employ. But let us delay looking at definitions until after we have looked at a listing of possible types of values, and for the moment employ a simple all-inclusive definition -- a value is anything of importance to the person.

Below are listed a variety of types of human values. Likely there are other types, perhaps a number, as we have not tried to uncover all possibilities (and to our knowledge no systematic list exists). There is nothing final about the categories -- they could be named and organized in different ways, are not completely independent of each other, and given values may appear in more than one category.

The special merit of a listing of this sort is that it may give one a concrete conception of the nature of human values and of the many different forms that they take, for otherwise the subject is so vague and contradictory that one may come away thoroughly confused. Too, most persons know of only a few specific values and may benefit from learning more of their extent. Their extent is so great as to be likened to a domain that stretches off into the hazy distance, its boundaries unknown.

Moral Values and Conscience

Because of their strength and importance the moral values head any list. Indeed, they are about the only values many people think of when asked their values.

There is no specific list of moral values though in total the number should not be great. Most obvious are those almost universally experienced as right, absolute (permitting no exceptions), and evokers of strong feelings of guilt and remorse at violations, such as honesty and truthfulness. From this small number of "musts" they shade off in strength to those that are experienced more as "shoulds" and "oughts" and involve some amount of needling of conscience at failure to practice them. Still others are held as standards of judgement and apply more to impersonal moral-ethical problems, such as those facing the entire community, than to one's own conduct, though if the problem also has personal significance then there will be the feeling of "I should" or "ought" here as well. These last are hardly distinguishable from the main body of values as most of these have the quality of being conceptions of the desirable with feelings of right-wrong, should or ought implicit.

Though a moral value will be experienced by the individual as a *personal* imperative, regardless of the behavior of others, actually morals are among the most evident of *group* codes. They emerge out of the necessity of peoples having to live and cooperate together in groups, having been established in any existing group long ago, and once established are taught with emphasis to each new generation of children. Individuals composing the group must be so socially shaped that they voluntarily direct their own behavior in ways conducive to group effectiveness and harmony and to avoidance of the upsetting and harmful. There is no alternative to this self-direction, for an arrangement of policing each other to enforce compliance with rules and customs would be utterly unworkable. (Actually, policing is provided in modern mass-societies such as our own, by policemen, prosecutors, and the like, and is considered necessary because so many people in such "disorganized" societies violate the moral-legal code. But its effectiveness is limited because only a fraction of violators are caught. More could be caught if more enforcers were employed, but soon a point is reached where it becomes unbearably costly to the society to maintain them.)

By the time we are old enough to be aware of what has happened usually we have become thoroughly "moralized" and are effective self-directors. But rarely would it be a case of feeling deceived by elders (unless it was felt that parents had overdone it and left one a handicapped adult with too strong a conscience), for usually morals are felt to be necessary or desirable for everyone.

Seen in terms of group welfare, certain moral values are essential in any group anywhere, others are desirable but permit some variation or exception without harm to group welfare, and some are unique to the given society and not really necessary to group functioning and survival but became established long ago as part of the group's beliefs, especially their religious beliefs, and continue because of those beliefs.

The first group, of essential morals, gain their imperativeness because they relate to problems that tend to arise in all societies and for which definite rules and norms must exist for dealing with them. So the rules and norms must be taught to the children with special emphasis, which results either in a strong sense of moral rightness or a comparably strong urge to do the expected thing. Maccoby (1980, p. 296-299) has compiled a list of eight such essentially universal problems. They are given below with brief identifying comment and spelled-out more fully under the moral values topic in Chapter 3.

(1) *Endangering self and others.* Careless, thoughtless, even playful, actions can lead to harm and injury, so in certain societies the children must be taught that the food and water supply is precious and they are to do nothing to endanger it. Elsewhere the teaching may be to avoid dangerous places or playing with fire.

(2) *Protection of health.* Threats to health are universal and the children must be taught how to avoid them, such as by carefully disposing of body wastes.

(3) *Property ownership.* Humans are possession-acquiring creatures and control of possessions readily become a source of discord, so children must be taught that certain objects are the property of others and not to be taken without permission, and taking without permission is theft and wrong.

(4) *Control of aggression.* Humans readily become angry and resort to forms of aggression, which can lead to far-reaching disruption of community functioning and retaliatory aggression, so the children must be taught that it is wrong to hurt others in the group and a grave offense to kill another.

(5) *Control of sex.* The mature sexual appetite also is strong, often is accompanied by such feelings as jealousy and possessiveness, and of course results in babies, so must be controlled and channeled in the interest of the group.

(6) *Self-reliance and work.* No society can function without each doing his share, so children will be taught to do their share of chores and aspire to be self-supporting adults.

(7) *Telling the truth and keeping promises.* Truthfulness and honesty are two obvious necessities if people are to carry on daily life together, so must be taught to the children.

(8) *Respect for authority.* Group living necessitates delegating authority or leadership, with the rest following that leadership, so the children will be taught to be obedient to parents, teachers, and others in authority.

Two other essentially universal problems, which produce associated moral values, are those of (9) *Care for elders*, which often involves respect for them as well, and (10) *Care for and protection of children*, necessitated especially by the long period of infant and childhood helplessness.

These ten types of moral values turn up in lists of commandments, virtues, and sins in the different societies of the world. For peoples in the Judeo-Christian tradition six of the Ten Commandments express them: Thou shalt honor thy father and mother; thou shalt not kill; thou shalt not commit adultery; thou shalt not steal; thou shalt not bear false witness (not lie); thou shalt not covet other's possessions.

The second group of moral values, those desirable but not essential for all, is nicely exemplified by the Seven Deadly (or Cardinal) Sins. They are: pride (egoism, vanity), envy (jealousy), lust (strong sexuality), sloth (laziness), gluttony (over-eating and drinking), covetousness (greed), and wrath (bad temper, ill-will). (As worded, all are negative values or *dis*values, and have the effect of producing a negative evaluation of the given behavior and a positive evaluation of its opposite -- modesty or humility in the case of pride.) It will be evident that each is a personal weakness which is harmful to interpersonal and group functioning in some way and any society would be fortunate to be free of the whole lot, but hardly a one is a critical defect and some amount of each can be tolerated.

Exemplifying the final group, of moral values unique to the given society and not really necessary to group functioning and survival, are the remaining four of the Ten Commandments. All are Moses' interpretation of the commandments of Yahweh, the Hebrew god, instructing the Hebrews on matters of religious belief and practice, including observance of the seventh day of the week as a holy day or Sabbath. The commandments are stated as moral imperatives and throughout Jewish and Christian history have had a strong moral emphasis; for example, failure to believe in God was a grave sin and could lead to excommunication, a virtual death sentence.

Though the given value typically was formulated far back in the past, it would have been transmitted from one generation to the next by parents, teachers, preachers, peers, and others, down to the present and to ourselves. Because of this generational mode of transmission the value could undergo slight changes in any generation and this be passed on to the next with the possibility of notable change over time.

Well into the present century there were (and perhaps still are in places) Sunday Blue Laws, derived from the commandment to observe the Sabbath, with some people feeling sinful and guilty if they worked or did anything "frivolous" on Sunday. All businesses remained closed and any manner of entertainment was forbidden -- the sports events, such as football, which are so prominent a part of today's Sunday would have been out of the question. While people today do not outrightly repudiate this and other of the religious commandments neither do many feel concerned about them and probably most do not even know they exist. The remainder of the commandments have varying strengths among people generally, with "Thou shalt not kill" (meaning not kill members of one's own group) as strong and illegal as ever, but "Thou shalt honor thy father and thy mother" much weaker to most and unmoving to many (and care of the elderly handled by pensions and other substitutes).

Though all of the Seven Deadly Sins continue to be negative values, all have lost the moral intensity they once had (imagine the shame one would have felt in earlier times at being accused of being lustful or slothful). Several, namely pride, lust, sloth, and gluttony, seem almost to have an accepted neutral status today (when called by more modern terms).

In Japan one can drop his purse or leave a parcel lying anywhere and invariably have it returned, so high and universal is their standard on theft. That we marvel at their level of public honesty tells its own story as to comparable levels here, though it would be a great mistake to overgeneralize -- some here are just as honest as the Japanese. It is the diversity here that is striking and alarming. Williams (1978, p. 37) reports from his sociological research that, in his judgement, here in the U.S. there has been some decrease in the binding power of such "absolute" values as honesty, but a probable increase in the effective implementation of humanitarian values.

Reflecting Williams' finding, it is probably correct to say that people hold different "honestys" (and comparable other moralities) for different situations, so might feel it unthinkable to be dishonest with a relative or friend but quite all right to break the law by under-paying taxes or deceiving the buyer when selling an item ("let the buyer beware"). A few years ago a young investment banker, who was making a million dollars a year and had $10 million in the bank, was arrested for making insider stock trades (i.e., had confidential information about a company not available to other investors), pleaded guilty, and was sentenced to prison. When a cross-section of American people were asked by a national opinion-polling organization (Harris, 1987, p. 109-11) if they would do the same thing if they had the chance 53% -- a majority of those asked -- said they would buy the stock, too, even if they knew it was illegal to do so. Further, the percentage rose to 64% of those earning $50,000 a year or over, as would 61% of all men, 60% of college graduates, 61% of those now owning stock, and 58% of "Yuppies." So the more affluent and privileged the people were, the more likely they would be to engage in insider trading. Indeed, even among the minority who said they would not engage in insider trading, 37% said the reason was that the "tip" might not be any good, and only 37% could bring themselves to say that "its just plain wrong to do it."

Another qualifier should be drawn in here. Throughout history people have employed "we" and "they" categories, with the morals applying only to interactions with members of "our" group (the "in-group") but not the "out-group." Probably the most obvious example is that of killing. Likely all groups regard attacking and killing members of their own group as the gravest of crimes, often punishing with death, but that same group might have a centuries-old tradition of attacking and killing members of neighboring groups, and modern "civilized" nations continue the practice by indiscriminate killing during wars (we saw new examples of this in the bombing during the recent Middle East war). A recent issue of the *Journal of Social Issues* (vol. 46, #1, 1990) is devoted to moral exclusion and injustice and the issue editor, Susan Opotow, says in part:

> Moral exclusion occurs when individuals or groups are perceived as outside the boundary in which moral values, rules, and considerations of fairness

apply. Those who are morally excluded are perceived as nonentities, expendable, or undeserving. Consequently, harming or exploiting them appears to be appropriate, acceptable, or just. This broad definition encompasses both severe and mild forms of moral exclusion, from genocide to discrimination. (p. 1)

Even as old morals fade and change, new emerge. A good example is the ongoing emergence just now of the new (yet very old) ethic of "conservationism." We are being urged to conserve water (especially here in the arid West), electricity, heating fuels, gasoline, trees (timber resources), wildlife, clean air (that is, avoid polluting), and to recycle everything possible. Each reader may note influences of the sort that have been acting upon him in recent years and what the personal effect has been so far. My own observation has been that there have been few or no outright messages saying "you should (or must) conserve"; that is, no declarations that it is a moral matter. Nor do I recall highly-placed figures, such as president or governor, urging it and giving it an aura of the imperative by their attention. But the several public utilities steadily urge conservation in their mailings and advertisements and justify it in the public interest. Similarly, the newspapers from time to time will carry reports urging conservation and for the same reasons. The environmental organizations continually stress the need for conservation and justify it on several practical and ethical grounds -- protecting our health, welfare of future generations, conservation of scarce natural resources, preventing extermination of wildlife, and assuring enough for everyone. It is this appeal to sense of practical necessity and duty, rather than declaring it a moral imperative, that seems to be the essence of this new ethic, with individual conscience coming in as a consequence of the sense of necessity and duty. Then, to the extent that one of these forms of conservation becomes a public issue, as when water or fuel becomes scarce to the point of requiring rationing, sharing then becomes a community moral matter and violators openly accused of immorality (as by the accusation, "What if everyone wasted water as you are doing?").

Though the total number of one's strongly held moral values may not be great, they are experienced as moral imperatives and accompanied by strong feelings. Because of this intensity of conviction and strength of feeling they often produce complex psychodynamic reactions, such as conflict, feelings of guilt following certain thoughts or acts, self-condemnation, and punishment of violations, and defensive rationalizations to handle the felt misery at violations. "Conscience" names this entire active process as we experience it.

These same moral values may also produce strong feelings of condemnation of others for their behavior.

Individuals will of course differ in the specific morals held and may differ significantly in their intensity, with some persons having a blindly dictatorial, punishing conscience, keeping them in misery much of the time. Others, to the other extreme, having so weak a conscience that there is little hesitation to do a questionable thing nor any self-reproach afterward. This person may profess noble morals, and do so sincerely, but only a deep feeling of rightness-wrongness leads one to live them consistently, through temptation, threat, pain and punishment, as when one is compelled from within to speak truth even when he has done wrong and faces punishment. Weakly held moral values permit so many "overlookings" (not recognizing the violation) or rationalizations-to-make-acceptable that there is not real conscience.

The following are examples of possible adult moral values. As worded they have a certain neutral blandness and the reader should mentally alter them to supply the right personal emphasis, as "I *cannot* be greedy" or "I *must* be honest" or "No one *should* hurt another."

One should (must) not be greedy.
    "   "   not hurt or kill another.
    "   "   be brave and fearless (not cowardly).
    "   "   not overeat (not be gluttonous).
    "   "   be faithful to mate.
    "   "   be truthful (not lie).
    "   "   be honest (not be dishonest).
    "   "   be self-controlled (not rage).
    "   "   be respectful and considerate to parents.
    "   "   protect his children.
    "   "   be helpful to others.
    "   "   be considerate toward others (not be disrespectful, impolite).
    "   "   not be sexually promiscuous (not be lustful).
    "   "   treat others fairly.

Behaviors and Traits of Others

What do you value in the way of behavior in the other person -- perhaps self-assertiveness, dependability, daringness, self-effacement? This category gives us the largest number of possible values, for hundreds or thousands of ways of behaving of other persons are subject to potential positive or negative valuing by someone (but not all by the same person!); and we seem predisposed to form judgments about others as to whether good-bad, admirable-deplorable, wise-foolish, smart-dumb, or other. This group of values has been placed here, following the moral values, for a number of these traits are subject to strong moral judgments (good-bad).

The research of Allport and Odbert (1936) on traits is applicable here. They went through a standard dictionary and took out all of the adjectives which appeared to describe characteristic or typical patterns of individual behavior -- that is, traits.

This yielded a first list of about 18,000 terms! However, upon closer inspection they felt that some were doubtful as true trait names, so were eliminated. Others were eliminated because they described temporary moods and activities, hence did not qualify as trait names. A third group were eliminated because they appeared to involve judgments of personal conduct rather than simple neutral descriptions. Their final list of reasonably neutral trait names came to 4500 -- still a very large number! All 4500 traits are potentially subject to valuing by someone.

While this is a long enough list of possible values, it can be increased because many of the behaviors falling in the eliminated list of temporary moods and activities also are subject to valuing -- examples: affronted, agitated, angry, appeasing, attentive, ashamed, annoyed. Similarly, many of the behaviors falling in their eliminated list of judgmental terms obviously are subject to valuing, for it was the valuing implicit in the terms that led to their rejection -- examples: adulterous, ambitious, amiable, angelic, appealing, aristocratic, articulate, asocial, attractive.

A comment of Allport and Odbert is especially pertinent relative to our concern with values, "In spite of our efforts to locate only neutral terms in Column I [their final list of 4500 trait names] some of the terms appearing there do seem to imply censorial judgment. In America to say that John is self-assured, inventive, or decisive is to praise him; in some societies he would stand condemned. . . ." "Praising" and "condemning" are but expressions of values, and the authors are recognizing how easy it is for traits to acquire values, how readily disposed we are to evaluate.

A good exemplification of personal traits is this list of twenty, which come indirectly from the Allport-Odbert list. The reader might wish to choose the several that seem most and least important to him:

Adventurous	Easy going
Ambitious	Imaginative
Broadminded	Independent
Capable	Intellectual
Cheerful	Logical
Clean	Loving
Courageous	Obedient
Forgiving	Polite
Helpful	Responsible
Honest	Self-controlled

Ideal Self

Just as we hold values toward the traits of others, so we hold them toward ourselves as well -- how I would like to be (my ideal self), how I strive to be, what gives me satisfaction when I seem to be that way. Also important are negative ideals -- how I don't want to be and source of self-dissatisfaction when I seem to be that way. It is a safe guess that everyone experiences these values, though with notable individual differences, and apparently all experience some self-dissatisfaction at perceived shortcomings. For certain, they play a large part in the lives of troubled-maladjusted persons, sometimes being the very essence of the inner distress, and they gain so much importance because this person tends to discount his strengths ("good" traits) and magnify the weaknesses, misperceiving the traits themselves and harshly judging because of perfectionistic values.

Examples of positive ideals are: self-accepting, courageous, intelligent, warm, good athlete at x̲ sport. Examples of the negative are: boastfulness, defensiveness, dominating, impulsive, impatient.

Interpersonal Values

Interpersonal values are one's conceptions of the desirable in relationships and interactions between persons. Many of the same traits will appear under this heading as in lists of ideal personal traits of others, above, because so many of those traits are seen and evaluated in social interactions with other persons.

Examples of such values are:
Being treated with respect
Granting the other autonomy or independence
Giving the other support
Being admired
Doing things for others
Letting self be used by the other
Avoiding discord at all costs
Respecting the privacy of the other
Complete candor and no secrets
Respect and obedience for authority
Helping the other grow
Establishing who is leader and who follower
Being tolerant of the failings of the other
Using the other for one's own ends

Marital Values

Marital values will include many of the above interpersonal values, for of course marriage is an interpersonal relationship. Additional marital values might pertain to such things as children (family size and child rearing practices), religion and church, recreations, social life, size of income. (If the disposition is fairly specific, such as belief in the desirability of church attendance, it is more properly called an attitude rather than a value.)

Sex (sex-role) Values

A special group of values are those relating to the sex-roles and behaviors of each of the sexes and the relations between the sexes. The behaviors involved are but special forms of personal traits and interpersonal relationships. These values have received much attention in recent years because of the women's liberation movement. They may be held by persons of the one sex toward own-sex status and behavior, either for self or for own-sex generally. Or, they may be held by persons of the one sex toward status and behavior of the opposite sex. Examples might be one woman's feeling that it is right for women to defer to men and another's feeling both sexes should be equal in all regards -- in the home, occupationally, and in public life; and one man's feeling that women should be feminine and another's feeling that both sexes should behave much the same way and do exactly the same work, no matter how strenuous or dangerous.

Child Rearing Values

Assume that you are about to become a parent. As you contemplate rearing your youngster, what sort of person would you like her or him to become? Perhaps obedient, God-fearing, or industrious?

There have been significant shifts in these ideals in the past half-century. Alwin (1987) reports that the parental emphasis on teaching children obedience has given way to a preference for autonomy or thinking for oneself as a trait that will prepare children for participation in adult society. Compared to parents of the mid-1920s, today's parents have almost reversed the order of importance in which child rearing goals are ranked. In the famous Middletown study of 1924, forty-five percent of the mothers ranked *strict obedience* as one of three most important qualities; 50 percent chose *loyalty to the church*; 30 percent chose *good manners*. *Independence* was chosen by 25 percent of mothers, and *tolerance* by only 6 percent.

Fifty-four years later in 1978, a new generation of mothers had virtually opposite child rearing goals. Only 17 percent of mothers chose *strict obedience* and 22 percent *loyalty to the church* as most important. Now 76 percent endorsed *independence* -- the ability to think and act for her/himself, and 47 percent chose *tolerance* of the opinions of others.

A national U.S. survey (Harris, 1987, p. 47-50) presented to a sample of adult Americans a list of thirteen traits that might be desirable for children to have. Heading the list as most important to develop was "A child should be honest," selected by 28 percent. In second and third place were "A child should have good sense and sound judgment" (19%) and "A child should obey his or her parents well" (17%). The next two, at 8%, were "A child should learn to be considerate of others" and "A child should learn to be responsible." Two others, at 4%, were "should try hard to succeed," and "interested in how and why things happen."

These results seem to contradict somewhat the Middletown follow-up findings in that "good sense and sound judgment," which is about the equivalent of *independence*, is essentially equal in percent of acceptance to *obedience* ("obey his or her parents"), and, indeed, one interpretation of such data has been that another trend emerged in the 1980s, away from the permissiveness and autonomy of the 1960s and 70s, to one of some amount of control, provoked by a practical need for control. As Alwin has commented personally, "For years, my wife and I have urged our kids to think for themselves. Now when we want them to do something, we have to appeal to their self-interest, their sense of fairness and logic. But sometimes its frustrating when you want them to go along with you." Only a minority of parents have the patience, skill, and dedication to use this strategy. Assertion of authority comes more naturally.

But the question asked by the pollsters invites two different interpretations; one leads the respondent to picture a child and to answer with the traits desirable in a child. The other pictures a child-becoming-an-adult and answers with the trait's desirability in an adult. In another phase of the above national opinion survey respondents were asked to choose which one of six qualities would be most important in preparing a child for later life. Now, 26 percent chose "a child should be able to think for himself or herself" -- that is, be independent or self-sufficient. In second place, and chosen by only 11 percent, was "a child should learn to obey." (Third was "to help others when they need help," at 7 percent, and fourth was "learn to work hard," at 6 percent.) So training for independence or self-sufficiency is still considered to be most important for the adult.

Results comparable to the American shift to independence are reported from Europe where, for example, German pollsters in 1951 found *self-reliance* and *obedience* to be about equal at 28 and 25 percent, but by 1983 *self-reliance* had jumped to 49 percent while *obedience* had dropped to just 9 percent.

The above-mentioned traits will serve to exemplify this category of values.

Goals of Life and Ways to Live

This category is made up of a variety of conceptions of the desirable and is a very important group of values. As goals, they motivate us toward their attainment; as ways to live, they tell us that this is a right and worthy way of spending our lives. For example, service to fellowman might be conceived to be an eminently desirable life goal and a most worthy way of spending one's life. With some of these values the goal or end attainment is the more prominent (e.g., becoming famous); with others the way to live, the daily activity, is the more prominent, sometimes with little or no goal quality present (e.g., creativity).

Harris (1987) reports that when a national sample was asked to choose which of three goals is their greatest single source of happiness *good health* was chosen by 46 percent, closely followed by satisfaction from *personal achievement*, at 44 percent, with *great wealth* chosen by only 6 percent. Harris adds, though, that other evidence indicates that not having enough money can quickly unravel a sense of satisfaction with one's condition. Older people, working women, the less well-educated, single people, those without children, and low-income people all say they are less happy now than in the 1970s (p. 41).

Some goals and ways relate directly to oneself, such as: security and safety, enlightenment, enjoyment-pleasure, advancement in career, self-development, closeness to nature, letting oneself be used, or creativity.

Other goals and ways relate to valued states of affairs that apply both to oneself and others -- to the community or people generally, such as: a world at peace, national security, solving man's problems, economic prosperity, preservation of the traditional customs, equality and tolerance.

(Incidentally, Rokeach employed this differentiation into the two types in assembling the 18 values of the "terminal values" portion of his *Values Survey* questionnaire.)

Values To Be Realized in One's Occupation

More specific than life goals are things one would like to realize in his/her occupation. They may enter into actual vocational choice or motivate a person now settled in an occupation, or just be part of the picture that one carries in mind of the ideal work situation no matter what the present job reality.

It used to be that most workers wanted good pay and security from unjust firing. But priorities have changed. Harris (1987) reports that this was evident when a national sample was asked to choose which one of five major work attractions was most important to them. Well at the head of the list, and singled out by 48 percent, was that "the work be important and give you a real feeling of accomplishment." Far below this as most important was "good chance for promotion," at 20 percent, closely followed by "good pay" at 18 percent. Still farther down were "no danger of being fired," at 7 percent, and "shorter hours and lots of free time," at 3 percent.

Suppose you are a mature person who has worked at various occupations and are now ready to settle into a lifelong career. What will you look for in a career -- what are your occupational values? Here are some possibilities:

Accomplish something (write a book, treat ailments, make discovery, build
      something, etc.)
Grow as a person (learn, mature, broaden)
Develop warm interpersonal relationships (daily human contact and sharing,
      friendships)
High productivity (set records, produce more, higher company income)
High personal income
Opportunity for travel, vacations

Variety, new experiences, change
Low-key work and freedom from tension, strain, pressure
Security of employment and income

Values Assigned to Occupations

Not to be confused with values to be realized in an occupation, the preceding type, we also form notions as to the worth of different occupations, whether we consider entering them or not. The value assignment is being determined by more specific values or personal meanings, such as the prestige associated with the occupation, or its income level, pleasantness-unpleasantness of the work, level of intelligence or skill required, characteristics of work associates, and other. As examples, what sort of value would you assign each of these occupations: teacher, bartender, tennis professional, engineer, check-out clerk, truck driver, delivery person, politician?

The number of existing occupations runs into the thousands so potentially there are that many to subjectively assign value, but anyone's list will be but a fraction of that and entire groups of hundreds of occupations may be assigned to a single evaluated category in one's mind, such as "clerical jobs," "white collar work," or "skilled labor."

Political-Economic Structuring of Nations

Some of people's strongest values are held toward political-economic theories and actual structurings of nations, so much so that they engage in political action of various sorts and in the extreme take up arms and give lives to preserve or attain a given structuring arrangement. We are able to name only a few such structurings -- autocracy, socialism, capitalism, monarchy, communism, theocracy, democracy -- and the names themselves may not kindle much feeling. But all holding values toward these will have fuller subjective images of them together with more specific values such as those listed below, and it can be seen from the listing that some of the most important values of life are included; no wonder they motivate so powerfully.

Freedom of expression	Law and order (stability and safety)
Freedom of movement	Assured employment and income
Occupational choice	Cradle-to-grave security
Right to vote	Opportunity for individual initiative (laissez-faire)
Equal opportunity	Security from external threat
Wealth-promoting	Freedom from choice and responsibility
A predictable existence	Community and personal growth promoting

Man's Relation to Nature

Three broad value possibilities exist as to man's relation to nature -- nature should be considered more important, more valuable than man; nature should be used for human ends; and nature and man have equal rights and compromises must be found. Within these, more specific values are possible.

This domain of value is very much before us today as it becomes more and more evident that man has for millennia followed a largely unrecognized ethic of using forest, prairie, ocean, sky -- every aspect of nature, for his own ends, but cannot continue to do so and exist on the planet. In the years ahead we will see pronounced changes both in recognition of this reality and in associated values toward nature.

Though it all seems new and surely nearly everyone still holds to the value that nature should be used for human ends, nearly a century and a half ago Victor Hugo anticipated current developments when he wrote:

> In the relations of humans with the animals, with the flowers, with the objects of creation, there is a whole great ethic scarcely seen as yet, but which will eventually break through into light and be the corollary and the complement to human ethics . . . (from *En Voyage, Alpes and Pyrénées*)

One of the principal roots of today's environmental ethics is Aldo Leopold's brief essay "The Pond Ethic," which appeared in his *A Sand Country Almanac* (1949). There he proposed that human conduct be guided by the ecologist's concept of a biotic community. "A thing is right," he wrote, "when it tends to preserve the intensity, stability, and beauty of the biotic community. It is wrong when it tends otherwise." Thus, tropical deforestation, ozone depletion, and the slaughter of whales are ethically wrong. Not because such actions may be wasteful, socially unjust, or harmful to humanity (all values in their own right), but because the nonhuman, even nonliving elements of nature, have intrinsic value (Borrelli, 1989).

This value position was echoed by the naturalist David Attenborough, at the conclusion of his recent TV series, *The Living Planet,* "We have no moral right to destroy other forms of life!" A remarkable assertion, and one that should give second thoughts to those of us who have always operated on an opposite assumption. And note how he has made it an issue of morality, in effect invoking the highest of judgements (short of the Divine).

Esteemed Persons

It is appropriate to regard certain persons as objects of value. One sub-group would be persons having some closeness to us, such as child, spouse, parent, or close friend, and perceived as having a certain preciousness or worth to us. The other sub-group would be public figures, past or present, who we admire or esteem, who we feel have enriched the world by their presence, and whose traits and behavior deserve emulation. A common way to assess this esteem is to ask a person which of a list of notable persons she/he would most wish to be like. A few examples of notable persons, past and present as perceived by one or another evaluator: Jefferson, Gandhi, Madam Curie, Einstein, Plato, Bach, Rembrandt, Elvis Presley, Martin Luther King, Gorbachev, Mother Teresa.

Interestingly, certain living persons may become valued objects. The possibility is suggested by Japan's "living cultural treasures." Just as old shrines, temples, castles, and the like are national treasures, so they have designated certain living persons as national treasures. Apparently all are older persons who possess some knowledge or skill that is unusual and in danger of disappearing when they die -- weavers, wood-block print makers, carvers, potters, and the like.

Valued Total Patterns of Life

This type of value was suggested by the work of Charles Morris (1956) who conceived of different patterns of life, which he called "ways to live," that individuals and whole groups come to value as the good life. Thirteen such patterns were formulated, each presented by a paragraph-long description, as exemplified by *Way 1* below, describing a way of life involving the preservation of the best that man has attained. Others describe carefree enjoyment, sympathetic concern, self-control, group participation, etc.. Though each description focuses on the activity of the one person, with nothing said of associates, neighbors, or community, the implication throughout is that others will live as the one does, hence describes whole patternings of society as well.

Going through and reacting to (evaluating) such a list of ways to live is a stimulating exercise and one might be surprised at how definite his views are as to ideal ways to live.

In Chapter 3 some actual ideal communities -- heavens on earth -- out of the past are described.

Of course Morris' list does not include all possible ways to live and others might be created from these by tearing them apart and recombining into one's own conception of the ideal pattern of person and society.

Morris' *Way 1* is reproduced in full below, followed by single sentences describing the other twelve, though in their brevity they do not begin to do full justice to each.

WAY 1: In this "design for living" the individual actively participates in the social life of his community, not to change it primarily, but to understand, appreciate, and preserve the best that man has attained. Excessive desires should be avoided and moderation sought. One wants the good things of life but in an orderly way. Life is to have clarity, balance, refinement, control. Vulgarity, great enthusiasm, irrational behavior, impatience, indulgence are to be avoided. Friendship is to be esteemed but not easy intimacy with many people. Life is to have discipline, intelligibility, good manners, predictability. Social changes are to be made slowly and carefully, so that what has been achieved in human culture is not lost. The individual should be active physically and socially, but not in a hectic or radical way. Restraint and intelligence should give order to an active life.

2.   Cultivate independence of persons and things.
3.   Show sympathetic concern for others.
4.   Experience festivity and solitude in alternation.
5.   Act and enjoy life through group participation.
6.   Constantly master changing conditions.
7.   Integrate action, enjoyment and contemplation.
8.   Live with wholesome, carefree enjoyment.
9.   Wait in quiet receptivity.
10.   Control the self stoically.
11.   Meditate on the inner life.
12.   Chance adventuresome deeds.
13.   Obey the cosmic purposes.

Standards of Judgement

Do you carry about in mind some evaluative notions, some standards of judgement, that come to the fore whenever you find yourself in certain situations. For example, imagine yourself an older person who lived through the long years of the Great Depression and since has had to "pinch pennies" to get by. Now you might be predisposed to perceive certain situations in terms of costs and possible wastes and to judge some things as too costly (wasteful). Specifically, such things as someone's new garment or new auto, another's choice of vacation, or another's tastes in foods, to name a few, might all be judged too costly, hence wasteful.

While this "cost-waste" standard of judgement is one of the most obvious, there are numerous other possibilities, as suggested by these questions that one in effect might ask oneself as part of the act of perceiving any object: Is it compatible with my religious beliefs (if not, its wrong)? For what is it useful? Is it dangerous, will it harm me? Is it a threat to my selfhood (am already insecure)? Is it novel or is it like what I am used to (I can't stand much novelty -- too disturbing)? And a timely question -- is it environment polluting?

This category most certainly will overlap others, for some of these specific standards of judgement will be found among other types of values.

Valued Sensory-Perceptual Experiences

Some of our most certain values have to do with subjective experiences. These are values in the sense that one feels "This is what gives me joy," or "this is what makes life meaningful," "I value this."

Specific possible valued experiences are these:

Gustatory sensations, as from certain fruits or prepared dishes

Sights and sounds of nature, as out in forest or at seashore

Aesthetic experiences of beauty and symmetry

Listening to music

Playing games, body movement

Sights and feels of human associations

Altered states of consciousness, as by drugs

Altered states of consciousness through meditation

Excitement, thrill, uncertainty, risk

"Sitting in the sunshine" -- repose, contentment, reflection

Aesthetic Values

A rather special type of value is the aesthetic. It is manifest whenever one makes a reaction or judgement toward an object having aesthetic qualities. Examples would be one person's valuing compositions or structures of simple line, another favoring complexity; one values abstraction or symbolism, another literal or life-like representation; one likes simple folk-type music, another the more complex classical music; one values bright color in painting or garment, another prefers subdued colors; one values evidence of tension, activity, and movement in sculpture or dance, another values flow and serenity. It might be objected that there is no need to call this "value," that "liking" or "preference" would serve. But the disposition acts as an *enduring standard of judgement* or guide in aesthetic situations.

In pure form, the valuing is a reaction to the aesthetic merits of the object as perceived by the observer, devoid of additional evaluative coloring. But evaluation often enters in to determine the judgement. To a person or group who value traditional forms of expression, a very novel creation may be judged negatively just because of its novelty. As another example, surely many a person over the centuries has reacted negatively to portrayals of the nude human body because of a belief that it is wrong or sinful to display the body.

Activities and Involvements That Give Meaning to Life

This is but a special form of valued activity. Frankl (1962) in his *Man's Search for Meaning* has theorized that all of us must find meaning in life, else a depressing emptiness will be there. A phenomenal number of sorts of activity and involvement can and do supply meaning to the millions, including such ordinary things as going to work daily to support self and family or, for a homemaker, looking after one's growing family and keeping them fed and healthy. But certain persons are more prone than most to experience meaninglessness, among them older persons. For many of these, the very daily activities that gave meaning to life are no longer there -- perhaps no longer employed or employable, children grown and gone, vigorous interests and recreations no longer possible, spouse, relatives, and friends now gone, etc.. It is easy to begin to feel that life is without meaning, become depressed, perhaps commit suicide.

But finding new meaning in life is always possible. For one it might take the form of service to others (as in doing volunteer work in a community agency), for another involvement in church and religion, another cultivation of new interests or developing new friendships, etc..

Whatever the activity, likely it will be experienced as meaningful or valuable, hence a form of value.

Deeply Personal and Interpersonal Values

Various psychologists, especially Rogers (1964) and Maslow (1959, 1964, 1967, 1971), have assumed the existence of personal growth tendencies in all of us, including in persons who at the moment appear to be thoroughly unhappy and maladjusted because torn by conflicts, anxiety, and low self-esteem. They have observed that when these persons have a chance to explore their lives and dig into their troubled feelings, as by penetrating discussions with an interested counselor, they begin, ever so slowly, to experience new positive feelings toward themselves and the persons in their lives, and toward their lives generally. Increased feelings of self-acceptance and decreased self-damnation and worthlessness usually are at the heart of the process of change. It is common for the person not only to feel better, but also to put a value label on these strange new feelings -- "I feel more competent and I like what I am feeling." The valuing helps the person keep working at the painful task of changing and serves as an inner guide, telling him when he is progressing and when standing still. As Rogers (1964, pg. 166) says in part,

> One's self, one's own feelings come to be positively valued. From a point where he looks upon himself with contempt and despair, the client comes to value himself and his reactions as being of worth.
> Deep relationships are positively valued. To achieve a close intimate, real, fully communicative relationship with another person seems to meet a deep need in every individual, and is very highly valued.

Generalizing beyond the seriously troubled person some of any person's values may be but partially articulated, more sensed or felt than spelled out, but when finally actualized are experienced as meaningful, as having intrinsic worth, much as Rogers is suggesting. Possible examples might be these (they blend into each other):

Self-acceptance; self respect
At ease; comfortable with life (free from anxiety)
Companionship; intimacy
Feelings of security
Feeling accepted
Capacity for self-expression
Feeling loved and loving

Motive-Derived Values

Any major motive may create a value simply because the object wanted or needed by the motive has inherent value because of the wanting. Since motives are numerous, so too will be this class of value, but as we suggest in Chapter 2, it is not necessary to regard every motive as a felt value, and is desirable to be quite critical in the matter. Motives may be divided into the two broad classes of abundancy and deficiency motives, producing their corresponding positive and negative values. Examples of the positive would be a conscious valuing of food, shelter (warmth), safety, pleasurable sensory experiences, bodily comfort, games, novelty and exploration, friendship, esteem, self-esteem. Examples of the negative would be a conscious negative feeling (disvaluing, avoidance) toward hunger, cold, and misery, danger, pain, sensory deprivation, physical and mental confinement, conflict and hostility, feelings of inferiority, experiences of failure, feelings of shame, fear-anxiety, and depression. (Various of these have appeared under preceding headings.)

Temperament-Dictated Values

Some of a person's values may come from the way his mind or personality works -- from his manner of approach to the world. One person may be so constituted as to see the world through aesthetic eyes, seeing pleasing forms, colors, compositions, and harmony everywhere. He need not be an artist at all; it is just his nature to find the artistic-aesthetic experience intrinsically valuable. Another may have an inquiring, analytic mind, always asking "why?" and always seeking answers. This theoretical approach may be intrinsically meaningful for this person. Another is a social being, a "people lover," who finds daily interaction with other, helping and cooperating, both natural and worthwhile. This line of reasoning about values takes its departure from the writings of Edward Spranger. Broadly, his thinking was that each person comes to interact with the world with a certain preferred orientation. He proposed six such orientations, the above aesthetic, theoretical and social orientations, plus economic, religious, and political orientations. The economic person is oriented toward what is useful so is practical-minded and readily becomes involved in such worldly things as making and building, commerce, and earning and investing, finding all of this personally meaningful. The religious person is always grasping for unity -- for a comprehension of the cosmos as a whole and a placing of self in that all-embracing totality. The effort in this direction, even if immediately frustrating, is inherently satisfying and valued. The political person is oriented toward power, influence, control. The "game" of politics, or power-seeking within group or organization, is stimulating and the gaining of personal power, influence, and renown experienced as desirable.

Engaging in these forms of behavior does not automatically make them valued. There must be an experiencing of them as personally valued (meaningful, worthwhile, useful).

If such value types as these six exist at all it is certain that others do as well. Though a questionnaire (the *Study of Values*) based on the six has long existed, it is more an interest than a value questionnaire and does not outrightly demonstrate that such value orientations exist. However, most appear to be strong possibilities and deserve a search for them in living persons.

Evidence of another sort for temperament-derived values comes from two long-term personality studies conducted by White (1975):

> A final visit to Chatwell and Merritt will illustrate this point [of diversity in life patterns]. Chatwell, having a high activity level and a talent for argument, soon came to attach important value to initiative and competitive assertiveness. At crucial points these preferences steered his action so that he moved into a career in which such values were of central importance. Family values were also important to him, but deference toward superiors and skill in making himself liked by those who worked under him were qualities it was easy for him to neglect. These qualities were of great significance in Merritt's working life. More placid and less assertive than Chatwell, he came to place high value on a friendly, cooperative relation with people, qualities that were ideally suited both to him and to a middle executive position in the business world. Necessarily neglected, in order to realize these values, was ambition to rise to the top and make big decisions. But Merritt, who also valued family life and certain interests of his own, refused to let his career enslave him and was content not to be everything. (p. 515)

Retrospective Valuations

It is common for older people, in their 60s or 70s to look back over their lives and do some sort of "summing up" -- decide how they feel about the way their lives have been spent, now that they are nearly over and have no more time to make corrections nor additional lives to relive. If fates or circumstances have dictated everything, then of course little evaluation is possible; but if one had been making choices as the years passed then a summing up is possible. In any case, a valuation can be placed on the different aspects of one's life.

The findings of a single famous study exemplify nicely. Just after World War I Lewis M. Terman began a longitudinal study of gifted school children. Though Dr. Terman died in 1956, the study still continues, and the surviving participants are now in their 70s and 80s. In 1972 the group of men and women were questioned at average age 62. As Robert Sears (1977), author of the report on the men comments, age 62 seemed a good time to ask these men to focus on both the past and future. With a long life of accomplishment already behind them, they would be in a position to evaluate its joys and sorrows, its successes and failures, its *might-have-been* as well as its *was*.

Satisfaction was assessed with respect to six areas of life experience: occupation, family life, friendship, richness of cultural life, total service to society, and joy in living. Two questions were asked: How important was each of these goals in life, in the plans you made for yourself in early adulthood? and, How satisfied are you with your experience in each of these respects?

Now looking back, at age 62, they reported that as young men they gave highest average rank to *family life*, followed closely by *occupation*, and then a bit lower *joy of living* (the remaining three all had positive ratings but notably below the highest three). Note, though, that we easily can be influenced in our recollection of goals by present values; as young men their actual goals might have been somewhat different. For the second question, as to how satisfied they *now* are with past life's experiences, again *family life* gave greatest average satisfaction, with *joy of living* slightly less, and *occupation* in third place (*friendship* is a close fourth, with the other two notably lower but still strong). As a group of gifted children these individuals had a full measure of good fortune in life. As Sears comments, "Looking backward, these men had not held joy in living as a major goal, but at age 62 they felt they had had a lot of it." (p. 121) (See P. S. Sears and Barbee, 1977, Holahan, 1981, and Tomlinson-Keasey et al. 1986, for the parallel report on the women, and see Shneidman, 1989, for the most recent report on the men).

Values Relating to Death

Three distinct groups of values relating to death have come to our attention. The first are conceptions of what a person would be willing to die for. Examples of possibilities are to die for country, science (advancement of knowledge), a leader, own ethnic or fraternal group, a principle such as truth or liberty, or a relative (to save his life). The second are values relating to the manner of dying. Possibilities are: face death stoically, go with dignity, go fighting, slip away quietly, be cheerful to the end. Third are conceptions of how the person would like to be remembered. Examples here are: as a patriot, devoted wife, conscientious employee, never a quitter, a ladies man, an artist.

Material Objects

This heading is included just to recognize that a very large category of the valued is material objects. Behavioral scientists usually do no concern themselves with such values, leaving them to the economist, though now and then such objects as food, home, money, automobile, television or hi-fi set may be included in our values questionnaires.

Limited-Domain Values, Including Institutional

These are values specific to some group or situation such as school populations, work groups in shop or office, boys gangs, military units, and prisoner groups. In each situation the specific values operate to produce judgements and determine conduct among the interactors. The category was suggested several years ago by debate in the press over the ethics of intercollegiate sports, particularly football. At the time there had been another scandal at a leading football school over illegal payments to players and giving of grades without the players attending classes, and the question was raised in the press, what should be the goals -- the values to be realized -- of intercollegiate athletics? Some of the answers proposed included: education first, sports second; teach sportsmanship; shape young citizens; teach ability to look out for oneself and get along in the adult world. But an actual unspoken value in many of the athletic programs is "win at any price," including just using the young men for the purpose.

A good related limited-domain example is suggested by the question, what values should be realized by our educational system -- training for occupations, liberal education (not occupation-centered), character development, all-round personal growth, develop critical minds? This question is raised again and again because schools have such an important role in modern society and always there is disagreement among those concerned as to goals.

Institutions are limited-domains and *institutional values* came to my attention while searching the values literature, and otherwise would have been missed because of their special nature.

From time to time an article would be encountered that mentioned the values of a given institution, usually in the context of a comparison of the values of the institution itself, the professionals composing the staff, and the "clients" who had to deal with the institution and its managers. For instance, there are a number of reports pertaining to mental health services which contrast the values of the institution (clinic, mental hospital), professionals (administrators, psychiatrists, clinical psychologists, etc.), and persons seeking assistance with problems. Other articles discussed comparable value differences as seen in business and industry, schools and colleges, military units, social service agencies, police departments, jails and prisons, churches, and other institutions.

A special institution is the family, whose values would be those held by the family as a group (as was mentioned above).

Institutional values are usually more implied than spelled out, so we are unable to give many specific examples. A common one appears to be that of accomplishing the mission for which the institution was created, thus a school's would be that of turning out educated persons, a hospital's that of caring for the ill and perhaps producing recoveries, a service agency's that of doing as much as possible within its budget to reduce distress or to get clients back to gainful employment, or a police department's that of enforcement of the law and keeping the peace. Many institutions will be driven by the value of accountability, of accomplishing something for the money spent. Some will value, explicitly or implicitly, institutional self-preservation or continuation. Often strongly implied by the writers of the reports is that the institution's values may have harmful consequences for the individuals who must interact with the institutional giant, that such values as accomplishment of mission, accountability, and orderliness of procedure (following the rules) can lead to insensitivity to individuals and their unique needs and differences, and to a frustrating and harmful rigidity.

Of course institutional values are not held by a superhuman monster, The Institution. They are "held" or enacted by living persons composing the institution, ordinarily its governing board and/or administrative officers. The official's own personal values may be somewhat different, but in his role as agent of the institution he may feel bound to carry out the official values.

Social-Class and Sub-Cultural Values

These are values that are specific to members of a social class or sub-cultural group. In this country the social classes are not very distinct, for a number of reasons, so not many values will be distinct to the given class. But in a country where classes are distinct, class members tend to occupy different occupations and have different income levels, live in different neighborhoods, send children to different schools, and in general, live in different worlds, each with its own array of distinctive attitudes and values. However, some differences in social class values have been reported for this country.

A pertinent example of such values is the child-rearing values of lower- and middle-class, or upper and lower socioeconomic statuses (SES), since we have already reported above on child-rearing values generally. Summarizing findings previous to about 1970, Maccoby (1980, p. 400-401) reported that lower SES parents are more likely to stress obedience, respect, neatness, cleanliness, and staying out of trouble. Higher SES parents are more likely to stress happiness, creativity, ambition, independence, curiosity and self-control. (She also reported that lower SES parents are more controlling, power assertive, arbitrary in their discipline, and likely to use physical punishment. Higher SES parents talk to their children more, reason with them more, and tend to show more warmth and affection.)

Kohn (1963, p. 288) reported finding much the same parental values as these and that there are characteristic clusters of value choice in the two social classes: working-class parental values center on conformity and external proscriptions, middle-class parental values on self-direction. To working-class parents it is the overt act that matters: the child should not transgress externally imposed rules; to middle-class parents, it is the child's motives and feelings that matter: the child should govern himself. Incidentally, both groups of parents shared many core values, honesty being a good example, with working-class giving it a "trustworthiness" coloring and middle-class a "truthfulness" one.

Kohn also has a good discussion of why each class held its respective values, mentioning in part that with the end of mass migration from Europe there emerged a stable working class, uninterested in mobility into the middle-class, but very much interested in security, respectability, and the enjoyment of a decent standard of living. Working-class parents wanted their children to conform to external authority because the parents themselves were willing to accord respect to authority, in return for security and respectability. Their conservatism in child rearing was part of a more general conservatism and traditionalism. In contrast, middle-class conditions of life both allow and demand a greater degree of self-direction, hence middle-class parents can and must instill in their children a degree of self-direction that would be less appropriate to the conditions of life of the working-class (p. 291-92).

But we reported above, in the general presentation of child-rearing values, that there has been a remarkable change in child-rearing values in the last half-century, with training for *independence* and *tolerance* increasing strikingly, and training for *strict obedience* and *loyalty to the church* having a notable decline. None of these studies divided the data into SES percentages, so we are unable to report extent of value shifts by each of the two SES categories outrightly, and must infer. But there is no doubt that the greater part of the shift has been in the working-class for as we have just seen, middle-class parents already valued independence. Alwin (1987) suggests three possible explanations for the shift. First, changes in the structure of the American family might encourage greater autonomy within families, especially for women and children, with all family members, including children, encouraged to make decisions for themselves. Second, it is likely that this trend away from preferring obedience is related to the expanding importance of education in our society. Today's parents not only have more schooling than their parents, they may also see further educational attainment as necessary to their children's ability to succeed in an increasingly technological and complex world. The more education people have, the more likely they are to value autonomy rather than conformity in children. Third, the changing characteristics of one or more subgroups of the society may account for a significant part of a social trend such as this. A pertinent example is the Catholic subgroup, which as a late-arriving immigrant group moved into the working class of Eastern industrial cities, lived the working-class values, and continued traditional obedience to the Church's teachings. But studies of Detroit Catholics have shown a trend away from obedience to institution and family authority and toward increasing independence for family members. "These changes are perhaps best understood in terms of changes in the American Catholic church and the gradual assimilation of Euro-Catholic ethnic groups into American society." (p. 4)

Though class boundaries are indistinct there are a number of sub-cultures in the U. S. today, a consequence of open immigration laws and the arrival of enough immigrants from certain countries to form ongoing communities. Good examples are the Vietnamese and Mexican communities. Each group brings its own customs and values from the native country and continues them here. But they tend not to persist for more than one generation because assimilation to the general American culture is so rapid. The Vietnamese are inheritors of the ancient Chinese Confucian ethic which idealizes loyalty and obligation to family, clan, superiors, and other human relationships. As one woman put it, "We were taught to love our parents more than life itself. Parents were more important than the man or woman you loved." This ethic stands in sharp contrast to the American ethic of individualism which values individual freedom to do what is best for self and make decisions without seeking advice or approval of others. One is free to act solely in self-interest short of injury to others or violation of law. The Vietnamese is enmeshed in a network of human relationships and seeks approval of family and others before acting. He may experience desires for personal goals but always there is the sense of the greater good of family or group and were he to act solely in self-interest would suffer ostracism from all sides.

Society-Wide Valued Activities

These are activities that are valued by virtually everyone in the entire society. Every society has its valued activities. Nearly all members share the value, so the value itself usually is implicit or taken for granted. Everyone is motivated to perform the given activity, they reciprocally reward each other for effectiveness in the activity, and thus keep the value and the motivation going year after year, often generation after generation. Here is a single example, taken from a recent anthropological report on the people of Tonga, a Polynesian island culture in the South Pacific (Marcus, 1978). Note that excellence in such ordinary activities as dancing, fishing, talking, farming, and athletics are valued and hence a source of motivation and reward:

> The following are common activities or objects of value in Tonga, which constitute the substance of rivalry for higher relative social status between individuals or between groups: the demonstration of a superior social skill that is both conventional and culturally valued such as dancing, fishing, talking, farming, athletics, and managing social relationships in the form of exchanges of goods and services; the distinctive performance of conventional obligations and responsibilities such as generosity in hosting, sponsoring feasts, and giving, on occasion, tributes to church and the kingship, where quantity is a marker and validation of relative social status among givers; the acquisition of valuable objects or resources such as land, church or government office, a noble title, a European-style house, more recently a car, or the accomplishment of a significant act such as marriage with a high-status woman or gaining overseas university degrees, where the means of acquisition or accomplishment have been indirect, secret, and obscure to public view, while the results are manifested as a coup, revelation, or surprise. (p. 243)

Dramatic examples of society-wide values are to be found in the anthropological literature because whole peoples over centuries may evolve strikingly different ways to live. One may value warrior exploits of bravery and daring, even to the extreme of the warrior's anticipating losing his life in battle while still young and vigorous (so that in death his skull can be put on display and all can see that the teeth are still white and complete). Another may value the opposite, peaceableness and cooperation. One may idealize (value) a meek, self-effacing, subservient sort of woman, another a woman who is self-assertive and aggressive and ready to fight back in the frequent marital quarrels, and even though she usually gets the worst of it in the battles, she is self-satisfied and respected by the husband for her spunkiness.

Simply because it is difficult for the members of the given society to recognize their own culture-wide values, because of being so immersed in them, like a fish immersed in water and unaware of the water, it is difficult for us to recognize some of our own values (but those that have been singled out and frequently restated will of course be exceptions, such as our idealization of *democracy*). One likely possibility is *self-reliance*. Hsu (1961), who grew up in china and therefore has an outsider's objective perspective, has argued forcefully that self-reliance is the most fundamental of American values. As he says, "The American core value in question is *self-reliance*, the most persistent psychological expression of which is fear of dependence. Self-reliance . . . has been inseparable in America from the individual's militant insistence on economic, social, and political equality. American self-reliance is a militant ideal which parents inculcate in their children and by which they judge the worth of any and all mankind." (p. 217) Likely the reader will find no reason to disagree, but our point is that he may be noting the possibility for the first time, because of the immersion. Be that as it may, the concept was presented in a "ways to live" questionnaire to American (and Indian and Japanese) college students (Kilby, 1971). About half of them, of both sexes, gave it strong acceptance (rated it either "very" or "quite" valued) but placing it well below several other ways to live (openness to change, self-development, friendship and affection, and solving of [national] problems) in a set of twenty values. So though it fell clearly among the half-dozen most valued, it did not have the *experienced* importance that Hsu says it in fact has among us. If he is right in his reasoning that it is so fundamental (and he may be in error), then it would qualify as a example of a value not fully recognized by us.

Universal Values?

Both philosophers and social scientists long have wondered whether certain values are held in common by all peoples. The very shared quality of being human suggests it and one at once thinks of such basics of existence as food and water, safety from danger, protection from heat and cold and avoidance of disease and death as being valued by all. Also, as was suggested at beginning of the chapter, certain types of moral values tend to occur almost universally because of their resulting from near-universal community problems. But perhaps all of these have been so basic as to have been taken for granted and the question has been as to the universality of less obvious values, more "of the mind" or "of the spirit."

An excellent example of the possibility of a certain sort of universal value has been the theoretical formulation of Florence Kluckhohn. Kluckhohn (Kluckhohn and Strodtbeck, 1961) postulated that certain questions or problems for which some solution must be found arise among peoples the world over. She identified five such universal questions: (1) What is the character of innate human nature? (2) What is the relation of men to nature (and supernature)? (3) What is the temporal (time) focus of human life? (4) What is the modality of human activity? (5) What is the modality of man's relationship to other men?

The answers or solutions are what Kluckhohn has termed "value orientations." This is a somewhat different concept from "value," which may be defined as a conception of the desirable. The value orientation involves the desirable plus beliefs about the object and is intended to recognize the combined, inseparable operation of belief and value, of "is" and "ought." Clyde Kluckhohn has written, "Since value elements and existential premises [beliefs] are almost inextricably blended in the overall picture of experience that characterizes an individual or a group, it seems well to call this overall view a value orientation . . . ." (1951, p. 411)

F. Kluckhohn has further reasoned that the number of answers or solutions to the questions that people discover is not unlimited, but rather falls within a limited range of possibilities. As may be seen in the chart below, the range is only three possibilities for four of the five questions, with only the "human nature" question having more. Specifically, the *human nature* question yields answers of either evil (man innately evil), mixture of good and evil, neutral (neither good nor evil by nature), or good, with each further subdivided as to whether changeable or unchangeable. For example, the traditional Judeo-Christian answer has been evil but perfectible. Because she has included in "nature" both the natural world and supernatural forces, the *man-nature* question yields answers of either subjugation to nature (man the victim or pawn of nature or gods), harmony with nature, or

Orientation	Postulated Range Of Variations					
human nature	Evil		Neutral	Mixture of Good-and-Evil	Good	
	mutable	immutable	mutable	immutable	mutable	immutable
man-nature	Subjugation-to-Nature		Harmony-with-Nature		Mastery-over-Nature	
time	Past		Present		Future	
activity	Being		Being-in-Becoming		Doing	
relational	Lineality		Collaterality		Individualism	

mastery over nature (man capable of coping with and overcoming the forces of nature). The *time* question yields answers favoring either the past (life focused toward the past), present (living in a timeless present with little concern about past or future), or future (things will be better or goals will be realized in the future). The *activity* question yields answers of either being (spontaneous expression of what is assumed to be "given" in the human personality), being-in-becoming (activity toward realization of potential -- self-realization), or doing (activity resulting in accomplishment, usually of an externally measurable sort -- "getting things done"). The *relational* question produces answers of either individualism (individual goals have primacy over group goals), collaterality (welfare of the present group has primacy), or lineality (group goals plus continuity of the group itself have primacy). Going back to the definition of value orientations, note that these answers involve primarily a system of beliefs about the way things are, but also conceptions as to the way things should be, the way people should live. Relative to assessment, an implication of the listing is that since the number of answers is not large, means can be found of learning the answers of peoples around the world.

Kluckhohn's final assumption is that all alternatives of all solutions are present in all societies, but are differentially preferred. That is, rather than a single answer being found among a given people, all possible answers are represented in the outlooks of different individuals and subgroups (ethnic, religious, occupational, regional, class, etc.) of the society. But they have different strengths of preference. Beyond wishing to recognize the fact of variability itself, she wishes to clarify the relation between *dominant* and *variant* value orientations. The variant orientations are not just "loose ends" or the outlook of the odd and deviant. Rather, the value orientations of a culture form an interlocking network of dominant (most preferred) and variant orientations, with the variants either permitted or required by the complexity of the social structure. Too, dominants and variants will be in constant slow evolution, as time passes and the society changes, with perhaps a variant of today becoming the dominant of tomorrow, again requiring that they be conceived of relatively and dynamically. The implication here for assessment is that a variety of values is to be expected in any group, and what is to be noted are percentages which indicate major values of the group, together with those indicating minor values having some strength of numbers.

This is a useful theory since it assumes that the universal aspect of value orientations lies not in specific orientations but in the questions or problems all humans must face and in the limited number of possible answers for each -- usually three. Too, since our natural tendency would be to assume that but one value orientation, one answer to each question, would have to be held by virtually all members of a given society in order to qualify as culture-wide, this tells us to expect variability, in the form of dominant and variant value orientations.

The above assumptions were employed by Kluckhohn and her research associates as the systematic basis of a study of the value orientations of five communities of the American Southwest but those findings will not be reported here.

CHAPTER 2

NATURE OF VALUES

Definitions of Values

"Value" is a widely used term with a number of meanings. As Charles Morris has commented, it is one of the Great Words of our language, its meanings multiple and complex. In addition to its varied and changing connotations in ordinary speech, it is a technical term in philosophy, economics, mathematics, phonetics, music, art, and the three behavioral sciences -- anthropology, sociology, and psychology. Within certain of these fields there are competing definitions, notably in economics, philosophy, and the behavioral sciences. Obviously we must define it if we are to use it.

All of the technical meanings except those of the behavioral sciences may be ignored here. So let it be understood that everything said in these pages is limited to values as held by persons and groups of persons. Even when so limited there is possibility of much confusion. Williams (1979) begins his chapter by stating, "The term 'value' has been used variously to refer to interests, pleasures, likes, preferences, duties, moral obligations, desires, wants, goals, needs, aversions and attractions, and many other kinds of selective orientations." (p. 10) Numerous books have been written on the subject but often the reader comes away more confused than enlightened because the author has not defined his terms and has used the concept so loosely and broadly that his meaning cannot even be inferred. Generally speaking, values may be defined so broadly that any object wanted by the person is a value (is valued). Or, they may be defined narrowly as to include only judgmental, evaluative dispositions.

Dictionary meanings tend to stress the worth or desirability of something to the person. Thus, American Heritage Dictionary gives "a principle, standard, or quality considered worthwhile or desirable." And Webster's New Collegiate, "The quality or fact of being excellent, useful, or desirable; worth in a thing." "To rate in usefulness, excellence, etc.; to place in a scale of values; as, to value honor above riches."

In an excellent, thorough chapter on values, Kluckhohn (1951), offers this widely-quoted definition:

> A value is a conception, explicit or implicit, distinctive of an individual or characteristic of a group, of the desirable which influences the selection from available modes, means, and ends of action. (p. 395)

Or, reduced to essentials, values are "conceptions of the desirable." That is, values are beliefs as to what is good, best, and right, and their opposites -- bad, worst, and wrong.

"Desirable" is the key word and Kluckhohn chooses to give it a limited evaluative meaning. The following nicely states his view, "Value, conveniently and in accordance with received usage, places things, acts, ways of behaving, goals of action on the approval-disapproval continuum." (p. 395) In other words, if consciously experienced, a value is a felt sense of what is best (or worst), of how things ought (or ought not) to be, of what is right and good (or wrong and bad). Kluckhohn, in agreement with John Dewey and others, contrasts "the desirable" with "the desired." The desired may be free of feelings of better or worse -- may even be at odds with what is felt to be right -- whereas the desirable implies that a judgement, a valuation has been made. Kluckhohn says the cue words are "right" and "wrong," "better" or "worse," (though he might as well have included "should" and "ought," and their opposites, so commonly are they used to express sense of right and wrong). Going further, Kluckhohn says in effect that the desirable has an aura of rightness about it -- "a value is felt and/or considered to be justified . . . ."(p. 396) "The desirable is what is felt or thought proper to want. It is what an actor [person] or group of actors desire -- and believe they "ought" or "should" desire . . . . ."(p. 396) However, he cautions that "desirable" should not be interpreted too narrowly, for it is not restricted to what is commonly designated as the "moral" (conscience). Here are several examples of such values, as held by one or another person: unconventionality is good; self-expression is better than high income; one should be cooperative (non-individualistic); self-indulgence is wrong; one should live this life to the fullest; industriousness is right and good.

Smith (1964) also reviewed the subject and, in agreement with Kluckhohn, also defined as "conceptions of the desirable."

While not offering an outright definition, Scheibe's usage implies that the different forms of motivation are values or create values, when he writes that value judgments suggest the operation of wishes, desires, goals, passions, valences, or morals (1970, p. 41-42). And throughout the book "motive" and "value" are essentially synonymous. As an example, he mentions that value lists are of two types, internal (personal) and external (ecological), with lists of *motives* being examples of the internal type (p. 47).

Scheibe's definition is rather typical of that of a number of writers, especially writers with philosophy backgrounds. These writers seem to have been impressed with the obvious role of the different sorts of motives in human affairs so reasoned that the "needing" or "wanting" of a motive -- its essence -- automatically creates valuing.

von Mering's title, *A Grammar of Values* (1961), might suggest that the book is a comprehensive listing of types of values. It is useful, does present some value types, and has ample exemplification from interviews with residents of several Southwestern communities to make the types concrete; but it is another source that could prove confusing. The dispositions being studied are termed "value orientations," and are assumed to be functional fusions of belief and value -- that is, inseparable combinations of what one experiences as fact or reality (what "is") and what ought to be. This is a reasonable approach since values often have ideational content -- what one experiences as the reason or justification for the value -- and the two are inseparable. But so much of the presentation and the quoted interview material is over on the belief side, with no accompanying valuing, that the reader may begin to wonder, is this what is meant by "value"? (The "value orientation" is a useful concept and surely more researchers should be investigating the belief content -- the personal "why I feel this way" -- of values, as this is an important part of the disposition.)

Since psychology traditionally has employed the concept "attitudes" rather than "values" the latter is not well known among psychologists and, for many, values are what the values questionnaires cover, two of them especially. The oldest, the *Study of Values*, which was based upon a theory of six broad orientations toward the world, was prepared at a time when hardly anyone knew anything about values and for a quarter of a century we just assumed that these were what was meant by values. Later the Rokeach *Values Survey* (1967) was published, became even better known, and has been widely used. It was a great improvement in that it posed two sets of values of eighteen each, expanding horizons to at least 36 values. But Rokeach contributed to the continuing narrowness by limiting his definition of values to modes of conduct (instrumental values) and end-states of existence (terminal values). He assumed the number of values to be relatively small; specifically, he estimated that the total number of terminal values of a grown person to be about a dozen and a half, and the total of instrumental values to be several times that number, perhaps five or six dozen (p. 11). For persons unfamiliar with the extent of values, it was natural to assume that the eighteen of each type in the questionnaire were the extent of values.

Williams (1968, 1979, p. 16) defines values as "criteria or standards of preference." This says no more than that the person is led to prefer one kind of object rather than another. (Though he does not enumerate objects, surely the term should be used broadly to name whatever can be preferred to something else, such as physical things, persons, colors, emotions, self-concepts, thoughts, symbols, and forms of physical activity.) He does state that, explicitly or implicitly, persons are continually regarding things as good or bad, pleasant or unpleasant, beautiful or ugly, appropriate or inappropriate, true or false, virtues or vices. This is a broader definition than that of Kluckhohn because of its inclusion of the pleasant-unpleasant and beautiful-ugly.

While these several conceptions by no means cover all to be found in the literature, they do suffice to exemplify the diversity of definition, and it is understandable why the uninitiated may become confused as to the nature of values.

But values are so important a human disposition that they demand the clearest possible conception as to their nature and extent and sharp differentiation from other dispositions.

There is much in favor of limiting values to evaluative dispositions, as in the Kluckhohn definition, for it identifies the major form of valuing and clearly demarcates it from other dispositions. But it appears to be too narrow for use in understanding and describing all the valuing of individuals (as opposed to the possibly less-detailed need of the anthropologist). At the cost of a notable loss of clarity of conception, it is proposed that in addition to those beliefs as to the right and best, should and must (evaluative values), also included are beliefs as to the worthy, significant, and important (worth values), beliefs which may be relatively free of feelings of right or best, should or must. This addition is consistent with dictionary meanings of the term. Here are examples which may make this form of valuing clear:

I may personally and intensely value things aesthetic, perhaps to the point of feeling that forms of harmony and beauty supply the whole point of existence for me, yet never have a feeling that this ought to be the way of things for everyone or otherwise label it as "best" or "right," and certainly have no feeling that I *should* be aesthetic. The very value itself arises not from a judgement of desirability but from the implicit worth of the activity. That is, because aesthetic experiences give me joy and satisfaction I find the aesthetic life to be inherently meaningful, rewarding, and fulfilling -- hence implicitly worthy. Of course I approve of it and feel very favorable, so it is a personal "good," though not a moral one. Comparable examples would be a person's valuing rich human association and friendships, a life of the spirit, or a life of the intellect.

I may value given forms of life work, let us say teaching or biological research, feeling them to be worthy ways of spending a life and evoking my full dedication, again without a sense of "should" or "best."

I may value certain things because I feel them to be important to me, and perhaps to others as well, such things as, for example, enlightenment (as in

Buddhism), sex-appeal, an assured supply of food and necessities, a hi-fi set. But again I do not label them right or best.

I may value an institution or organization, such as a university or public interest group, because I feel its activities are meritorious.

I may value forms of conduct in others (a sense of humor, say) and subjectively classify it as admirable, but not feel that one should or ought to be that way.

I may value certain persons, perhaps my child or my wife or a friend, without any sense that I should or that it is good or best to do so. They just have intrinsic worth for me. I value my own life and well-being without feeling it right or that I should. I may value human and animal life generally without feeling that I should, though here surely the more usual case is to value human life because it is a moral "must" and to be indifferent toward animal life.

It may be noted throughout these examples that the inner something which gives the object its value is a sense of its importance, meaningfulness, admirableness, or esteemability -- its worth to me generally.

Even where worth is the sole basis of the value, these values move very close to the evaluative because the sense of the worth of the given thing, with its implicit approval, results in a subjective label of "good," and this "good" easily gets converted into a generalized "good" and into feelings of "right," "better," and "best." Also there is a selectivity, for only certain things have worth, so in a non-judgmental, preferential sense some things are better than others.

The two types may also be difficult to separate as to origin. In several of the examples it was suggested that the worth was implicit. In others some underlying value might have been supplying the experienced worth, perhaps that of service to fellowman, advancement of knowledge, pleasure, or security. This might be based on worth or on an earlier-acquired evaluation ("one *should* behave this way"), or a combination of the two.

So while there appears to be merit in recognizing the two classes of value, evaluative and worth, because of their different nature and origins, it would be a mistake to keep them separate, for they do interblend. Rather, they might be pictured on some sort of continuum as this:

Moral Imperatives	"Right" with "Should"	"Right" or "Best"	"Right" and Worthy	High Worth	Lower Worth
	Evaluative Values			Worth Values	

On the far left might be placed the moral values with their powerful connotation of "right" and imperativeness. Next would come the values described by Kluckhohn as having in effect an aura of rightness. Next would come the broad array of dispositions that one experienced as right, best, true, or good. Following would come those dispositions that combine elements of "evaluation good" with "worth good." Then would come the broad array of worth values, varying from those experienced as of great importance to those of minor importance.

Let us use here, then, the definition that values are conceptions of the desirable or the worthwhile (and their opposites). This will include that which is subjectively felt to be worthy, important, better or best, good, or right (and their opposites). (As a shorthand, we can continue to refer to the whole as "conceptions of the desirable," since "desirable" has both the evaluative and worthy meaning.)

Clarification of "Conceptions"

We have just defined values as "conceptions" but this does not mean that they are always clearly represented in consciousness. Rather, they vary from clear representation, through degrees of generalness and vagueness, to not being consciously-articulated at all.

But whatever the degree of clarity, a genuine concept-formation process appears to have been necessary, for the object has to be symbolized to self in some way. There must be a subjective meaning, a concept, for such things as, say, "industriousness," "security," or "pleasure" if these are to be given value. Possible synonyms for "concept" are "belief," "disposition," "construct," "felt sense," and the just-used "subjective meaning"; together these should serve to describe what we have in mind.

Value concepts tend to be generalized, in the sense that valuing of food and negative valuing of hunger are general concepts, the general class of edible objects having been concepted as a result of specific hunger and food experiences. This general concept-formation process will occur even if poorly symbolized; there can still be a "felt sense" of the thing. Note especially that virtually all the value concepts that appear in our assessment devices and in learned-discussions are generalizations -- examples: clean, honest, self-actualizing, communistic, self-esteem, anarchistic. The generalizing tendency recognized, not all value-concepts are general. Perhaps the perfect example out of history is the specific category of food, salt. Its value became so formalized in many parts of the world that often it was used as money. Another example would be a valuing of the love of a specific person rather than love in general.

Values tend to "abide," rather than to be "of the moment." They are relatively enduring dispositions. They do evolve and change, but typically not suddenly. However, some may be of short duration, arising because of a specific momentary structuring of the life situation, and subsiding when the situation changes. Perhaps our best fictitious example is the desperate words of King Richard, in Shakespeare's Richard III, cried out as he stands unhorsed on the battlefield, "A horse, a horse, my kingdom for a horse!" (If the reader will excuse analysis of the statement, he is expressing both a desperate motive to regain a mount, and in his "my kingdom for a horse" expressing its value.) Certainly real life gives us comparable examples, especially when health or life seem threatened and suddenly well-being and life itself become very precious.

Universal group values raise a special question as to whether all values involve concept formation. These are values which are so widely accepted by the members of the group -- and the group invariably is an entire society -- as to be virtually universal. Such values ordinarily have existed in the society since time immemorial, hence a person born into the group grows up in a value milieu that is as omnipresent as the air he breathes. The values are absorbed unconsciously in the growing-up process and are lived throughout a lifetime without awareness that they are values. And of course everyone's behavior is patterned by the values. Examples of such values abound in the anthropological literature for such values are among the most evident things about a society to the visiting anthropologist, and are the basis for defining culture as being composed of values in large part. Examples would be the valuing of the warrior life by the Sioux Indians of the American Great Plains; the valuing of a total pattern of life characterized by mildness and peacefulness, self-control, and cooperativeness by the mesa-dwelling Pueblo Indians of the American Southwest; the valuing of much human interaction -- sociability -- by the Mountain Arapesh of New Guinea; and the valuing of family continuity, respect for elder, and reverence for ancestors in old China.

The question, then, is, if people are activated by values of which they are unaware, where is the "*conception* of the desirable"? Two things may be said in reply. The first is that, as we have already said, concepts may be present even though not symbolized and even in these dramatic instances of blithe unawareness this still might be the case. Kluckhohn favors this explanation as he poses the question "can a *conception be implicit?*" and answers that some of the deepest and most pervasive of personal and cultural values are only partially or occasionally verbalized, that an implicit value is almost always potentially expressible, especially when put into words by an observer and then agreed to (or rejected) by the person, and that verbalizability is a necessary test of value.

While agreeing of course that values can be implicit, I am inclined to favor another rather simple explanation in this case. It is that the person becomes involved in a network of more specific attitudes, goals, human interactions, and rewards which result in a living of the value without an articulation of it. That is, though the Sioux warrior might be unable to put into words that he valued a warrior life, he would be expected by everyone from childhood to prepare to be a warrior, as a young man he would desire to raid enemy camps to steal horses and if necessary fight with defenders, he would admire older men who had attained fame as warriors, and he himself would sit at the campfire after successful raids and with the approval and admiration of others "count coup" -- recount his warrior exploits. The value obviously is implicit throughout. No concept, as such, is needed. In comparable manner the Pueblo child would learn by example and teaching specific acts of peacefulness and self-control; later in daily adult interaction he would be expected to behave according to the group norms (which embody the values) and would face censure if he deviated.

Relation of Values to Other Dispositions

Attitudes. Values and attitudes are so closely related that it may be asked whether there is a need for both concepts. Anthropologists have always used "value," but psychologists, beginning in the 1930s, used "attitude" and have so continued up to the present, with "value" coming into use only in recent years.

Attitudes are enduring dispositions that involve a concept (belief, meaning) of the object, have a "for" or "against" quality (have valuation implicit), involve some amount of feeling-emotion (are not cold beliefs), and motivate and produce an action tendency -- as, to vote a given way. They vary from person to person in how clear the concept is and how strong the feeling (sometimes being more feeling than meaning), and may have little or much motivational power with little or much action resulting.

Much the same characteristics describe values.

By convention "attitudes" name dispositions held toward specific things, such as a political party or candidate, a current fashion, a specific job, or a specific group. "Values," in contrast, name dispositions held toward general things, so might be held toward socialism or other general political ideology, or toward standards of dress rather than a specific clothing style. The more general an attitude the more it becomes a value; the more specific the value the more like an attitude.

The one key distinction and justification for two concepts rather than one is that many attitudes will be based on underlying values. For example, many people developed attitudes against building nuclear-energy plants when they learned of the dangers involved in disposal of the atomic wastes. On the face of it the attitude may seem self-contained, with no value involved. But when we ask why danger was the determining factor in adopting the attitude we realize that one of the most obvious and basic of values is involved, that of valuing of human life. This supplying of basic assumptions as to the desirable is a fundamental role of values, and we need a clear conceptual means of recognizing these foundations of our judgments and attitudes.

However, it would be a great mistake to assume that values are at work every time a person expresses an attitude. Rather, many attitudes are borrowed ready-made from others with no ideational or value foundation. Also, some attitudes are the result of such needs and psychodynamic processes as hostility, anxiety, and ego-defense.

While social psychologists have tended not to stress the difference between attitudes and values, a notable exception has been Rokeach, perhaps the most active of all social scientists in doing research on both dispositions. His thinking is presented in several places (1968, 1973, 1979(a), 1979(b)), with a concise statement in the last of these. His main points are that the conceptual difference between the two is conveyed when we say that humans have thousands of attitudes but only dozens of values, that values are deeper as well as broader than attitudes, that values are standards of "oughts" and "shoulds" whereas attitudes are not, that values are determinants rather than components of attitudes, that values transcend objects and situations, that philosophers, theologians, anthropologists, sociologists, historians, and therapists think it more important to understand people's values than their attitudes, that moral dilemmas involve questions of value, that inter-group and intrapsychic conflict involves questions of value conflict rather than attitude conflict, and that different social institutions specialize in inculcating and transmitting different subsets of values rather than attitudes (p. 272). Rokeach is telling us that if we wish to stress the difference between the two there is plenty of justification for doing so.

At the point of doing attitude-value research usually it is not possible to separate the two dispositions nor is there a need to do so, and ordinarily it makes little difference which term is used -- if specific objects are involved likely it should be "attitude," if general then "value." (The obvious exception would be studies that attempt to discover values that underlie specific attitudes.)

Again, because of this similarity, results of pertinent studies on either topic have been used in this book. Psychologists have accumulated a considerable body of information on attitudes that is not duplicated on values; its use fills some of the gaps.

Motivation. The one mean problem created by broadening the definition of values to include the worth values has to do with motivation. In brief, some motives (needs, desires, drives) create valuation of the needed or desired objects, hence values. But should all motives, just because of their "wanting" quality be considered to be values (valuings)? If so, then we have two duplicating concepts, inevitable confusion, and a danger of stretching the value concept so thin as to greatly reduce its meaning and usefulness. At times we might even find ourselves saying that a given person values (wants) something that he disvalues.

It is especially because of the interaction of strong motives and the moral values that the distinction must be maintained, for otherwise we would find ourselves denying or distorting one of the most real conflicts of human existence. Classic examples are the valuing of honesty while experiencing the powerful motive for money and possessions; valuing of sexual propriety and loyalty to mate while experiencing sexual lust; valuing restraint in eating and drinking while hungering for more food; valuing ego-restraint while impulsively boasting and self-aggrandizing. Not only are these motives not valued, often they are disvalued and a source of self-dissatisfaction and guilt.

There is considerable discussion in the literature on the relation of motivation to value. Kluckhohn (1951, p. 424) comments that if one approaches the explanation of behavior in a psychological framework, it is easy to confuse value with motivation. David Aberle, in an unpublished memorandum to Kluckhohn (p. 424) comments in part:

> Whatever we mean by a value, the area of values is apparently difficult to circumscribe. The examples ordinarily used have a tendency to fall into one or another area that is already being successfully exploited under some other head. Descriptions of the values of an individual shade off into, or are readily absorbed by, such notions as motivations, conscious and unconscious; goals, goal-orientations; meanings, and the like.

Some writers, such as Scheibe above, have assumed that motivation is the source of value, that what is desired automatically is valued. Others, notably Kluckhohn, have reasoned to the contrary that "the desired" is to be differentiated from "the desirable." Of course much of the disagreement turns on differing conceptions or definitions of values, with writers such as Kluckhohn defining values solely as evaluative dispositions, hence necessarily excluding "the desired."

It appears possible to differentiate value and motive and to limit the extent of valuing in motives by granting that all motivation involves valuing, but only a portion of it produces conceptions of the desirable, the form of valuing with which we are concerned here. That is, all forms of motivation produce at least implicit valuing, but only a portion of it produces conceived (experienced) values. The distinction may be elaborated as follows:

(a) All significant forms of motivation produce at least implicit valuing, automatically.

Table 1 (taken from Krech, Crutchfield, and Livson, 1974, p. 459) presents a listing of some of the principal human motives and a perusal of it will give us examples of specific motives (though necessarily these are general relative to the more-specific motives of actual persons). All motives on the page may be assumed to create implicit value in their objects, the needing-wanting of the motive supplying the value, with no necessity for a felt sense of importance. Because implicit, the valuing itself will be unconscious and in a real experiential sense there will not be any valuing. That is, the needing-wanting will be experienced but no additional sense of valuing. Since the objects of these forms of motivation do not attain the status of experienced conceptions of the desirable, they do not qualify as values in the sense that we are using the construct here, and may be eliminated from further consideration, and the total of motives also qualifying as value sources thus significantly reduce.

TABLE 1

THE HUMAN MOTIVES

Listed in this table are some of the principle human motives, classified under the general aims of survival and security (deficiency motives) and satisfaction and stimulation (abundancy motives). Under these general headings the motives are further classified according to whether they mainly pertain to the body, to relations with the environment, to relations with other people, or to the self.

	Survival and Security (deficiency motives)	Satisfaction and Stimulation (abundancy motives)
Pertaining to the body	Avoiding of hunger, thirst, oxygen lack, excess heat and cold, pain, overfull bladder and colon, fatigue, overtense muscles, illness and other disagreeable bodily states,etc.	Attaining pleasurable sensory experiences of tastes, smells, sounds, etc.; sexual pleasure; bodily comfort; exercise of muscles, rhythmical body movements, etc.
Pertaining to relations with environment	Avoiding of dangerous objects and horrible, ugly, and disgusting objects; seeking objects necessary to future survival and security; maintaining a stable, clear, certain environment, etc.	Attaining enjoyable possessions; constructing and inventing objects; understanding the environment; solving problems; playing games, seeking environmental novelty and change, etc.
Pertaining to relations with other people	Avoiding interpersonal conflict and hostility; maintaining group membership, prestige and status; being taken care of by others; conforming to group standards and values; gaining power and dominance over others, etc.	Attaining love and positive identifications with people and groups; enjoying other people's company; helping and understanding other people; being independent, etc.
Pertaining to the self	Avoiding feelings of inferiority and failure in comparing the self with others or with the ideal self; avoiding loss of identity; avoiding feelings of shame, guilt, fear, anxiety, sadness, etc.	Attaining feelings of self-respect and self-confidence; expressing oneself; feeling sense of achievement; feeling challenged; establishing moral and other values; discovering meaningful place of self in the universe.

Source: Krech, Crutchfield, and Livson, 1974, p. 459.

(b) Some motivated behavior results in conceived values.

Any motive in Table 1 may now be considered relative to the question, is this motive likely to produce implicit value solely, or be consciously felt (conceptualized) as well? Of course, our answers will be purely speculative, yet the exercise of going through the whole may prove insightful. Take motivation to "avoid interpersonal conflict and hostility" (third group down under "Survival and Security"). Avoidance of interpersonal tension and conflict is important for most of us and we are led spontaneously to do various things in daily human interactions to maintain smooth relationships; so at least it has implicit worth or value. But is it likely ever to be more than this -- a felt value? If one *feels* that smooth relationships are desirable (and/or conflict undesirable) then we have an example of a *conceived* value. Further, with this motivation it would not be unusual for a person to feel that interpersonal conflict is *wrong* or *bad*, which gives us an *evaluative* value.

Quite many of the listed motives lead me to speculate that *usually* they will produce only implicit value, with perhaps "avoiding over-full bladder and colon" the most obvious possibility. Yet any one of us might be led by circumstance (a dearth of toilets) or bodily condition to put high on a list of personal values "freedom from over-full bladder or colon" and most certainly approve providing of toilet facilities everywhere. In general, most or all of the motives on the page could produce conceived values, given the right circumstances.

This possibility of a conversion from implicit value to conscious may be explored a bit further. When motives create conceived values it is the specific quality of the experiencing that creates the value. That is, it is not the motive outrightly that does it, but what happens in the process of carrying out the motive. To take a simple example, let a person become hungry (as though for the first time) and be led to start imaging food and means of getting it and engaging in actual food-seeking activities. Let us suppose that the food is found and consumed without delay. The whole sequence is completed without conscious valuing arising. But now let us assume that food is not immediately obtained. Now with the passing of time the experience of hunger becomes stronger and food acquires increased worth; as a result of some number of experiences of being somewhat hungry the person could be expected to form a general concept of the value of food. The implication of the example is that persons who have been hungry with some frequency will value having an adequate supply of food, whereas persons who have never been really hungry will give it little value. Additional examples might be these: First, a person with low self-esteem would be motivated by these feelings to seek recognition and admiration, but since these needs tend to be insatiable, would experience a lack of recognition and might, in interview or on questionnaire, assign esteem high value, whereas a person who is high in self-esteem would have any esteem needs so readily met as to have no occasion to come to value esteem or those human interactions that are ego-protecting and self-enhancing. Second, a young person who has grown up in a period when the country has been free of war and threat of war may place low value on world peace and national security because his safety needs have been so easily met, whereas people who have experienced war and its attendant fears may give peace and security high value. Research evidence of a comparable sort was Rokeach's (1970) finding that poor people give "clean," among other goals, a much higher relative ranking than do well-off people. Rokeach's interpretation was that the poor value it higher because they have had less cleanliness in their lives.

An example of special interest here is the hunger for water (thirst), perhaps the most important of all life-maintaining needs. Yet because it is so essential, ordinarily households and communities make arrangements to have water always available, with the consequence that one could go through life always having his water need met (just temporarily feeling thirsty) and never form a conception of the desirability of water!

Our example of the person coming to value food happens to represent the ideal case of motive producing value, for we may assume that he has acquired a general valuing of food (a concept of its value), even though his hunger drive will wax and wane depending on recency of ingestion of food. Thus the example gives us a clear separation of the two phenomena, motive and value. It is this *abiding* of value, no matter what the momentary motivation, that is the hallmark, the proof as it were, of value here. We would expect it to continue (more or less available to awareness) even if the person went for long periods without becoming really hungry. But where the motive itself is general and continuous (though not necessarily in the forefront of attention all of the time), then motive and value seem indistinguishable. A possible example would be the person's hungering for attention and admiration, which is present continuously, and is at once an insecurity-caused motive and an important (valued) goal.

It is to be hoped that by some such analysis as this the relation between the two phenomena, motive and value, can be clarified and the category of motive-caused values strictly circumscribed. But even when so circumscribed, the number of motive-caused values still will be relatively large.

(Though employing somewhat different reasoning from ours, Rokeach (1973, p. 20) has argued that there is a difference between motive and value. "Values are the cognitive representation and transformation of needs . . . ." That is, it is not the needs as such that are values, but the needs as conceptualized. He does not elaborate on how the conceptualization takes place, but does add that once the needs become cognitively transformed into values they are capable of being defended, justified, advocated, and exhorted as personally and socially desirable. For example, needs for dependence or conformity may be cognitively transformed into values of obedience, loyalty, or respect for elders. Aggressive needs may be transformed into values of ambition, honor, family or national security. He is suggesting here the possibility of considerable alteration from the original need in process of conceptualization.)

Interests. Interests are positive dispositions toward given activities, vocational or avocational, such as fishing, teaching, rock-climbing, and physics.

Values relate to interests in two directions; first, interests may produce values; second, in the reverse direction, values may be the basis of interests.

Interests are a specific form of motivation, the feeling of interest, the involvement with the object or activity, being the motivation. As motivation, it creates implicit value, just as do other forms of motivation, as explained above -- simply put, interest-in is implicit valuing. Whether the interest will also become a conceived, a felt, value will depend upon the person's experiencing. My neighbor is interested in cycling and most certainly regards it as a personally valuable activity. I am interested in painting and also attach considerable conscious value to it.

Modern Maturity Magazine (vol. 31, #1, 1988) invited its readers, who are mainly older persons, to tell what they wanted in the way of second careers. A great variety of choices were given by those who responded; here are a few examples: helping people, lead an expedition to largely unexplored swamps of tropical Africa, city planning, use computers to teach preschool children to read and write, be a nurse's assistant, work with animals or people anywhere outdoors, improve care of nursing-home patients. All of these are expressions of interest, but should they also be called values? Of course the question would have to be answered for each person. In general, it is suggested that were we there observing each, we first wait until the person has tried the new activity, to see whether the interest was realistic and whether it continues, and then look for additional evidence of feeling of worthwhileness or importance or meaningfulness of the new activity before calling it a value.

The second form of relation is that of broad values creating specific interests. Interests can have several different causes, among them values. We have already suggested, as an example, how a value such as service to fellowman could underlie an interest in teaching. Probably most people wonder why anyone would be interested in so dangerous and arduous an activity as rock climbing. An ego-need to prove something could be the explanation, but a valuing of courage and endurance could also supply the explanation.

In general, values have a very important role in interests, particularly the vocational, and the subject deserves attention elsewhere in its own right.

Valuing

Values logically lead to the activity of valuing. Hence it would seem that values are the basis of all valuing. Not so! Every time we are called upon to make a choice an act of valuing takes place. If the choice is a major one and there is time to reflect then doubtlessly values are the basis of the choice, as in choosing jobs, or mates, political parties, religions, or life philosophies. But life is filled with day to day choices, many relatively unimportant or even trivial, such as whether to buy a blue or green garment, yet ordinarily there is at least a momentary valuing -- do I want this or that -- before choice. I suggest that this act of valuing be kept separate from values, that it not be assumed that values are the basis. The opinion comes from self-observation. I began with the assumption that values were involved in all such real choices, however minor, where one does indeed weigh this and that. But as I noted the great variety of choices that I was making I became aware that so many were merely a weighing of the immediate alternatives and did not involve my values.

Valuing the Values

A considerable part of the material on values seen in the press is actually a two-part thing, a valuing of the values. That is, the worth or merit of any given value is being judged relative to some valued end, usually the welfare of the group or society, or the person himself. For example, a person or group might value "doing your own thing" (engaging in self-expressive activities without concern for the approval of others). Now the question, as asked by anyone (columnist, social scientist, educator, public official, citizen) is, is doing your own thing good or bad relative to some standard of judgement (value)? The standard of judgement might be whether it is total-society harming or improving, or whether personal-growth promoting or stunting, or hurtful to others or enhancing, or even moral or immoral (it might be judged licentious).

At any time, somewhere, some values are under attack. It is to be expected, part of attacking whatever is contrary to some person's or group's convictions and values. A good example was the attack on "middle-class values" during the civil rights agitation of the late 1960s. Overnight middle-class values began to be blamed for continued racial discrimination and resistance to granting of civil rights to blacks, though the specific offending values never were identified. It came as a surprise because social scientists have always understood that middle-class persons generally, with their better educations, liberal values, and freedom from the frustration of day to day competition for jobs and income, were the most liberal portion of the population and in the forefront of change. Such in fact was the case here, too, but the advocates of rapid change were frustrated at the slowness and needed something to blame.

Though we are not concerned here with such evaluations, it is important to recognize what is happening, for this two-step valuing-the-value complicates our subject and can leave anyone confused or with a mistaken conception of the nature of values.

Object Values

Though our concern is with values held by persons and groups, there is another meaning and form of value that if not understood can cause confusion. Too, it deserves appreciation in its own right. Morris (1956, p. 11-12) has called this "object value" because the value is assumed to lie out there in objects, not inside persons, and enters lives only indirectly. The most obvious use of this meaning is by the economist in his description of the value of goods and services. For example, autos, houses, and clothes all have given monetary value and these values can be treated as objective facts with little regard for the wants and needs of possible users. Similarly, the workings of the entire economic system can be described with little mention of the consumer. But these values ultimately are connected to the wants and needs (values in broadest sense) of potential users and the value of the auto would drop to zero overnight if gasoline ceased to be available to power it.

Morris' concern was with object values of a less obvious sort and he made up a simple example to show the connection between personal and object value. Suppose a person who has diabetes seeks the advice of a dietician as to the appropriate diet for his ailment. He prefers (values) a certain diet, but the dietician tells him that this diet is not in fact the right one for his health and prescribes another as the right one (which has object value). That is, the healthy diet is valuable in the realistic or "true" sense, even if it is not valued by the person. Of course the dietician could be wrong in his understanding of the effects of given foods, so the "true" diet, with its object value, may not really be known.

The general implication of this concept is that various things or states of affairs have value for the person or group, whether this is appreciated or not, and with some frequency it will not be.

Let us just paraphrase Morris' example to bring out the broader implication of the concept. Let the setting now be ancient Athens and the interaction be between Plato and his friend and "patient" Crito. Crito is explaining that for a long time he had suffered from a "sickness of spirit," a sense of pointlessness and lack of meaning in life (comparable to the patient's diabetes), but had recently begun to go out socially and mix with people and attend dinners and life now had meaning, and he now valued a convivial life (comparable to the diet valued by the patient). "Dr." Plato (now in the dietician's role) tells him that his present valued way of life will not be adequate for long, the meaninglessness will return and only a life that strikes a balance between the three parts of his nature (mind, heart, and appetites) will really work, so he must combine in proper proportions intellectual activity, vigorous action (as by gymnastics), and socializing and other pleasures of body and senses. Here these three human qualities are the object values, for Plato is describing how people actually are, hence this is what Crito must do to live the true, real, or good life. But like the dietician, Plato could have been wrong about the true and real; at least for the last 2300 years thinkers have been proposing other formulations of the real or actual person.

Aristotle disagreed somewhat with his teacher, Plato, and reasoned that the real and true goal of life is happiness, but only a life of the mind brings true happiness. His reasoning was that the striking superiority of man over animal is his power of thought, and as the growth of this faculty has given him supremacy, so, its development will give him fulfillment and happiness (a nicely reasoned statement of object value, but, as with Plato, not necessarily true in fact).

Both of these examples point to a logical connection between values as the subjective sense of the right and desirable and the way things actually are. If we functioned in a perfectly logical way we should seek to know how things actually are -- the real or true -- and shape our values to reflect this reality. But as Plato's and Aristotle's differences exemplify, the real is not readily known, particularly that involving human welfare, and human values often have irrational origins. In another place Aristotle remarked that "it is the things which are valuable and pleasant to the good man that are really valuable and pleasant." Here he is telling us how the real is to be identified and the evidence, the proof, is the good man's experiences. But if the qualities of the good man are uncertain how is he to be known? Perhaps it is the manner of experiencing the valuable and pleasant that identifies the good man, a nice circularity! Maslow (1959) has written that as a result of study of self-actualizing (effectively functioning) persons we now know something of the human potential and can reflect this in our values.

Value consequence. Closely related to or but an aspect of object value is value consequence. Though our approach here is one of treating any personal value in a neutral, non-judgmental way, personal values do have consequences and reality itself renders judgements (reality is object value). So, in the above example of doing your own thing (quite apart from valuing-the-value), the consequence of everyone doing his own thing might be a sort of social anarchy, with one inconveniencing, irritating and hurting others, and in the end no one able to fully express himself.

Another example, this one of grave import with far-reaching consequences is our valuing life and physical well-being. When someone falls ill we hope that doctors can save his life and restore him to health. When someone is injured we hope his pain can be reduced promptly and his body fully repaired. We are depressed when we learn of someone's dying of an incurable disease and approve of the spending of millions to try to find a cure. We welcome each new scientific advance that promises to reduce disease and prolong life. Thousands of persons are involved in medical research and billions of dollars spent annually on health delivery services. Consequence of all this effort is that many more children today are spared the formerly fatal childhood diseases and reach adulthood in good health, fewer women die of childbirth complications, fewer soldiers die of battle wounds, fewer people die of infectious diseases that formerly ravaged whole populations, fewer workmen are lost to fatal injuries, and more and more old people live longer as their ailments are brought under control. Such is the consequence of our valuing life and physical well-being.

But another consequence is an ever-increasing population, both nationally and world-wide. Soon -- whether tomorrow or a half-century from now -- the carrying capacity of the earth will be exceeded and catastrophe will follow. Realistically, we should stop saving and prolonging lives now, but who is in favor of it?

Historical Background

From earliest times people have been concerned with questions of value and virtue -- What is the good life? Who is the admirable person? What is virtue? What is the just society? And since the time of the Greeks a major branch of philosophy has been that of ethics.

At the height of Athenian cultural development Pericles, Athens' great leader, delivered an oration praising their city; each thing praised represents a valued quality and the total gives us a good impression of Athenian (and Greek) civic values.

"Our government is called a democracy," he said, "because power resides, not in a few people, but in the majority of our citizens. But every person has equal rights before the law; prestige and respect are paid those who win them by their merits, regardless of their political, economic, or social status; and no one is deprived of making his contribution to the city's welfare. . . . In our public dealings we have respect for our officials and the laws which protect the helpless and those unwritten laws whose violation is generally regarded as shameful.

"But we do more than this. We have provided for the happiness of our people many creations: athletic games, contests of various sorts, festivals throughout the year, and beautiful buildings to cheer the heart and refresh the spirit as we see them every day. Also we enjoy imported goods from all over the world, which add to the attractive variety of our life.

"As far as preparing for war is concerned we are much better off than our enemies. Our city is open to the world, and we have no regular deportations to keep foreigners from learning what might be of use to an enemy. For we have confidence in our native resourcefulness rather than in mere military strength. Our enemies have a rigid system for cultivating courage from their youth onward, but we, doing pretty much as we please, are as well prepared as they when danger arises. . . .

"We love beauty without extravagance, and wisdom without weakness of will. Wealth we regard not as a means for private display but rather for public service; and poverty we consider no disgrace, although we think it a disgrace not to try to overcome it. We believe a man should be concerned about public as well as private affairs, for we regard the person who takes no part in politics not as merely uninterested but as useless. We reach decisions on public policy only after full discussion, believing that sound judgment, far from being impeded by discussion, is arrived at only when full information is considered before a decision is made.

"To sum it up, I claim that our city is a model for all Greece and that here more than anywhere else a man can become independent in spirit, versatile in accomplishment, and richly developed in personality." (Quoted from Angell and Helm, 1981, pp. 252-253)

Over the centuries there has been concern especially with morality, which is understandable since wherever humans interact, which is everywhere, problems arise as to how one should treat another, as to the rights and welfare of each. Wittingly or unwittingly, the strong easily may take from the weak, the clever exploit the simple, men dominate women, captors enslave the defeated, and so on; and when people begin to interact in groups these inequalities become compounded. Plato aptly describes the problem (as paraphrased by Durant), and his analysis is as true today as in Greek times.

Men are not content with a simple life: they are acquisitive, ambitious, competitive, and jealous; they soon tire of what they have, and pine for what they have not; and they seldom desire anything unless it belongs to others. The result is the encroachment of one group upon the territory of another, the rivalry of groups for the resources of the soil, and then war. Trade and finance develop, and bring new class-divisions. "Any ordinary city is in fact two cities, one the city of the poor, the other of the rich, each at war with the other . . . ." (423). A mercantile bourgeoisie arises, whose members seek social position through wealth and conspicuous consumption: "they will spend large sums of money on their wives" (548). These changes in the distribution of wealth produce political changes: as the wealth of the merchant over-reaches that of the land-owner, aristocracy gives way to a plutocratic oligarchy -- wealthy traders and bankers rule the state. Then statesmanship, which is the coordination of social forces and the adjustment of policy to growth, is replaced by politics, which is the strategy of party and lust for the spoils of office. (1927, p. 27)

Human interaction also forces the emergence of codes of personal morality and we find worldwide in the history of most societies much the same moral virtues as taught by the Greeks and by the Hebrews and Christians, such as avoidance of injury and killing, observance of marital vows, respect for other's property, respect for elders and care of elderly, honesty and truth-telling, and care and protection of children.

Early in Greek history the concept of justice was formulated and became the focal point of judgement of any behavior, goal, or social-political arrangement. Justice is itself a value, but of a very special sort because of its use as an all-encompassing standard of judgement. We should pursue its history a bit for it features prominently in contemporary theory of moral development and research.

We might automatically assume justice to by synonymous with equality but that would be a projection of our own values. Over history there have been different conceptions of justice. At one point Plato has Thrasymachus declare, "I proclaim that might is right, and justice is in the interest of the stronger . . . . The different forms of government make laws, democratic, aristocratic, or autocratic, with a view to their respective interests; and these laws, so made by them to serve their interests, they deliver to their subjects as 'justice,' and punish as 'unjust' anyone who transgresses them . . . . For injustice is censured because those who censure it are afraid of suffering, and not from any scruple they might have of doing injustice themselves." And in another dialogue (Gorgias) Callicles denounces morality as an invention of the weak to neutralize the strength of the strong. "The weak distribute praise and censure with a view to their own interests; they say that dishonesty is shameful and unjust, meaning by dishonesty the desire to have more than their neighbors, for in light of their own inferiority they would be only too glad to have equality. . . ." (Durant, p. 25)

This was not Plato's own conception of justice, and he may have put the words in the mouths of the two simply as a means providing contrast with his own conception; but the position has had its advocates over the centuries. Machiavelli defined virtue as intellect plus force and is famous for his advice to the ruler to use any means necessary to further his own ends, be it deception or whatever. More recently the doctrine has been more or less correctly associated with the name of the 19th century philosopher Nietzsche. Another writer expressed the idea neatly when he said that "a handful of might is better than a bagful of right."

These other interpretations permit Plato to pose the questions: What is justice? Shall we seek righteousness or power? Is it better to be good or to be strong?

One might think that Plato, as a noble Athenian, would equate justice with practice of democracy and equality, but such was not the case. Pericles delivered his oration at the end of the first year of the long Peloponnesian War and soon after that Athens fell into a decline. Even before the war had begun Athens had begun to "bully" smaller states and became feared and hated, the war ended in defeat and chaos, and this was followed by the corrupt dictatorial rule of The Thirty. Plato lived through this terrible time, and through Socrates' being democratically condemned to death by his fellow citizens, so emerged with a strong distrust of popular democracy.

His blueprint of the ideal or just state, the *Republic*, was conceived in the light of these events, not only as a means of assuring justice for all but also as a means of assuring a stable state that could continue indefinitely. The society was to be made up of three groups of people: a small group of leaders at the top -- "guardians" -- who have spent a lifetime in preparation for their now-spartan role as wise, experienced leaders and who themselves owned nothing; an intermediate class of well-trained soldiers who also own nothing (the guardians are drawn from this group and given special training); and a third group composed of the large remainder of the population who engage in agriculture, commerce, and industry and in general keep the society functioning in the practical sense. The guardians regulate trade and industry for the welfare of all but within these regulations the artisans and workers of the third group are permitted to own property, marry and have families, indulge themselves with food and merriment and in general live much as present-day materialistic and pleasure-seeking people do.

Plato's definition of justice is simply this: the having and doing what is one's own. This seems not to say much. As Durant (p. 47) remarks, after so much delay we expected an infallible revelation. What does it mean? Simply that each person shall receive the equivalent of what he produces, and shall perform the function for which he is best fit (having in mind the three classes of callings). A just person is a person in just the right place, doing his best, and giving the full equivalent of what he receives. A society of just men would therefore be a highly harmonious and efficient group, for every element would be in its place, fulfilling its appropriate function like the pieces in a perfect orchestra (Durant, p. 47).

And in the individual, too, having in mind the three different aspects of mind, heart, and appetites, justice is effective coordination of the three parts, each in its fit place and each making its cooperative contribution to behavior. Each individual is a cosmos of desires, emotions, and ideas; let these fall into harmony and the individual functions effectively as a person and member of the society; let them lose their proper place and function, and disintegration of the personality begins. All evil is disharmony: between man and nature, between men and men, or between man and himself (p. 48).

So returning to Plato's simple definition of justice, it is not a literal equality between all, but an equality in light of people's natures and roles and it is not democratic at all yet has the virtues of an ideal democracy because of the wisdom and fairness of the leaders.

Jumping over the centuries we come to Immanuel Kant (1724-1804) and his concept of moral law as the determinant of morality and justice.

Kant came on the scene when the thinking of the three British Empiricists, Locke, Berkeley, and Hume was strong. Locke was the one who described the mind of the child as a *tabula rasa* -- latin for a blank slate, meaning that the child begins life with nothing there in the mind, with experience (learning) the origin of all that one knows, including his moral standards. Nothing is innate. Previously the Rationalists had assumed that there were certain innate qualities common to man, though they were still searching for these eternal truths. Locke and other Empiricists challenged this, saying that each person may learn a different moral code and that there are no universal rights and wrongs.

Kant had no argument with the idea that specific facts and beliefs come from experience, but he felt there were a number of innate structurings of the mind and these have the function of organizing what experience is bringing into the mind and dictate our ways of thinking. As a single example, Hume had assumed that any experience of an object causing something to happen (perceiving a cause-effect relationship) is due solely to event A always being followed by event B, leading to an *inference* of a cause-effect relationship. Kant reasoned that Hume was assuming too much, that the capacity to reason cause (to) effect was already possessed (*a priori*) in the intellect.

Kant was even more convinced that there is a comparable innate foundation for morality. To him the most dramatic reality of our experience is our moral sense, our inescapable feeling in the face of temptation that this or that is wrong. Even when we yield to temptation, the feeling of wrong is there nevertheless. This sense of moral duty or necessity is there not because of any teaching, but simply because it springs forth from one's inner nature. It has an imperative quality and is experienced immediately and directly as true and binding.

More formally stated, there is an *a priori* (innate) rational principle which makes moral judgements inescapable, universal in form, and absolutely necessary to any explanation of the moral dimensions of life (Robinson, p. 271). Further, that same rational principle produces an *intention* to do good; moral acts could not take place without there being a prior intention. To acknowledge this intention, the *fact* of intention, is to acknowledge simultaneously a *freedom of the will*; but the very freedom is limited by the felt requirement that the will *make moral law* (perform moral duty).

This predisposition to moral judgement and the imperative will-to-moral-duty that springs forth from within Kant called the "categorical imperative." It takes different forms or may be stated in different ways. One of the clearest is in the form of three rules or maxims (Titus, p. 164-165).

The Principle of Universality. "Act in conformity with that maxim which you can at the same time will to be a universal law." Or, stated in clearer terms, "Choose only as you would be willing to have everyone choose in your situation." More simply still, since this is but a formalization of the familiar golden rule, "Behave toward others as you would have all others behave toward you." Our actions should come not from impulses and desires but only from a principle that can be applied universally. Kant used the example of a man who, after a series of misfortunes, contemplates suicide. When he attempts to universalize such behavior he realizes at once that it cannot be universalized, for if everyone were to commit suicide humanity would disappear.

The Principle of Humanity as an End, Never Merely as a Means. "Act so as to use humanity, whether in your own person or in the person of another, always as an end, never merely as a means." People, as rational beings, are ends in themselves and should never be used merely as means to other ends. Physical things may be used as means, but when we use a person simply as a means, as in slavery or commercial exploitation or false friendship for selfish ends, we degrade him and violate his being as a person.

The Principle of Autonomy. The moral laws that a person obeys are not imposed upon him from outside. They are the "laws which he imposes upon himself." The sense of duty and the reason which a person obeys come from within; they are expressions of his own higher self.

Though Kant apparently never uses the term "justice," employing "moral law" instead, the first two principles of the categorical imperative clearly are principles of justice.

It is possible to employ the categorical imperative as basis of almost any moral system, without also accepting Kant's reasonings about the innate basis of morality, since actually its essence, especially as stated in the golden rule, is found in ethical systems worldwide. In this century John Rawls (1971) adopted its essence and fitted it into his moral values formulations. More recently, the psychologist Lawrence Kohlberg, needing a means of evaluating the quality of moral reasoning, adopted justice as his standard of evaluation and employed the categorical imperative as criterion of justice.

The Kohlberg theory is amplified in succeeding chapters, together with research findings. In brief, he uses *justice* as the ultimate standard of judgement in deciding the stage of moral reasoning of any person, child or adult. But since justice itself can be given different meanings, as we have just seen, he accepts the categorical imperative, as just spelled out, in broad definition and further defines it with such more specific concepts as *fairness, equality, reciprocity,* and *democracy.*

That is, the question is asked, what is this person's explanation of the just solution to a particular moral dilemma?

Kohlberg (1976) says that in essence moral conflicts are conflicts between the claims of persons, and principles for resolving the claims are principles of justice, "for giving each his due" (p. 183). At every moral stage there is a concern for justice, but at each higher stage the conception of justice is reorganized.

For sake of completeness it might be mentioned that the doctrine that pleasure or happiness is the greatest good in life has always been popular. It had several names in ancient times but since the time of Jeremy Bentham and John Stuart Mill, in the nineteenth century, has been called "utilitarianism." Mill's utilitarianism "accepts as the foundation of morals, Utility, or the Greatest Happiness Principle, that actions are right in proportion as they tend to promote happiness, wrong as they tend to produce the reverse of happiness." Mill accepts the general position of Bentham, who used the phrase "the greatest happiness for the greatest number" as the essence of good. Utilitarianism is mentioned here because the criticism is sometimes advanced that Kohlberg could or should have used it in place of justice as his standard of judgement of moral maturity, or at least that justice is not the only possible criterion of maturity.

Summary Comment

The meaning of "value" as a personal conviction and evaluative disposition is understood by all, including the layman, and ordinarily the context indicates that this is the meaning being used. This is the rock-solid meaning of the term and justification for its continued use, no matter what its abuses. When writers use it loosely with other meanings, as they often do, then there is confusion and the term becomes almost useless. Additionally, when used with the broader "worth" meaning, as proposed here, the number of sorts of value becomes great and the boundary between value and related dispositions, especially interests and motives, often is unclear. If we are to have a useful concept, writers must state their meanings, and where there is doubt as to whether a disposition should be called "value" the question must be asked, is there a felt sense of importance, meaningfulness, significance, worthiness, or synonyms of these, for these are the defining qualities.

CHAPTER 3

ROLE OF VALUES IN LIVES

Values profoundly influence our lives. They are part of the very reality that each of us experiences daily. They give structure to a life and point the way into the future. They help supply meaning to existence. They create specific motives, influence how we will perceive things, and help determine our thinking. They are prominent in the major choices of life -- of mates, friends, occupations, and social groups. They are implicit in our conceptions of the good life. They produce lifelong commitments and they may dictate how we will die. But they also may be part of a well tailored mask, a professing of lofty ideal with no commitment and no practice. Let us look at the role of values in lives.

In the presentation below values are treated first as group-wide phenomena, in order to bring out their role in group functioning; then we narrow down to look at their additional role in individual lives. Of course all are held by individuals and the experiencer may have little awareness as to whether one of his values is held by few or many others. But the extent of sharedness does make a difference. The sharedness of group values produces a group dynamic that is absent with values held by but one or a few persons, and the group dynamic in turn produces a distinct individual psychodynamic. This can be brought out as we proceed.

Group-Wide Values

Values as Part of Group Structure

Social scientists recognize several group processes that occur simultaneously when people come together and begin interacting and form stable groups. These processes are called collectively "group dynamics," and involve such things as reciprocal communication and emergence of stable channels of communication (not everyone will talk with everyone else), emergence of leadership and a variety of other roles in the group, and emergence of rules and norms that govern member's behavior together with methods of enforcement.

Among the rules and norms that emerge are values, and the dynamics of their emergence are somewhat as follows: (a) reciprocal communication of the emerging value among group members; (b) reciprocal encouragement to practice the value; (c) reciprocal pressure to conform to the value and reciprocal reward for living or practicing the value; (d) reciprocal imitation throughout; (e) consensual validation of the value; and (f) a group-defined reality overall which gives the individual that often necessary assurance that all of this is "true." Examples might be a boys' athletic club valuing "fair play," a lodge or college fraternity valuing the mutual support of "blood brotherhood," or a professors' organization valuing "freedom of inquiry." In general, shared values will emerge in any newly-formed, enduring group and be a central part of the group's cohesiveness. Contrarily, emergence of difference of values is a sure source of discord and splitting of groups.

Granted many individual exceptions, these processes together tend to make group values more prominent, influential, and enduring than values held by one or a few persons.

Values as Part of the Groundplan of Existence

Beginning at the most basic level, society-wide beliefs and values together supply the groundplan of existence for each of us. Together they tell us what is "real" and what is good and ought to be. Each of us thinks he is reading reality directly when he perceives trees and mountains, wind and clouds, animals and humans. But actually a significant part of that reality has been culturally colored and defined, with the desirables and undesirables ("goods" and "bads") predefined. One people will say to its children that the birds and beasts are God's creatures and must be respected (they have value), another people will tell them that the creatures lack souls and were put on earth by God solely for man's use -- kill as many as you wish! One's perception of the animals will embody these meanings with their inherent values.

Here is an excellent example of that reality-building process taken from the anthropological literature, that of the Hopi Indians.

The Hopi are a pueblo-dwelling group of American Indians who live on mesas in northeastern Arizona. It is an arid environment, the rainfall scarce and uncertain, the growing season short with the possibility of killing frosts early and late in the crop cycle, the winters cold and the summers hot. Hard work is necessary, life arduous, and crop failure and famine always a possibility.

Continued contact with Euroamerican culture has of course changed their beliefs and values somewhat, but as of the early decades of the present century their outlook was distinct. Their conception of the world -- the universe -- was of a balanced system with the gods, nature, and man contributing to the welfare of each other and of the whole by the exchange of service. If each did his part the world would continue its smooth orderly course. In this system, men's ritual activities, prayers, and conduct had to be correct to maintain the universe in a harmonious state, particularly with regard to the movement of the sun, growth of crops, rainfall, and animal and human reproduction (Aberle, 1967, p. 95).

Their conception of the ideal society mirrored their conception of the universe. The people should be cooperative, peaceful, self-controlled, and conservative. Doing the new or different or radical thing had no place -- it only served to upset the balanced system. So they valued tradition and quiet orderliness and doing things the time-honored way. Similarly, anger and violence were condemned, for in anger the thoughts were bad and displeasing to the gods, and the violence upsetting to the smooth functioning of the social system. And there was no place for individualism or self-assertion. No one tried to gain renown and boasting would have been among the most disvalued of acts. It was well understood that one should be industrious, well-controlled in thought and action, and should blend himself into the group endeavor. Unlike so many societies, self-assertive leadership was not valued, and leaders were chosen by a sort of automatic promotion or seniority system, and practically pushed into leadership roles.

Their beliefs about the role of man in the universe and in society found expression in their conception of the ideal person:

The ideal individual can be summed up by the term *hopi*, usually translated "peaceful." It includes the values: (a) strength -- physical and psychic, including self-control, wisdom, and intelligence; (b) poise -- tranquillity, "good" thinking; (c) obedience to the law -- cooperation, unselfishness, responsibility, kindness; (d) peace -- absence of aggressive, quarrelsome, or boastful behavior; (e) protectiveness -- preserving and protecting human, animal, and plant life; (f) health. These make up the Hopi "one-hearted," good personality.

In order to contribute maximally to community well-being, the coming of rain, the success of farming, and the like, every individual should live up to the ideal code in action and in thought. If even one person has a "bad heart," rites will fail. That is why the announcement of a ceremonial is accompanied by the Crier's admonition to cease all quarrels.

The polar opposite of the *hopi* individual is one who is *kahopi* -- not Hopi. Such a person may show any or all of the following qualities: "lack of integrity, quarrelsomeness, jealousy, envy, boastfulness, self-assertion, irresponsibility, non-cooperativeness and sickness" (Thompson 1945:545). The extreme development of these characteristics is the witch, the "two-hearted" individual, who is antisocial, lawless, an agent of illness and death. (Aberle, 1967:95-96)

Culture-wide Beliefs and Values Produce Motivation

It will be evident from the above examples that culture-wide values and beliefs are determining so much of the specifics of daily behavior, determining not only how things will be perceived but also many of the more important motives, which in turn produce specific behavior. The general formula is that the implicit values define for everyone what is important; all are telling each other what is important by word and act; all therefore are motivated to do the important things; they encourage each other by their reciprocal approval of the valued activities; and by their approval and admiration they reward those who do the valued things. Observation of the reward encourages others to perform the valued activity, and thus the cycle continues endlessly, the value constantly reaffirmed and the resulting motivation kept constantly alive. The several cultural examples given previously of the Sioux (p. 37) and the Tongans (p. 25) and the Hopi above all demonstrate this.

A striking additional example comes from pre-revolutionary China, as reported by Hsu (1967) in a book aptly titled, "Under the Ancestor's Shadow." Centuries ago the Chinese evolved the conception that the dead enter a spirit world, there to remain for a long period of time before eventual rebirth on earth. While in the spirit world the given spirit may either be tortured and damned in a sort of Chinese version of hell (and later be reborn a lowly animal or miserable human), or be treated well and have a comfortable life in a city of the dead, or even be made an honored official or sort of divinity of the spirit world and spared rebirth entirely. The Chinese came to believe further that the fate of the spirit in the other world is in good part determined by the prayers and other observances and acts in its behalf by living sons. Failure here would cause the spirit to be damned.

These key beliefs made sons valuable -- indeed, invaluable! -- but not daughters, and made continuation of the family line indispensable, for its termination would mean that no longer would there be a male descendant to act on behalf of all the ancestors. (Daughters at marriage become a part of the new husband's family and no longer considered to belong to their family of birth or to have any role in it.) But not only did these beliefs dictate the value of sons, and daughters, and family continuance, they dictated a whole series of more specific values, beliefs, and motives, and indeed went far toward determining an entire way of life -- the living lived under the shadow of the ancestors. Hsu mentions, for example, that there was no romantic tradition as we understand it, for the purpose of marriage was not to find a love-mate and life's companion for the son, but rather to find a mother for his children; hence an estrangement existed between the sexes. (But there is a romantic tradition in Chinese literature going back thousands of years.) Getting sons was so desperately important that it overshadowed everything. And pity the poor wife who did not bear sons, for she became utterly superfluous, soon to be replaced by someone who could, and not wanted back by her family and emphatically not by another husband. Were this not tragedy enough, she faced the certainty at death of an eternity of misery for there would be no sons to pray on her behalf.

Group Values Supply Consistency and Predictability

Society-wide and other group-wide values help to supply the consistency and predictability that we require of each other if we are to live and work together. There can be no personal security and no stability of social organization where each person acts impulsively and solely in terms of self-interest. Kluckhohn (1951, p. 400) poses the question "Why are there values?" and answers that the reply must be, "Because social life would be impossible without them; the functioning of the social system could not continue to achieve group goals, individuals could not get what they want and need from other individuals in personal and emotional terms, nor could they feel within themselves a requisite measure of order and unified purpose. Above all, values add a measure of predictability to social life." Seen in terms of the individual, the consistency and predictability is giving the person some sense of security, meaningfulness or purpose, and future direction.

We can best appreciate the importance of shared values in group life if we picture a condition where people live together in the same neighborhoods, cities, and countries but lack common values. Such conditions do exist and in part this is what Durkheim had in mind when he named the form of social disorganization often seen in modern societies "anomie" (anomia). It would take us too far afield to try to describe such anomic communities or to account for why they exist. Suffice to say that when a person lives in such a setting of absence of shared values he may find his neighbor guided by values opposite his own with the resulting possibility of disagreement and public clash; he may be unable to join with others in solving community problems for want of agreement as to goals; he may be disturbed by the fact that there seem to be so few universal values and may be confused about life's purposes; and he may feel frustrated, anxious, and discouraged at his own lack of direction and at the lack of common purpose in the community.

Timely exemplification of what happens when a portion of the population does not live by key values of the majority comes from a recent report on crime in California (*San Jose Mercury News*, 25 March, 1990).

The key moral values of any society are considered so important that they become formalized as laws, with punishments for their violation. Some societies put offenders to death or cut off hand or foot (or otherwise maim), depending upon the seriousness of the violation, but societies in the European tradition have tended to rely heavily in recent times upon imprisonment. Six crimes compose the California Crime Index -- homicide, rape, robbery, aggravated assault, burglary, and motor vehicle theft -- and these fairly well exemplify the serious crimes of modern societies; half of them are against persons and half against property (theft). (But absent from the Crime Index are forms of dishonesty, especially "white collar" crime, such as taking money from others by deception -- fraud and embezzlement. There are always enough people in our communities who will resort to forms of white collar crime that special agencies exist at community, state, and Federal levels to try to prevent and prosecute it.)

About two decades ago certain politicians sought to get elected by taking a "get tough on crime" posture. Since there was considerable crime, the public responded with a demand to get tough on criminals, and more punitive laws were passed and flexible programs curtailed. Soon existing jails and prisons were filled and jail-prison construction programs begun. Over the past ten years California has tripled its number of jail beds and filled virtually all of them. Despite a $3.2 billion prison construction effort now underway, a new study shows that $5.2 billion will be needed by 1994 for even more prisons, jails, and youth facilities. From 22,500 inmates in 1979 California's state prison inmate population has grown to 86,000 today. By 1994 it is expected to grow to more than 136,000 and total in jails, prisons, and youth facilities to more than 249,000, which is more than the population of most cities in the state   (A significant portion of these incarcerations is made up of drug convictions, which is a very different class of crime, however harmful to person and community it may be. No separation as to type of crime is given in the report, though it is reported for the six crimes of the Crime Index that during the past year homicide was up 8.2 percent, aggravated assault up 11.4 percent, rape up 3 percent, robbery up 14.7 percent, burglary up 1.3 percent and motor vehicle theft up 11.7 percent.) Officials are quoted as saying there is no longer sufficient money available, nor is there time to build jail beds fast enough, to take care of the influx.

Though we are not concerned here with the causes of this state of affairs nor with possible remedies, it is pertinent to mention the opinion of Barry Krisberg, president of the National Council on Crime and Delinquency, that imprisonment is not very effective either as a deterrent or corrective. It is frightening only to those who have something to lose. The growing underclass from which most inmates come has little to lose, especially when only a tiny percentage of lawbreakers is ever caught. Notable here is that he doesn't even mention moral values as entering into the person's decision; probably for these people a general value of honesty doesn't exist (though the assumption of "honor among thieves" appears to have some validity, which is to say that anyone has a selective code of values rather than a general absolute one.)

In summary of the role of group-wide values, they are helping supply the groundplan of existence and hence helping to determine each individual's conception of reality, with all that this implies as to the causation of behavior; they are helping determine how things will be perceived; they are producing daily and life-long motivations; they are supplying stability and consistency to groups, and security, meaningfulness, and direction to individuals; they are supplying part of the ideological fabric that holds a group together; and they are supplying each new member of the group with an array of desirable and undesirable objects and ways to live.

Additional Role of Values in Lives

In addition to the above functions of values in lives, we may narrow-down to the individual level and mention some of the above again from a more individual point of view and add others.

The Predisposition to Evaluate

Probably the most common, if not also the most important, role of values is as standards of judgement. As Kluckhohn (1951) has observed, surely one of the broadest generalizations to be made by a natural historian observing the human species is that man is an evaluating animal. Always and everywhere men are saying, "this is good," "that is bad," "this is better than that," "these are higher and those lower aspirations." Like spectators standing at streetside watching a parade pass by, we watch the things of life that come our way and evaluate them -- the actions of leaders and nations, the sexual-moral conduct of characters seen in movies or on T.V., the actions of neighbors and acquaintances, the actions of organizations and corporations, and especially the actions of prominent persons in sports, entertainment, and public life. We seem to have a predisposition, a need, to evaluate.

A manner of empirical support for the generalization is found in the research of Charles Osgood and his associates (1957). They found that the predominant reaction of people worldwide to stimulus concepts was an evaluative one.

They presented lists of concepts (words, ordinarily) to respondents and elicited a reaction by having the respondent check-mark pairs of adjectives. Many different adjective pairs were used in the research, but the following will serve to exemplify: good-bad, pleasant-unpleasant, positive-negative; strong-weak, heavy-light, hard-soft; fast-slow, active-passive, excitable-calm. The first three pairs are evaluative in nature, the next three pairs express a general reaction termed "potency," and the final three pairs a general reaction termed "activity." The adjective pairs were spaced on the page such that respondent could indicate degree of reaction, such as very, quite, or slightly good, or bad (also neutral), and the pairs were randomly arranged so that the evaluatives were mixed in with the "potency" and "activity" pairs. Hundreds of concepts were used in the research; the following will exemplify: peace, doctor, rage, heart, horse, bread, rain, pain, mind, color. That is, respondents would indicate for *peace* how good or bad, strong or weak, hard-soft, fast-slow, passive-active, etc. it is.

Though people responded somewhat differently to each concept, the striking finding was that the strongest, most consistent, most frequent reaction was evaluative, as exemplified especially by "good-bad." Apparently it is most natural for us to make an evaluation of things rather than to respond in terms of other qualities. In daily life these evaluations become the basis of specific attitudes.

Here are a few examples of valuations, as taken from von Mering (1961). All are comments (judgements) made by residents of the Rimrock area of New Mexico when queried about their fellow area-residents, the Navaho Indians. The topic under discussion at this point is whether the Navaho should have equal rights, and these residents are showing by their comments that they take the value *equality* for granted as right and true but attach qualifications relative to the Navaho (p. 126):

1) Equality -- that's something you can't just flatfoot give to 'em. They have to kind of acquire it for themselves. It's going to take time. (H #3, S #7)

2) What I think, if they clean up and then come to a dance and behave -- then they've got just as much right there as you have. Nobody in his right mind can think different; -- now would they? (H #4, S #10)

3) Well, I wouldn't -- I wouldn't be in favor of giving them the same right as we have to vote at the present time, but after they are educated, then I think they should have a right to vote as we do. (H #4, S #11)

In another discussion *equality* (equality of opportunity, equal chance, a "fair shake," etc.) for the Navaho is again being discussed, but this time no qualifications are expressed (p. 144):

4) I believe if you take a Navaho, and send him to school and give him the same opportunity that you had when you were in school, on up, and put him out under the same conditions you are, that he'd have an about equal chance. -- Whether he don't wash himself much or his clothes look different got nothing to do with it. (H #1, S #1)

5) If one of 'em had a farm right here, he'd be just as much into that program as we were. Certainly he would have just as much right -- just as much say. (H #2, S #6)

6) I believe that's the main thing they need, as far as that goes, is to be treated just like anyone else -- someone who's got freedoms and rights. (H #5, S #14)

7) I don't believe -- they can ever have any economic security without equal rights. (H #5, S #13)

The valuing process may produce no more than a subjective "that's right," "this is wrong," but it may produce much more, for values often are sensed as very important "goods" and "bads," "rights" and "wrongs." One may be led to publicly criticize and condemn (or compliment and praise), physically attack, agitate for (or against), contribute money and time, and in the extreme take up arms and join with other in defense of what is experienced as the essence or reason to be of life itself (or in opposition to what is experienced as the negation of life itself).

Moral Values and Conscience

As explained in Chapter 1, certain moral values are necessary for group functioning, as a means of leading each individual *voluntarily* to do what he must if the group is to carry on its daily activities and to survive over time. From anthropological sources Maccoby (1980, pp. 296-299) compiled a list of problem situations that tend to exist in all societies for which definite rules, often in the form of moral teachings, are prescribed. The list was outlined in Chapter 1 and deserves amplification here.

1. Endangering self or others. The safeguarding of the food and water supplies of the group is an absolute essential in many groups in the world and this is impressed upon the children from an early age. Among nomadic desert tribes every member must cooperate in conserving and protecting the precious water supply, and no child in playful moment can be permitted to pull the corks from the goatskin bags that carry the water. Among pastoralists the herds must be carefully tended and protected; among farming communities gates to fields of ripening grain must be carefully closed. Children are also trained not to play with fire and in cities not to play out in dangerous streets.

2. Protection of health. The specific rules emphasized will depend upon the group's theory of disease. Among one people there will be great fear of supernatural beings as bringers of disease and death and children taught to avoid certain activities at risk of their lives. Societies that attribute disease to contact with bodily wastes teach their children to dispose of their feces and may teach strong aversions. In societies that are aware of the transmission of germs by mouth, children are taught to cover their mouths when they cough, not to put soiled objects in their mouths, and not to spit on the sidewalk. As knowledge of effects of pollution of air and water become known, polluting increasingly become a moral issue and polluters blamed for releasing contaminants into the air or public water supplies.

3. Respect for property. Though societies differ in how much property is communally owned and how much individually owned, all have some individual property, even if it be no more than items of personal adornment, clothing, handbags, tools and weapons, or the like. Children must learn to distinguish objects belonging to others and learn the concept of ownership and the meaning and wrongfulness of theft. When property is communally owned strong values may be attached to proper care and use of this property.

4. Control of aggression. Humans readily are aroused to irritation, anger, and aggression of different sorts -- attack, fighting, injury, and killing. So an important part of moral training is teaching control of aggression. Of course its control is never complete -- one may become enraged and aggressive in spite of strong internal prohibition, and all societies must provide means of trying to redress the wrong when it happens, as by punishment, monetary payment, banishment, or other. Typically the moral taboo on attack applies only to members of one's in-group -- family or clan, tribe, or nation, and harming and killing members of designated out-groups may even be morally required. But there is an ethic shared by some members of modern nations which regards all life as sacred and abhors all killing. The inhibition of aggression within the group usually extends to avoid damage to the self-esteem or possessions of others, as well as physical injury.

5. Control of sexual activity. The mature sexual appetite is another strong motive and throughout history societies have imposed some control on its expression. The most obvious reason for its control is that it leads to babies, and each child must be cared for, fed, and protected for many years before it can fend for itself. There is of course a limit to the number of children a mother can care for; doubtlessly the institution of marriage arose to provide a mate to share the burden, but with that came rules limiting sexual activity to the couple. The community has always had a stake in the matter, for growing and gathering food tends to be a group enterprise and where food supplies are limited, as has often been the case, the arrival of another mouth to feed becomes a concern of all. A related reason for control is to assure that a second child is not born too soon after the first, for the mother may not be able to carry two children about with her as she engages in the sometimes heavy labor of gathering, digging, and cultivating. (Gransberg, 1973, reports on the comparable problem of caring for twins and finds from an analysis of twin infanticide in various societies that the practice of allowing one infant to die is typically found in societies where mothers have heavy work loads or where they have a minimal amount of help.) All societies have prohibitions against intercourse between close blood relatives, and apparently against close marital relatives as well, such as between mother-in-law and son-in-law. Because it is a strong motive and readily becomes a part of such feelings as attraction and affection, jealousy and possessiveness, there is always the possibility of "mistakes" leading to personal tragedy and community crises, such as a man or woman falling in love with another's husband or wife or two men becoming involved with the same woman and out of jealousy one attacks or kills the other. So, for various reasons young persons are taught moral rules governing sexual activity.

6. Self-reliance and work. Mature individuals are expected to contribute to their own support and that of family or other social unit. So children are taught to ask for help only when necessary, to help with chores when they are old enough, and to learn skills that will contribute to their own self-support when they are grown. Though other moral values in the list are of more importance, surely many a parent worries that her/his child may grow up lacking initiative and lazy unless special attention is given to developing ambition and initiative in the growing child.

7. Telling the truth and keeping promises. This is an absolute essential for social interaction, for lacking it others cannot assume the correctness of anything said or rely on promises, and community life simply could not go on. Societies will differ in their emphases. In industrial societies, which operate by intricate coordination of the time schedules of many different people, failure to keep promised appointments will lead to censure. In simpler societies the exact moment of fulfilling the promise is unimportant but supplying the exact amount of the promised object, such as the number of cows promised as bride price, may be. Among ourselves there are subtle understandings as to permissible deviations from literal truth-telling, with the "white lie" considered to be a socially desirable deviation; we may wonder as to its extent in very different societies.

8. Respect for authority. Most social groups have some sort of authority structuring where one person has power to make decisions and give orders and others are expected to respect and obey the leader. These arrangements will differ greatly depending on the size and complexity of the group, with, at the one extreme, a small band of tribal hunters obeying a single leading hunter and, at the other, a modern city with a hierarchy of authority figures -- policemen, police chief, mayor, judge, etc. -- to be obeyed. All groups have to have leadership structuring if they are to function effectively. Extended families have a head, tribes have chiefs, nations have leaders or rulers, armies have officers, classrooms have teachers. And of course the members in all of these groups must cooperate or obey or otherwise follow the leadership if the group is to function. So children must be taught to show respect or deference toward persons in authority and to comply with demands. While societies differ in how rigidly they enforce obedience to authority, almost all teach their children deference toward their parents and toward certain authority figures outside the family, and this teaching continues up into adulthood. Among ourselves, a sense of duty or obedience to duly constituted authority may be the essence of this (adult) morality.

In Chapter 1 two additional commonly-occurring moral values were mentioned: (9) *Respect and care for elders*, and (10) *Care for and protection of children*. Since Maccoby did not regard her list as inclusive, undoubtedly other common problems and their associated rules and values might be found. The list suffices to tell us why moral values must exist. But it should be noted again from

Chapter 1 that not all of the moral values of a society, ours specifically, are necessary for the group's survival.

Clarification of "Conscience."

Finding myself uncertain as to the meaning of conscience and its relation to moral values, dictionaries were consulted. Since "conscience" is a loosely-used term, others may be uncertain as well. The main question is, are moral values and conscience the same thing?

Popularly, "conscience" is often used loosely for the whole moral nature of the person. A more specific meaning is that it is the total of one's distinct moral values. In this sense, conscience has no real existence and the term is used simply as a shorthand when wishing to refer the entire class of moral values.

English and English (1958) have one of the clearest definitions: "Conscience is defined as the more-or-less integrated functioning of a person's system of moral values in the approval or disapproval of his own acts or proposed acts." Stated in other words, they are saying that moral values are the substance or content of conscience; and conscience is the functioning, the psychodynamic of the moral values. There is also the assumption that the moral values form a system -- have some manner of inter-relationship, the operation of which is part of conscience. This formulation is good in recognizing both the specificity of the moral values and their dynamic role.

(Incidentally, both this source and *Oxford English Dictionary* mention that an earlier assumption was that conscience is an innate or divinely implanted faculty enabling one to judge correctly on moral issues. Whether divinely given or not, the capacity for conscience is innately supplied, else none of us would have one, and how appropriate to regard it as the voice of the Divine within each of us!)

This definition serves to identify the basic function of conscience, that of approval or disapproval of our acts, but there is much more to this psychodynamic process, whether the whole of it be called "conscience" or not. Exemplary of its complexity are the two possible extremes of conscience, the troubled-neurotic person with too much conscience and the psychopathic person with too little. Troubled-insecure persons often are criticizing and condemning selves for moral failings and feeling guilty, but this activity of conscience will not be due to their having been taught numerous strong moral values in childhood. Rather, their feelings of insecurity and inadequacy cause them to adopt perfectionistic standards which doom them to moral shortcomings, and, additionally, they are predisposed by their inferiority feelings to be looking for things about themselves to blame. At the other extreme, some persons lack any sort of conscience and have no capacity for remorse or guilt at obvious moral transgression, such as harming others, yet in most cases have been exposed to about the same morals-shaping influences as others, and are quite aware of the morals of the society and will describe themselves as moral persons (both of these extremes are described further in next chapter). Even within the normal range, there will be interesting variations in the functioning of conscience. A person may have a "strong conscience" in the sense that the feeling of "I should" and "I ought" or even "I must" -- the goading of that nagging feeling of duty, is there often and in regard to almost any moral concern that comes to mind. Thus when the annual appeal for contributions from one's alma mater arrives there is the feeling "I *should* help the college"; when reminded that autos are the main cause of air pollution, one thinks "I *should* own a smaller auto and take the bus more often"; when an announcement for a peace rally appears in the newspaper one feels "Its my *duty* to go and support so important a cause." The list of such feelings can become quite long. Sometimes there is an awareness of a specific value that must be honored, but at other times one simply feels a sense of duty, with no awareness of any value, though, to be sure, specific values are there somewhere in the background, defining for the person what is important. But the sense of duty over-arches all specific values and supplies their dynamism. The opposite of this person might be someone who has a full array of moral values and is certain of their rightness but conscience is so weak that the values often get compromised by other influences of the moment.

Possible additions to the complexity are certain values which have a very broad general nature, values such as justice and fairness, respect for the integrity of persons, doing the Divine will, respect for the rights of nature, and freedom and equality. With these the appropriate moral behavior often is not obvious and sometimes fine judgements must be made as to what, for instance, is the just and fair thing to do and as to what one's own moral duty is.

Using "conscience" loosely here to designate the whole process of the functioning of moral values, some general functions may now be given.

Psychodynamics of moral values and conscience. The moral values stand in a class by themselves because of their powerful nature, though certain other values of the person may also be powerful. There is no formal list of moral values, and each person's array will be somewhat unique to himself, but in a given society most persons will share certain ones and the total held by anyone will not be great. As indicated above, such values as honesty and truthfulness, avoidance of injury, industriousness, and fairness are widely held values among ourselves and likely are held widely around the world as well, as they are necessary if people are to be able to live and interact with each other and communities to function (it is the negative or "evil" form of these that best communicates their moral significance -- dishonesty, lying, hurting others, laziness, and being unfair).

As to their dynamic role, several functions stand out: (a) self-punishers for moral transgressions; (b) guides in anticipating and forestalling moral transgression; (c) self-rewarders for moral "goodness"; (d) guides in moral reasoning; (e) guides or motivators in reaching out and initiating action; and (f) standards of judgement of the behavior of others.

(a) *Self-punishers*. Though the essence of conscience is the self-judgement following a transgression, with its following emotion of guilt, troubledness, or other, it is well to formulate it as a complete sequence, beginning with perception as initiator, and reaction of some sort as terminator. Otherwise, if we picture its initiation at the point of judgement we may find ourselves employing too inflexible a formulation and incapable of accounting for the variability or adaptability that is always there. So to aid in conceptualization let us use this simple formulation: perception-interpretation (leading to) ➜ judgement-emotion (leading to) ➜ possible reaction. An example showing the sequence might be this: I get into an argument with my wife and become increasingly angry and start shouting; she ignores my arguments, which further frustrates, and in addition she accuses me of behaving childishly; in great irritation and frustration I hit her. Let it be assumed that I have a strong moral value against both losing my temper and hitting anyone, so my perception-interpretation of my own behavior is that I did lose my temper and hit in violation of values. I condemn (judge) myself for behaving this way and feel self-disgust. In further reaction I scold myself, keep coming back to my disgusting conduct and, feeling bad, resolve to try to avoid it again.

Because the perception-interpretation phase occurs instantly and unconsciously, seldom are we aware of its role, but in certain exceptional situations we may be reminded of its importance. A good example is perception of own conduct in situations of moral exclusion. As mentioned in Chapter 1, moral exclusion involves excluding other individuals or groups from one's "moral community," hence viewing them as outside the boundary within which moral values and rules of justice and fairness apply. The most obvious example is the excluding of persons labeled "the enemy" and thereby feeling morally justified in abusing and killing during war between countries, civil war, insurrection, terrorism and guerrilla warfare. The enemy gets treated better in declared war between countries than in civil war and insurrection, which often is unbelievably brutal, because international rules of war prescribe certain forms of humane treatment for prisoners of war. Which is to say that the prisoner of war is admitted back into one's moral community.

Another example of the role of perception is feeling guilt or shame as a result of criticism or accusation from others. Indeed, sometimes the perception of fault-finding is a misperception, resulting from one's misreading what is actually said.

The specific coloring of the central emotional state of conscience will vary from time to time. "Feelings of guilt" is the term most often used to describe it; at other times it might be described as feelings of remorse, self-disgust, troubledness, self-irritation, self-condemnation, and (mild) self-dissatisfaction.

On the reaction side, the miserable feeling of guilt spontaneously produces such reactions as self-castigation, self-punishment, reliving the incident and wishing to have done better, resolving never to repeat the behavior, doing something positive in compensation, apologizing and making amends, rationalizing the event to self so as to excuse and justify own behavior, and perhaps, in the extreme, if the misery is so great, losing memory of the event (repressing). Persons who tend to be very severe with themselves are the very ones who must resort to extreme reactions, such as repressing.

Main moral values have a strong, absolute quality, so much so that they are dictators of one's conduct with no choice or qualification. Suppose the value of fairness is strong with me. As a teacher the very thought of treating a student unfairly is repugnant, but suppose some circumstance leads me to treat someone unfairly. Then upon learning of it I feel very troubled, guilty, and remorseful, and those feelings motivate me to want to do what is needed to remove the harm. I have no peace of mind until it is done. But of course moral values do differ in strength or importance, this determining the self-perception, the self-judgement, and any reaction. I might, for example, value truth-telling, but in fact not regard it as all-important and find myself sometimes spontaneously exaggerating my accomplishments and defensively lying about my errors and faults. As I judge these failings I feel somewhat regretful, yet am quite self-forgiving, and soon have forgotten each violation.

Unlike childhood morals that gain their impelling quality from parental interactions and emphases, adult moral values gain much of theirs through their connection with the self-image. That is, one in effect will be saying to oneself "I see (conceive) myself to be an unselfish (or kind, sympathetic, equalitarian, helpful, etc.) person." From this follows an effort to behave consistent with this conception of self -- to be unselfish or whatever -- and some self-dissatisfaction at falling short, together with some self-censure of the sorts mentioned above (see Allport, 1962, p. 134-138).

(b) *Anticipating and forestalling.* Though we emphasize conscience as provoker of guilt, an equally important function is that of preventing disvalued thoughts and actions. So in my example above of hitting my wife, if conscience had been more effective, or the provocation less intense, I would not have become angry or had any impulse to hit. This is the *ideal role* of moral values and conscience (the touch of the Divine within!) and if it always functioned ideally we never would have occasion to feel guilty and condemn ourselves.

(c) *Positive moral behavior.* In our preoccupation with moral prohibitions it is easy to forget that all of the negative values have positive aspects (e.g. unfairness *and* fairness) and there are still other moral virtues. Though one may take for granted the rightness of honesty or fairness and make nothing of it to self when honest and fair, there may be times of feeling gratified at one's own valued behavior. Granted that self-praise can be sheer vanity, still the good feeling of a good act is quite as justified as the bad feeling of a failing.

(d) *Guides in moral reasoning.* While the main substance of conscience is the firmly established moral values, which produce a somewhat automatic, predictable reaction, conscience must also be seen as a flexible, adaptable process that comes into play whenever one encounters an issue, problem, or dilemma that provokes a moral reaction. The specific judgement that is made may never have been made before; rather is a result of *moral reasoning* about the issue while weighing two or more value considerations. And one's own behavior and welfare may not be involved at all, hence there is no possibility of a reaction of guilt (or self-satisfaction) as in the classical case. We shall see this exemplified in the topic below on people in moral interaction.

(e) *Motivators to action.* A fairly obvious additional role of moral values, as of values generally, is as motivators to action. The idealism, the sense of the right and just inherent in one or another value easily can mobilize one to action, to right the wrong, assure fairness, improve the lot of humanity, or whatever. The above moral reasoning may take one beyond a simple judgement, and on to action.

(f) *Judgements of others.* Though dictionary meanings speak only of conscience as self-judge, the moral values also affect perception of the behavior of others and, as just mentioned, how one will reason on moral issues that have no personal involvement. If respect and care for elders is strong with me likely I will be judging others with the same standard. We might wonder whether the person who has a strong conscience toward his own behavior is equally strong in condemnation of the same failings in others.

The category of moral values has no clear boundaries and, rather, shades off into other types of evaluative values, all being experienced as right, good, and true and having the motivational quality that one "should" or "ought" to behave this way. The main moral values appear to differ only in being experienced as more certainly right, are held with greater intensity, and may have more the quality of "must" than the more flexible "should".

Ideal Self-Concepts

The preceding topic proposed that some moral values become a part of the self-image; but the self-concepts are not limited to the moral and may be examined further. Each person holds a number of concepts as to his present nature -- one person might describe self as of medium stature, poor at figures, in good health but readily catches cold, a political liberal, interested in archeology, quite good at tennis, enjoys social gatherings, etc. (the list can get quite long).

Also held are concepts as to how one ideally would like to be; that is, valued traits. Some of these will have the quality of "ideal" or "perfect" -- to be the outstanding (perfect) pianist, the champion tennis player, the Nobel-prize-winning scientist -- and not assumed to be realistically attainable, but still idealized and valued nonetheless. Others will be much closer to daily behavior and function as standards against which we judge daily thoughts and acts -- perhaps to be considerate of other's feelings, to be a calm controlled person, to be more consistent in one's tennis game and win more often. Some will actually be attained in daily life, so will be a source of present satisfaction -- perhaps one values good health and is now living a health-promoting life, or values meditation and enlightenment and now meditates and has experienced some enlightenment, or values a good memory and now has a good memory.

Also held of course are negative or contra-ideal self-concepts, ideas as to how one would dislike being. One might exclaim to oneself with some vehemence, "I would hate to be a 'couch-potato,' my whole life wasted viewing the T.V.." When we think of the contra-ideals, the moral negatives readily come to mind, such as selfishness, dishonesty, greed, or laziness; but quite a long list can be assembled if less-extreme traits are included, such as disvaluing and avoiding boastfulness, defensiveness, dominatingness, impulsiveness, and impatience. Which is to say that quite many ways of behaving can be regarded by one person or another as undesirable and hence to be avoided and criticized in oneself when observed.

Just as certain of our values lead us to be judging the people and events that come our way, so these self-values lead us to judge our own behavior, at one moment feeling self-satisfied at valued acts and self-critical at another for disvalued acts. It would be interesting to know how often ordinary (normal) persons experience these self-evaluations, but I know of no evidence on the matter. For the moment, let us just guess that it occurs from time to time but is not constantly occurring.

Turning to effectively-functioning persons (who would be the extreme in the mentally-healthy direction), it is generally assumed by personality psychologists that they experience a rather good fit between ideals and actual behavior, so the times of self-dissatisfaction will be few and not devastating. Likely they do have their times of thinking that it would be nice to be able to create beautiful music or discover a cure for cancer (etc.) but they accept the fact that "I seem not to be the one chosen to do it." And they would not be expected to have much in the way of literal dreams of glory, where one daydreams of people flocking to admire one because he is the greatest pianist or greatest scientist, because these persons are reasonably accepting of own talents and skills and have little need to dream of glory, and are little preoccupied with self. But they do experience times of self-dissatisfaction and criticism since error and imperfection are the lot of all humanity and they are realistic about their mistakes.

At the other extreme we are certain that ideal-self values play a large part in the lives of troubled-maladjusted persons. Their insecurity leads them to be preoccupied with self generally and often leads them to have dreams of glory -- to idealize being acclaimed as "the greatest" at whatever activity is chosen. Worse, their standards for more ordinary daily behavior are so high and their judgements of self so severe and frequent that they have many times of self-criticism. Too, the self-criticism can be so severe that they may be damning themselves for past ordinary shortcomings. Even behavior in conformity with ideals, which should yield welcome self-satisfaction, tends to be distorted and discounted.

This constellation of behavior tends to keep itself going because the self-condemnation keeps the insecurity high, and the insecurity produces the high ideals and self-condemnation. Often in such a person there is a need to prove self outstanding, to draw acceptance and admiration, which may take the form of boasting and self-assertion (egoism) but this too is self-defeating.

During counseling ordinarily much time is spent in helping the person to change to more self-tolerant values and to perceive own behavior in a more realistic manner, and of course to change actual behavior. These are all interlocked and progress usually slow. (This thumbnail sketch of the troubled person may suggest more uniformity than is actually seen; these several reactions are typical, not universal.)

Individual Values as Motivators

Just as society-wide values motivate, so, too, do individual values. The given conception of the desirable is straightforwardly mobilizing motivation to live the given way or attain the given goal. Examples of such ways to live and goals were given in Chapter 1, among them to attain security and safety, develop self, and have a life of carefree enjoyment.

Typically these values pattern our lives for years or even for a lifetime, so gain importance by their duration.

But as important as the above types of values are in patterning lives, still the profound role of values in lives might be missed if no more were said. History is full of instances of persons devoting their lives to causes, sometimes enduring torture and suffering, and sometimes sacrificing their lives for sake of a value. The apostle Paul comes to mind as one who came to regard the new way of life, Christianity, as so important that he devoted the remainder of his life to its propagation, even in face of condemnation, attack, and imprisonment. The medical missionary, Albert Sweitzer, devoted his life to giving medical care to tribal peoples in remote areas of Africa, and Mother Teresa has done the same for the poor of Calcutta, India. The pages of the monthly newspaper *Amnesty International* regularly carry reports of persons in countries around the world who have been imprisoned, and often abused and tortured, because of their actions in behalf of such precious values as freedom of speech, equality, and democracy and against dictatorship, corruption, abuse, and exploitation.

Perhaps no better statement of the role of values in motivating action in spite of danger may be found than this brief one, written by an anonymous citizen of El Salvador in the midst of the turmoil, civil war, and murder and oppression by the military of that troubled country: "The opposite of fear is not courage. As I walk into danger or risk I carry my fear and doubt with me. But what keeps me from being overwhelmed by fear is conscience, the consciousness of what is right, the conviction of what I must do, the determination to be true to my conscience."

Comparable examples were the behaviors of Europeans who aided the Jews at the time of the Nazi persecution, always at great risk to their own lives. Fogelman and Wiener (1985) report the rescuers fell into two groups, those motivated chiefly by deeply-held moral values and those whose motivation was mainly emotional and based on personal attachment or identification with the victim (some combined both).

Rescuers of the first type felt ethically compelled to rescue Jews, while those in the second type usually personalized the situation between themselves and those they helped. They were less concerned about fulfilling abstract moral obligations than about trying to protect people from harm.

Fogelman and Wiener (p. 62) report that they could recognize value-oriented motivation immediately when they asked rescuers why they did it. Almost instinctively they would reply, "What do you mean?" as if there was no need to explain. Questioned further, such rescuers said matter-of-factly, "It was the right thing to do," or "I was only doing what a human being should for another human being."

The appeal to values in modern warfare. As we have seen, values are among the most powerful of motivators, sometimes overriding such basic motives as fear, pain, and hunger. Modern warfare requires mobilization of the efforts of whole populations, ordinarily requiring such sacrifices by the civilian population as higher taxes and reduced income, reduced supplies of food and clothing (rationing), long-hours of work, and often the danger of bombing, invasion, and loss of life. For the military forces there is of course the danger of attack, maiming, and death. Fear of attack will itself be a powerful motivator of defensive efforts, but for several reasons fear is not enough and an appeal to values may be the only way of producing the required depth of involvement and willingness to sacrifice on the part of the millions. To some extent the value-produced motivation arises spontaneously, as when young men feel moved by patriotism to enlist and others to volunteer to become air raid wardens. But this falls short of what is needed, especially to keep people involved after the early idealism of sacrifice has worn off, so systematic programs are initiated by governments to appeal to values and thus sustain the involvement.

A few instances will exemplify different aspects of the process.

At outbreak of World War I young Englishmen of the upper classes, university students especially, rushed to enlist and request active duty, but this eagerness was not out of antipathy for the Germans. The peoples of the two countries had long enjoyed good relations, there was much cultural exchange, they were able to visit each other's country without a passport, and the royalty of the two countries was closely interrelated. Patriotism, that blend of sense of duty and devotion to country, was the main value and motivation of these young men. Surely also many saw themselves as akin to the knights of old going off to risk lives for King and Country, and, the battle won, soon to return to the respect of grateful countrymen (for all expected the war to be short). Of course the same thing happened among the young men of Germany, France, Austria, and Russia. (See the report on Vera Brittain, at end of next chapter, for a good impression of the times and the war spirit of the young people of England at outbreak of WWI.)

Patriotism as felt toward the large modern nation-state is a fairly recent thing, as is also conscription. The two logically go together in that conscription can force the young man to enter the military but cannot assure that he has a willingness to fight; patriotism supplies that. At outset rulers probably systematically encouraged the patriotism in order to produce committed fighters, but it seems now to be largely self-perpetuating. The flag-waving patriotic orator on national holidays will be one of the most obvious perpetuators, but throughout the society there will be less-obvious encouragers -- history books, patriotic novels and films, teachers, parents, etc.. And for certain, at outbreak of war, there will be a great spontaneous reemphasis on duty and devotion to country in communities all across the land, with consequent effects on people's motivation.

In Europe, as W. W. I continued for four long years, the leadership of each country had to find means of keeping its civilian population hard at work and enduring privation, and its soldiers willing to enter the trenches and face the machine guns and bombardments. New appeals to values had to be devised and the issues sharpened. Inevitably, "our" side came to be portrayed as the savior of Western civilization, the protector of liberty, the preserver of Christianity. The enemy became bloodthirsty barbarians (the word "Hun," as used to describe the Germans, had this meaning), slayers of innocent women and children, godless infidels; and were they to win, our brave soldiers would be shot, our women despoiled, everyone enslaved, and a dark age would descend upon Europe. The appeal to values and to fear worked, but just before war's end French soldiers had had enough of the slaughter and refused to go forward to the trenches, German sailors mutinied aboard ships, and Russian armies joined the revolution.

Early in W. W. II President Roosevelt broadcast to the world the Four Freedoms -- freedom of speech and religion and freedom from want and fear. He delivered them with considerable eloquence and throughout the war they were repeated often. They were intended to inspire people everywhere to join the struggle in expectation of their realization at war's end. Later he proposed the organization that became the United Nations as a means of giving people a vision of world government where disputes could be settled without warfare. This idea, too, had wide appeal and surely inspired many a person to contribute to the war effort.

As we know, the Vietnam War split the country, and provides a good example of failure to evoke cherished values and unite the country in their defense. Few young men were inspired to enlist and effort to avoid the draft was widespread. There was no mobilization of the nation in face of imminent danger and no demand that everyone make sacrifices. It was "life as usual" even for the war's supporters. The only ones who were made to sacrifice were the young draftees. The only strong ideological appeal was of the danger of communism, but neither President Johnson nor President Nixon was a convincing advocate, Vietnam was far away, and many remained unconvinced of any danger.

The Mideast War proved to be remarkably brief but of course its length could not be foreseen, and President Bush had to plan his military offensive in anticipation of protracted warfare and high casualties. Too, he had to gain the approval of a Congress that was not solidly convinced of the necessity of military attack to force the withdrawal of Iraqi forces, rather than continuation of the embargo. So his task was to inspire the soldiers to risk their lives for a worthy cause, prepare parents to perceive the death of a soldier-son as for a noble cause and not merely to protect an oil supplier, and to convince congressmen of the rightness of his strategy. And unlike the situation in previous wars, he could not stress danger to homeland and threat to cherished American values, as there was no danger from Iraq on those scores.

In a televised address to the nation (28 Jan., 1991) he presented his appeal. Note in the excerpts below his use throughout of strong American beliefs and values to try to convince his audience.

Straightforwardly, he posed the approaching attack on the forces of Iraq as the "defining hour" for a historic battle between good and evil. This states the moral magnitude of the undertaking in crystal-clear terms.

Declaring that only the United States among the nations of the world has had both the moral standing and the strength to undertake this struggle, he continued, "We are the only nation on this earth that could assemble the forces of peace. This is the burden of leadership -- and the strength that has made America the beacon of freedom in a searching world." "Americans know that leadership brings burdens and requires sacrifice. The conviction and courage we see in the Persian Gulf today is simply the American character in action."

"We are Americans, part of something larger than ourselves. For two centuries, we've done the hard work of freedom. And tonight, we lead the world in facing down a threat to decency and humanity."

"What is at stake is more than one small country; it is a big idea: a new world order -- where diverse nations are drawn together in common cause, to achieve the universal aspirations of mankind: peace and security, freedom and rule of law. Such is a world worthy of our struggle and worthy of our children's future."

These last lines might as well have been taken from addresses by President Wilson, as he pleaded for the League of Nations at end of W. W. I, and President Roosevelt, as he gave his vision of the United Nations.

Bush concluded with a pointed appeal to the conscience of his viewers, "This we do know: Our cause is just. Our cause is moral. Our cause is right. Let future generations understand the burden and blessings of freedom. Let them say, we stood where duty required us to stand."

It will be evident that he resorts to considerable exaggeration in his description of America; no falling-short of ideals is mentioned. This is typical of such presentations and perhaps considered necessary if ideals are to be stimulated. But we may wonder at foreigners' perception of the address, with their more objective view of this country, especially the Arabs, who will know well America's long support of Israel at the expense of the Palestinians, depriving them of the above "peace and security, freedom and rule of law."

Values as Determiners of Choices

It was mentioned under an earlier topic that evaluations or judgements of people and things -- "this is good," "that is bad" -- are common human behavior. A common related role of values is as determiners of choices and decisions. Life is filled with occasions for choice; they cannot be avoided.

It was suggested in Chapter 2 that not all acts of valuing or choosing involve values. So many of the day to day choices are just of the moment and involve a momentary weighing of the two or more alternatives -- Shall I buy the tan or blue shirt?, Shall we go to movie X or Y?, Shall we vacation at Smith Beach or Jones Inlet? No enduring values underlie the choices.

But significant choices and decisions often involve values. Possibilities are: (a) *Choice of field of study, occupation or career.* Vocational interests are in part values and in vocational counseling an effort is made to help the counselee discover his values. Typical of studies on the matter was that of Rosenberg (1957). A nationwide sample of college students were shown a list of wants and values and each asked to consider to what extent a job or career would have to satisfy each of these requirements before he or she would consider it ideal. Having highest rating at 78% was *Use my special abilities and aptitudes*, followed by *Provide a stable, secure future* (61%), and, chosen by about half (48%), *Permits creativity and originality*. Lowest was *Provides adventure* (16%), *Has social status and prestige* (26%), and *Gives chance to exercise leadership* (32%).

(b) *Choice of mates*. Studies have found that the values of the other person are an important consideration in selection of a mate. The questionnaires used in computerized dating give values a prominent place.

(c) *Choice of friends*. As in the preceding, we are especially sensitive to values in forming enduring friendships.

(d) *Choice of political party* or other political affiliation or activity, including decision to vote for a given candidate. Political groups themselves support given values, so the individual may simply be picking the group whose values are similar to his own.

(e) *Choice of membership group*. As with the preceding, a common basis for choice is perception of the values of the group as matching one's own.

(f) *Decision to give financial or other support* to an organization or movement. Again as with the preceding.

Values Can Give Meaning to Existence

We have seen how group values can be supplying point and meaning to existence for whole peoples. Individual values can have the same role for each of us. Singly and in total they can be giving one a sense that life is meaningful, that I am here for a purpose and have my work to do, that daily activities have worth, that I envision a lifetime well spent.

Contrarily, where there is a dearth of values one might experience purposelessness, a wondering and questioning of existence, an emptiness, perhaps even as the Existentialists would have it, an agony of the spirit. It was just such a condition that Frankl had in mind when he wrote of the condition of meaninglessness and termed it a special kind of neurosis -- "noogenic neurosis."

Frankl's ideas deserve full reading, together with the narrative of his experiences in a Nazi concentration camp (see *Man's Search for Meaning*, 1962). In brief, he says there are three ways of giving meaning or finding value in life: creative meaning, experiential meaning, and attitudinal meaning. Creative meaning is found in creative and productive activity, such as serving others or engaging in one of the many forms of creative activity. Experiential meaning is found in receiving from the world, as in surrendering oneself to the beauty of nature. Attitudinal meaning is special and comes into play only in times of suffering and adversity -- and suffering if not also adversity is part of the common lot of humans. We cannot will away a disease or other misfortune, but we can take different attitudes toward it. We can let ourselves be crushed and destroyed by it or we can find meaning in it. Attitudinal meaning is the finding of personal significance in suffering (Frankl, 1962).

Values Expressed in Conceptions of the Good Life

It seems likely that everyone has a conception of the good life, however imaginary and impossible of attainment it may be. Its creation is effortless and for some it helps supply meaning to existence and may make present life more tolerable.

In the depth of the Great Depression of the 1930s a song titled "In the Big Rock-Candy Mountains" was popular. It was well suited to those difficult times when many were unemployed, penniless, sometimes hungry, and wandered the countryside looking for work, for it rather well described the poor man's utopia. In the Big Rock-Candy Mountains handouts grew on trees (food was plentiful and free) and you never had to work; the railroad box-cars all were empty and the sun shone every day; watchdogs all had rubber teeth and policemen wooden legs; the jails were made of tin and you could slip right out again as soon as you were in. The lines about policemen, guard dogs, and jails were appropriate because these wandering men sometimes resorted to petty theft, as of food, and daily rode the freight trains (empty box-cars), which was illegal but often their only means of transport, so they often were in trouble with the law. Too, it was a time of widespread dissatisfaction with the existing social order, because it seemed to have failed, with much anti-establishment sentiment.

Conceptions of ideal ways to live and ideal societies have existed since ancient times. Indeed, it is proper to regard descriptions of heaven (Christian) or paradise (Islamic) as ideal places to which one goes at death.

Holloway (1965) has aptly commented:

The Promised Land, the Golden Age, Heaven, and Utopia represent myths that are common to all mankind. Those peoples whom we suppose to have lived ideal lives compared with our own, themselves knew legends of better times, when all was ease and bliss. Similarly, each civilization and each century has its comparative golden ages. What the eighteenth century is to the present, the Renaissance was to the eighteenth century; and if the humanist scholars of the Renaissance looked back to a silver Rome and a golden Greece, the finest achievements of the Greeks themselves were inspired by traditions of an heroic age in which gods and men were sometimes indistinguishable, and all was veiled in legend half-accepted as fact. (p. 20-21)

Plato's conception of the ideal or perfect society, as laid out in the *Republic*, is one of the earliest to come down to us, but there were others in Greek times, Zeno's *Republic* for one. St. Thomas More, writing in 1516, gave us the word "Utopia," the name of an imaginary island where perfection in moral, social, and political life prevailed. His utopia was derived almost entirely from the Greeks and Plato.

Much of the reform within Christianity in Europe, beginning in about the eleventh century, was inspired by visions of a more perfect society, and the persecutions, as of the Waldenses and the Anabaptists, were caused as much or more by fear of the social changes advocated or actually practiced (such as community ownership of property and equal sharing of income) as by religious beliefs. Luther was as much opposed to them as the Catholic Church.

For nearly two thousand years men and women of the Christian heretical sects have attempted to live according to the precepts of the biblical Sermon on the Mount, for it has been perceived as describing an ideal manner of living (and surely about the briefest of such descriptions). Many of them, especially during the last three centuries have set up small societies of a communistic nature (Holloway, p. 8). Seventeenth-century Europe was full of such sects. Persecution, however severe, did nothing to diminish their fervor. But since Europe tended to be an inhospitable place for them -- there was as yet no political or religious freedom, no election, and no country in which the Church was disestablished -- they turned to the New World where there was religious and political tolerance, ample open space, land cheap or free, and each community able to live well-apart from disturbing neighbors.

By the nineteenth century they were firmly established and that century was the golden age of community experiments in America. Holloway says of them:

> Over a hundred communities, with a total membership of more than one hundred-thousand men, women, and children, were tried out in the course of the century. Some features of these experiments, whether they were sectarian or not, were more revolutionary than those of the much larger democratic and working-class movements in Europe, from which they differed fundamentally in that they attempted to dissociate themselves completely from established society. Instead of trying to change society from within, by parliamentary reform or by violent revolution, they tried to set up models of ideal commonwealths, thus providing examples which (in some cases) they hoped the world would follow. The ideal they sought, and often succeeded in achieving, included equality of sex, nationality, and colour; the abolition of private property; the abolition of property in people, either by slavery or through the institutions of monogamy and the family; the practice of non-resistance; and the establishment of a reputation for fair-dealing, scrupulous craftsmanship, and respect for their neighbours. (p. 18-19)

In a book aptly titled *Heavens on Earth* (1965) Holloway describes many of these communities.

Nearly all have ceased to exist. It would be useful to detail the founding, life, and demise of several, but that would take us too far afield. Some adverse influences came from outside the communities, such as the filling-up of the country with people and the consequent increasing exposure to external ("foreign") American cultural ways, and rapid industrialization, but notable were the divisive influences from within. Utopias begin as conceptions of the ideal society in someone's mind. As long as they remain in minds or on paper they can continue to be ideal or perfect, but the moment they begin to be actualized, reality, in the form of human imperfection, intervenes. Personal rivalries for power, conflicting views as to what should be community policy, religious schisms, "holier than thou" attitudes and criticisms of backsliders, failure of some to do their share, egoism, selfishness, and jealousy are some of the imperfections that tend to crop up again and again in such communities.

But notable in the communities that were created is how radical their ideals (values) and practices often were and how long they did continue before dissolution. Some might have continued far longer had the original members remained alive, for of course the original "dream" was in their minds; but new generations, both within and without, tended to be quite different in ideals and beliefs and had little desire to continue the communities.

Though few utopias are conceived and organized these days, it might be mentioned that ideals of a very practical sort are experienced by everyone -- ideals as to family life, level of income, job security, quality of housing, medical care, education and the like. Public opinion polling organizations regularly sample the public's attitudes toward these things by way of assessing public morale. Public officials find this information useful or necessary in making decisions. (See Campbell, Converse, and Rodgers, 1976, for a general report on the quality of American life, and see polling reports in newspapers and elsewhere for recent reports on goals or ideals.)

We are indebted to Charles Morris (1956) for his formulation of thirteen possible ways to live, about half of which are broadly derived from historic patterns of living, ideal or real. One may read them and decide which are his own conceptions of an ideal way to live (see pages 15-16, Chapter 1, above, for *Way 1* and headings of the other twelve).

Values as Foundations of Specific Attitudes

Another of the basic roles of values is as foundation of specific attitudes. By no means all of a person's attitudes will have value foundations; some are simply borrowed whole from other persons and still others result from ego needs, hostility, anxiety or other causes. But attitudes may have value foundations. I may, for example, value both human and animal life and so find myself adopting such specific attitudes as opposing war, supporting the U. N. children's programs, supporting the Humane Society, and favoring legislation and agreement to protect porpoises and whales.

A study by Smith (1949) is one of the few that has attempted to examine the relation between the person's values and his attitudes. A sample of 250 adult men in a New England community were interviewed twice. The first interview was designed to elicit a description of each man's attitude toward Russia, especially the nature of the main beliefs composing the attitude. The second interview was designed to gain information about each man's personality, including his values. Smith found that the nature of the central values of the person was important in determining the main aspects of his attitude toward Russia. For example, 36 percent of those respondents for whom "liberty" was a central personal value stressed "the lack of freedom and democracy inside Russia," as compared with only 17 percent of the rest of the respondents. This proved to be the only important difference between the two groups in their attitude toward Russia.

Rokeach (1973, p. 87-121) has published evidence showing that values probably were involved in or related to a number of specific attitudes of his respondents, but the nature of the research procedure does not permit us to say that the value of a given person produced the attitude. In 1968 a nationwide sample of American adults completed his *Value Survey*, which consists of two lists of 18 value terms, and also were asked their attitudes about a number of concerns of the day -- the Vietnam war, civil rights, religion, etc..

He found that the value concept *equality* was given a higher average ranking by persons who (a) expressed compassion (felt sad) at the recent assassination of Dr. Martin Luther King and sympathy for his wife and children; (b) expressed favorable attitudes toward such civil rights concerns as equal housing, education, and job opportunities for black Americans; (c) expressed similar favorable attitudes toward the rights of the poor for medical and dental care, adequate housing, and education (etc.); (d) expressed favorable attitudes toward student protest (which was primarily against the Vietnam war); (e) expressed unfavorable attitudes toward our continued involvement in the Vietnam war; and (f) expressed favorable attitudes toward the churches' being active in public affairs. In a separate study, Tate and Miller (1971) found that persons classified as intrinsically religious, as compared with the extrinsically religious, ranked *equality* higher.

The value concept *salvation* was given higher average ranking by university students who gave strong affirmative answers to the question, "How important is your religion to you in your everyday life?," as compared with students who gave negative answers (Rokeach, 1973, p. 111).

Rokeach found a number of other value concepts to be statistically related to the above attitudes but it is difficult to see connections. For example, those most sympathetic toward the student protests gave relatively higher rankings to *a sense of accomplishment, wisdom,* being *broad-minded, imaginative,* and *intellectual,* than did the unsympathetic; whereas the unsympathetic gave higher average rankings to *a comfortable life, family security, national security, salvation, true friendship,* being *clean, obedient,* and *polite* (1973, p. 106). Hardly any of these have a common-sense relationship to the student protest and in most cases the difference between the two groups of respondents, though statistically significant, is not striking. There may be patterns of personality make-up hidden in these tables of rankings that would yield fascinating insights and explain some of these results, but a different method of analysis would be needed to uncover them.

Unfortunately, knowing the person's values does not allow us to predict his attitudes. The same value may lead different persons to develop different -- even opposing -- attitudes. For example, individual freedom is a basic American value. In some individuals this leads to attitudes that one has a right to make money however one wishes, with no interference from government. But in others it may lead to attitudes that government must be used to protect the rights of individuals, especially from economic exploitation by clever, indifferent businessmen. As must be emphasized throughout, how the given value will affect attitudes will be dependent on such other things about the person as his other values, beliefs, and attitudes, and also by his temperament and wants and by such situational influences as his group affiliations.

Clarity of Values as Characteristic of Effectively Functioning Persons

It is generally believed that a well-developed set of personal values is conducive to better personal integration, effectiveness, and peace of mind. Studies tend to support the assumption. A number of earlier studies found that students who had more insight into their own values were thought to be better adjusted, more self-objective, and less given to rationalization. However, these evidences of a correlation are not to be interpreted as proving that the insight into values was cause of the greater effectiveness. We are better advised to regard the clarity of values as one characteristic of effectively functioning persons. In one thorough study of "soundness" in graduate students at a major university it was found that the sounder students showed four areas of effectiveness, one of which was "character and integrity in the ethical sense." These subjects gave evidence of being more dependable, serious, responsible, and tolerant. They had strong internally-determined principles (Barron, 1954, as cited by Allport, 1961, p. 279). In an oft-cited study of self-actualizing persons Maslow (1954) found fourteen notable characteristics in these effectively functioning persons, among them "ethical certainly." "None of the subjects was unsure of the difference between right and wrong in daily living. Expressed differently, they did not confuse means with ends, and held firmly to the pursuing of ends felt by themselves to be right" (Allport, 1961, p. 281). Allport, in his description of the mature personality, gives "a unifying philosophy of life" as one of six characteristics of such a person, and concludes that an integrated sense of moral obligation provides a unifying philosophy of life (Allport, 1961, 304).

People in Value Interaction

We have noted how humans are inveterate evaluators, passing judgement on most things that come their way. Some of our valuations are made in private, as when we react approvingly or negatively to things seen in newspaper or on television, without sharing the judgement with anyone else or informing another of the value. But other judgements are made in interaction with others, as in conversation around the dinner table, in classroom discussion, at neighborhood gathering, town meeting, club, or wherever else people gather and discuss issues and express values. In these interaction situations what is happening? Do people coolly and rationally exchange views, or do they typically express their values with some conviction and readily become emotionally involved in the interchange? Is there some influence on each other's values, or do they hold much the same position throughout? In general, do values tend to be rather set convictions, or are they somewhat variable depending upon the issue, with whom interacting, and personal characteristics of the holder?

One study of the question was done by Haan, Aerts, and Cooper (1985), specifically investigating moral values, which as we have seen are among the strongest and most important of values. Their overall purpose was to present a new theory of moral value interaction, termed the Haan "interactional theory," and to compare it with the leading existing moral value theory, the "cognitive developmental theory" of Kohlberg.

It was a two-phase study, intended to investigate (a) *moral development* and (b) *moral interaction* as seen by the two theories. Our review here is divided into the two parts, with the moral development phase treated in the next chapter on origins of values, and the interactional phase treated here. Since the interactional theory has much to say on moral interaction and the cognitive theory very little (it is primarily a theory of development), little will be said here on results of the comparison of the two. Later, when development is reviewed, the two may be compared and results presented.

Three groups of persons were used in the study -- four-year olds, high school teenagers, and university students of average age 19, but the main group was the university students. These students belonged to already-existing friendship groups and the groups were asked to take part in two types of morals-involving interaction: (a) group *discussion of moral dilemmas*, which permitted verbal expression of values; and (b) *playing moral games*, where personal values could be expressed in action. But none of the dilemmas was a personal one for any participant and no one was required to declare what he would do personally to solve it, so it was a somewhat detached form of moral reasoning rather than personal moral action. However, the dilemmas were quite typical of the moral problems that face groups and communities and the involvement shown by the students indicates that they were perceived as real.

The playing of moral games was intended to face teams, and their members, with actual moral choices and actions, specifically involving honesty or acting in good faith. But the honesty involved was a far cry from, say, keeping dishonest money; rather it was honesty manifest while playing a game, with only tiny amounts of money at stake, and some of the "dishonest" ones may have perceived their own behavior at the moment as clever game-playing rather than as dishonesty or bad faith. Even so, there was plenty of involvement, with feelings of moral outrage and condemnation by some at the dishonesty and bad faith of others. (The experimenters had no desire to test deeply-held morals, but if they had, ethical considerations limit what can be done. As was, even with these mild moral games there was enough serious involvement as to warrant a period of light-hearted "cooling-down" at end of each game so that hopefully no one would leave with troubled feelings.)

Because of the more impersonal, less serious nature of these moral problems, a number of things could be influencing the given student's moral reasoning or action, whereas if a deeply held personal moral value were involved probably there would have been much less variability of the sort described below (though this assumption deserves verification).

Though value differences may be the most obvious thing in a value interaction, ordinarily the interactors share much in common in the way of underlying meanings or assumptions, perhaps all assuming that fairness or justice or duty is the ultimate standard of judgement of any solution. Were this lacking, there would be little basis for discussion of alternatives or solutions. People's value differences arise from specifics -- specifics of the situation or problem and specific personal priorities, interpretations, and conclusions. This will be evident in the discussion excerpt below.

Moral values are experienced as important, sometimes even as self-evident truths or imperatives, so value interactions tend to cause people to become thoroughly involved. Several things commonly occur at once. Each person experiences his position as "right" and may have difficulty even "hearing" other positions. Only slowly, if at all, is there an opening. Moral values are in part emotion -- they are strongly felt -- so the involvement brings emotions with it, and interactors are experiencing emotion throughout, with emotion becoming an important determinant of everything that happens, be it irritation, exultation, dejection or whatever (and see below for more on this). And moral disputation puts people under stress as they find themselves becoming personally involved, perhaps challenged and under attack, and the whole interaction becomes one of everyone wanting to talk at once and everyone intent on having his point of view heard and appreciated (Haan et al., 1985).

These qualities make moral interaction a somewhat different thing from ordinary group discussion, and give special significance to such things as interpersonal relationships, nature of leadership, and the person's adaptive and maladaptive ways of handling stress. The effects of these are elaborated below.

Before analyzing the interaction further, it may give one an idea of what may be happening in any group value-interaction if a transcription of one of the group interactions is presented. This is titled the Peace Corps Dilemma. As the authors comment, the group continuously sidesteps the necessity of deciding (but they are not required to come to a decision). Nevertheless, there is plenty of assertion of values.

Discussion of the Peace Corps Dilemma

In the first session the discussion groups took up the issue as to whether Andrew, an only child, should go overseas on his scheduled tour of duty for the Peace Corps or stay with his widowed mother, who has just developed a serious, chronic illness. The exchange begins a few minutes into the discussion. Readers will want to notice the students' third-person position, their relationship to the staff leader, and the group's continuously sidestepping the necessity of deciding. (These transcripts have been light edited for readability; SL will refer to staff leader.)

SARAH: You can care and you can be with them but there is nothing you can do. They are dying and it's a fact.

LUKE: You may feel that way now (*interjections by Ruth*) but I am just trying to put myself in the mother's place. You know maybe I'd want to stay, too.

RUTH: I think the mother would be very concerned about her son's career. It's like -- I don't know -- it's like his going off to the Peace Corps would make him, you know, so much farther ahead in having -- I don't know -- a fulfilling life. Although I'd like my son near, I wouldn't feel like I would be doing my duty as a parent in keeping him with me.

JEREMIAH: First I want to say two things. He can go on this Peace Corps later. In other words, he can enter at any stage in his life. (*Interruption from Sarah.*) It is not like he is missing out on a once in a lifetime . . . (*interruptions*) well, just remember what you were trying to say, 'cause I just want to say something I've been trying to say. You can't save their life. But you're talking about while the person is alive you want to make it as comfortable as possible. You're talking about --

someone you love. It is not a physical thing and it is so much more important. Like those experiments with apes -- they put an ape in a thing without a mother (*interruption*) and the little monkey dies because there is not a physical person -- there is nothing there. And that is what happens when you put people in these convalescent homes. They are not getting any love at all. The whole -- they just have no will to live and they die. (*Several voices at once.*)

RUTH: As a mother I would feel burden knowing. . . . I'd feel the burden!

SARAH: I don't want to burden my children. (*Many talking at once.*)

RUTH: I wouldn't want my kids around. I would feel bad. (*Many talking at once.*) I would live my life in such a way that I wouldn't need my son here. I wouldn't. . . . I hope that I live my life independently.

LUKE: Are you sure of that?

MARTHA: (*to the man*) Are you going to expect them to take care of you? Are you going to expect them to take care of you when you are old?

LUKE: I think I will want them to strongly. . . . I am sure. I want them to take care of me . . . you know.

MARTHA: Of course you'll want them to . . . (*interruptions*). . . . Do you want them to give up part of their life. Okay, you've just graduated from college, you're still young. . . .

LUKE: He is an only child, yeah, right.

MARTHA: There is so much opportunity for him. Do you want to stagnate his life right now at this point in time?

LUKE: I'm pretty much undecided about this whole thing. I still feel very strongly about the mother thing.

SL: Abe, what do you think?

ABE: I just had the feeling why can't you accomplish something? Why do you have to go to these foreign countries to accomplish something? There are so many opportunities in the cities and even the Peace Corps operates in the United States (*interruptions*) a lifetime goal.

MARTHA: But what he wants to do is go to a foreign country.

RUTH: For someone else it might be to work for IBM and that might be personally fulfilling but for this guy he wants to be. . . .

SARAH: (*interrupts*) But can I just make one point? No matter how much love there is for the mother and how much love there is for the son -- in the son's mind he's being kept back. He may never admit it, but there does build up a sense of bitterness. . . . (*Others: Yeah!*) . . . and I don't want that.

SAUL: I think it depends on the individual.

JEREMIAH: It does depend on the individual. I think you're speaking for what you would want. (*Many people speaking at once.*)

SL: Let me interject a question . . . uhm, to those of you who have raised the point that you should do what you need to do. Does it logically follow from what you're saying that as . . . I am really asking this as an open question . . . that as people get older and are widowed and there is no husband or wife in the home and they get ill, are you saying they then should be put into institutions for care . . . I mean, is that the solution to the problem?

LUKE: No. (*Others: No!*)

SL: Then what is the solution then? How is she going to be taken care of and while you're also getting to do what you want to do? The problems are not mutually exclusive. How would you handle both of these situations? You are giving a lot of weight to the need for the individual to be able to go out and to live their life, but you are also concerned about what to do with people who are older and ill. How do you balance those two?

SAUL: First you could try hiring a nurse or someone to stay at home with her . . . that is a lot more personalized. It's not the cold nursing home.

DEBRA: But he might not be able to afford it. Do you know how much a full-time nurse is?

SAUL: Right, right. . . .

DEBRA: I tell you -- a lot more than a Peace Corps worker makes. (*Laughter . . . yeahs*)

ABE: I think his dilemma is a secondary part of the question. He should first decide whether he is going to go or whether he is going to stay and then if he is going to go, it is up to his mother to decide. Does she want to go to a convalescent home, does she want to have a nurse hired? If he stays, does she still want to go to a convalescent home? That's what I think. (*Sarah interjects: Yeah.*) I think that would be my solution. But first the question has to be answered by him alone, whether to go or to stay.

SL: How do you think he should answer?

ABE: I think you should stay.

SARAH: What about the bitterness that is going to build up in him?

SAUL: Why would there be bitterness?

ABE: There is not always going to be bitterness. (*Jeremiah: That's true.*) But you have to realize that these people are getting older and they always can't be as they were.

SARAH: And they lived their life and had their chance and it's your turn.

SL: How would you balance out the problem I posed to you a few minutes ago. Is there a balance between what you do with your life and what they want to do?

SARAH: I know I don't want to live to the point where I can't take care of myself. I don't want to see that day -- because I don't want to have anyone think they have to take care of me (*interruptions*).

SL: What I'd like you to do is to generalize beyond this one situation. Is the solution for Andrew and Andrew's mother the one you would recommend for the whole society?

RUTH: I don't think an older or ill person should go to the convalescent home. That should be farther down the line of alternatives. You know, first of all, if you can afford it, hire a nurse. If you couldn't do that, maybe your mother has an older friend and they could live together and look after themselves -- I think that would be an ideal situation and maybe it is unfortunate that *he* has no brothers and sisters that they could all help out together. But I don't think you should totally abandon her (*interruption*) altogether. Yeah, yeah. I don't think he should abandon her and stick her in a convalescent home and send her a check every month (*many interject agreement*).

SARAH: You know, there is like a contract and. . . . (*Ruth interjects: That's right.*)

ABE: There are -- has to go with a balance, you know. One grandmother may be perfectly fine in a convalescent home -- that may be what she thrives on -- interaction with these people of her own age that will replace the friends she is losing but it may not be right for a grandmother who just enjoys spending time with people 20, 30, 40 years younger -- it has to do with the situation. The best person to realize that would be the children.

JEREMIAH: But first of all, it depends on whether she's really to the point where she needs a nurse 'cause she may be really ill, then of course if you can't afford a private nurse the only alternative is a convalescent home as the cheapest way to go. It just matters that the son is there and that she is being taken care of and at a different level, more abstract, she knows that she is being loved more than if she just was in a place where they have hard floors.

MARTHA: Do you have any relatives in a convalescent home?

JEREMIAH: I have -- and both of them have suffered. We don't have the money to support them. I know my uncle did have money, but he wanted to live his own life so he sent a check and he thought that was love. I think that the whole question here is -- what are the morals we're talking about? What is most important in our lives? Is it our

work? Or is it our relationships with people -- our lives or whatever? (*Many interject.*)
ABE: I think it depends on the individual. (p. 159-164)

This dilemma is an excellent topic for discussion because two or three major values are involved. On the one side is the age-old moral value of respect and care for parents (one of the Ten Commandments) and on the other the strong American values of self-direction and self-realization (freedom to do as one wishes for one's own good without interfering obligations and the right to realize one's potential and have the best possible life). In many societies respect and care for parents is still strong and there would be no question as to one's duty; but here, especially among a group of young Americans who would tend to see the problem through the son's eyes, there is clear difference of values and it produces a lively discussion.

Haan et al. identify several things that are influencing the nature and outcome of the interaction: emotion, group interrelationships, personal traits and strategies, and specifics of the moral problem. These are sketched below.

Role of emotions. As mentioned, moral values are strongly held, often having the quality of absolute rights and wrongs, so all will have some amount of emotion as part of their very nature. When people begin to enter into moral discourse the emotion will be there as a prominent part of the interaction. Haan et al. say emotions are almost always part of dialogue, even when the dilemma is hypothetical. Also, that emotion is contagious, automatically producing a corresponding emotion in the other. People use their own and other's emotions about dilemmas as important signals. A person may communicate emotion, such as indignation, even before anything is said and signal a moral evaluation that has yet to be verbalized (p. 68).

In moral conflict, first motivations are often heated attempts to defend the rightness of one's own moral claims. At this early point emotion may be too strong, hence maladaptive, producing heated assertion, verbal attack, shouting matches, withdrawal in anger, and other failures of dialogue. But if there is mutual concern to address a problem, there follows a cooling-down, with less intense emotion, and effort at communication.

Interim emotions inform and direct moral processes and may, in fact, determine the moral balance that discussants achieve and accept (p. 146). However, this does not mean that people resolve moral issues solely by emotion. Instead, emotions accompany and enrich understandings, and they convey far more authentic information about a person's position in a dispute than any well-articulated thoughts. In ordinary circumstances, emotions instruct and energize actions. But in situations of great moral costs or stress, emotions can overwhelm and disorganize rational evaluations. At this point understanding of the issue and quality of moral action deteriorate (p. 147). (And see the section below on coping and defending for more on this.)

Recognizing another person's emotional state is a reciprocal act, and mutually experienced emotion is a reaction of empathy. In the Haan interactional theory, the process of empathy is assumed always to be a <u>central</u> feature within moral action. Empathy may not appear at the beginning of moral disputes, but, from this theory's point of view, it evolves in circumstances of good faith, and it must evolve if equalization is to be achieved (and equalization is assumed to be the essence of morality in this theory) (p. 147).

It will be evident that emotion has both a negative and positive role in moral values and moral interaction. Not only does it give "body" to morals but supplies the motivation to be moral -- feelingless beliefs are not enough to produce action. They make the dilemma important and therefore lead to serious involvement in the discourse. They may produce too much ardor at outset, but at end may supply a compensating glow of mutual satisfaction and relief at reaching a mutually satisfactory solution.

Emotion is given a prominent place in the Haan interactional theory because it is reasoned that emotion is always there and playing a crucial part, as we have just been saying; this is to be contrasted with any assumption that moral values are simply cool, rational convictions. "From the interactional view, two well-known characteristics of practical morality are inconsistency in the quality of the same people's moral actions in different situations and the emotions moral issues generate, both moral indignation and the glow of the good conscience. This practical morality cannot be understood unless this inconsistency and the role of emotions are explained. Studies of people's strategies of coping and defending when they face moral conflict should elucidate both of these phenomena." (p. 69) (See below.)

Nature of group structuring or interrelationships. How members of a group interact with each other will of course determine how effective they are and the outcome of the interaction. Much could be said by way of description of the interaction within any group. Especially important is the nature of the leadership. In this study there were no formally selected leaders and two patterns of informal leadership were identified -- *led* and *dominated* groups. The authors reasoned that when friends of the same age and status are faced with stressful moral problems, their reactions would be differentially affected by belonging to a group that was either dominated or led by one of its members. A dominated group will be one where someone is unusually forceful, speaks often, may interrupt others and show disrespect for their opinions, and in general dominates the group (and earns a rating of "dominating" by group members). In a led group the person(s) who manifests leadership is equalitarian in manner and receptive to expressions of opinion from everyone and respectful of all (and earns a rating of "fair" from group members).

The nature of these two forms of leadership has special importance in the Haan interactional theory because morality is defined as equalization among persons in moral dialogue. "By its very organization a dominated group violates the stipulation of the interactional theory that conclusions are moral only when achieved through moral processing. Dominated groups would have difficulty following the rules of interactional moral dialogue whereby all may speak, none should dominate, and anyone may veto. Moral ends are only accidentally achieved by immoral means." (p. 112)

The following is a summary of all that happened within groups under the two forms of leadership. In essence it is a report on group process or dynamics, not how they dealt with the moral problems. Led groups operated smoothly and consistently in an egalitarian fashion, and members took this experience very seriously. Dominated groups were perturbed, disjointed, and inconsistent; members clearly did not pull together and some were forced into becoming conformists, isolates, or antagonists (p. 126).

Although both kinds of groups were equally involved in the project, led groups were more able to suspend disbelief* and take an analytic attitude toward their own group's processes; they were generally less distressed, more communal in their functioning, and less resistant to the staff leader. More of their members took roles of social-emotional leader and less often took the roles of conformist, isolate, and antagonist. At the conclusion of the group sessions, led groups thoughtfully evaluated their experiences. More often they stated that they had been personally affected by the group experiences, and they talked more than the staff.

In comparison, the dominated groups, although observed to be equally involved in the group sessions, were less able to suspend disbelief and take an analytic attitude toward their group's processes; they were more stressed, hierarchical in their functioning, and resistant to the staff leader. Members more often took roles of conformists, isolates, and antagonists, and less often took roles of social-emotional leaders. Dominated students gave higher marks to their friends at the sessions' end for being able to handle themselves well in conflict. Their evaluations of the experience were handled with some cynicism; they denied having been personally affected, and the staff had to talk more during the evaluation to keep the discussion moving. (p. 125)

Suspend disbelief means willingness to commit oneself to the moral tasks even though this was a research situation.

Personal ways of dealing with moral interaction. Influential on the course and outcome of value interactions will be the specific behaviors of individual participants. In one interaction a given person might become defensive and ineffective but in another might keep cool and objective and be effective. The specifics of each situation will be mainly determinative of what one will do, but each person does possess an array of characteristic ways of behaving -- traits of personality -- so a person may be likely to behave a given way in most interactions. Haan et al. (p. 126-132) have used the convenient dichotomy of *coping* and *defending* to describe these situation-evoked and enduring ways of reacting.

Coping means using effective problem-solving behaviors, defending using ineffective. Ordinarily one spontaneously uses coping reactions, but if something about the interaction prevents effective coping, as when one is under verbal attack from others, one may be thrown on the defensive, feel threatened, become emotional, and begin to defend. Ten coping and ten defensive processes are identified (pp. 128-131). In general, feelings of threat and resulting defensiveness causes people to forfeit or restrict choices, are thrown back on old ways of perceiving and thinking which often are inappropriate to the present, thinking is "muddied" and overgeneralized, analysis restricted and faulty, and magic evoked to shed unpleasantness. These behaviors not only make the person ineffective but can be disturbing and irritating to others in the group and block arriving at balanced solutions.

Coping is possible because one is able to remain in self-control and has full use of his faculties, so is attuned to the present situation, the mind open to options, thinking relevant, feelings experienced but not disorganizing, and negative feelings endured and positive feelings enjoyed. It is assumed that moral skill is increased as the person takes part in moral dialogues, coping more and defending less.

As mentioned, moral exchange is often stressful and trying, leading to defense, but Haan et al. assume automatic processes occur in group interactions leading to recognition of each discussant's self-interest and to restoration of social harmony and movement toward mutually-accepted solutions. "Moral exchange is often trying, but full, accurate, and sincere dialogue about the legitimacy of each discussant's self-interest is expected as well as needed if social harmony is to be restored and enhanced." (p. 139)

In general, the students coped more than they defended. Consistent with the differences in functioning of led and dominated groups, students in led groups coped more and defended less. Few differences were found between moral-game-playing students and moral-dilemma-discussion students in coping and defending. An interesting theoretical question is whether moral action is due largely to specifics of the situation, and hence variable from one situation to another, perhaps coping in one and defending in another, or whether due largely to stable traits, hence consistent from situation to another. (One student in one group was by far the most effective coper throughout while another in the same group was consistently the poorest coper.) There was evidence of both here, with probably more variability than consistency, but uncertainties as to research devices indicate caution in drawing conclusions.

There were interesting sex differences in adaptive strategies, though the correlations indicate numerous exceptions. The men were more likely to cope by using intellectuality, logical analysis, playfulness, and concentration, and to defend by intellectualizing, rationalizing, projecting, and displacing. Women were more empathic and suppressed their feelings more; they also defended more by doubting, regressing, and becoming rigidly "socialized" (p. 136).

A major hypothesis of this research was that students' moral levels will be higher when they cope and lower when they defend. Effective moral dialogue requires that interactants fully and accurately exchange views about the legitimacy of each other's claim. This is the essence of social coping. Dialogue is of little use when one or all parties defensively distort or negate critical aspects of their mutual moral problem (p. 128).

Specific moral meanings and costs. Another determinant of the nature of the interaction and group effectiveness is the moral meaning of the given problem for each person. Some moral problems facing persons and groups are more easily resolved than others. What determines the moral meaning of an issue and its costs, the difficulty, in resolving it? Haan et al. reply that meaning and costs flow from three sources: the objective features of the dilemma, the nature of the interpersonal relationships, and the personal history and strengths and weaknesses of the participants.

Objective features are exemplified by such things as familiarity and timeliness of the issue, the specific issues of civil rights or environmental degradation being issues familiar to many people today. Another objective feature is whether physical harm to the "victim" is a possible consequence of one line of action, especially if the consequence is death. The possibility of someone's death usually resolves the issue at once because the ambivalence of all concerned is immediately reduced. No one wants unwarranted and avoidable death to occur; life is valued in all moral systems (p. 221).

Interpersonal relationship might be exemplified with a led group that is capable of pinpointing differences and achieving an equitable solution without delay versus a dominated group that becomes embroiled in mutual recrimination and finds solution elusive.

Personal history is well exemplified by reactions to one of the moral dilemmas used in the study, which involved a girl who needed money badly to complete college and received an offer from her professor to spend Thanksgiving vacation in the Bahamas with him in exchange for next quarter's tuition. This is a dilemma that has special significance to women and produced strong reaction among these college-age women who empathized strongly with the girl.

The general implication of these three determinants of meanings and costs is that each moral problem may produce a somewhat unique reaction in the person. Two dilemmas that appear identical to the observer may not evoke identical perceptions and interactions by the person. The researchers found considerable evidence of this specificity of moral behavior.

Effective moral action. We have just reviewed some of the major determinants of a group's moral interactions -- emotion, leadership, coping and defending, and nature of the problem. Now some of the consequences for level or quality of moral action for the group of college students may be listed:

(1) Moral situations of different costs or stressfulness had strikingly different effects on level of moral action. The person's level of moral action in one situation did not predict how he or she would act in another, even when the situations were similar. Stressful games, in which students generated moral difficulties of their own making, resulted in lower moral action levels; nonstressful games resulted in highest moral levels. Although discussion sessions produced similar levels of morality, higher levels occurred when the contents of the hypothetical dilemma were close to the student's experience and involved issues that they might face and could resolve in real life (p. 344).

(2) Almost without exception, the equable, moral processes of the led groups resulted in higher levels of moral action than the morally violating processes of the dominated groups (p. 344).

(3) Enough evidence was generated to suggest that the objective contents of moral dilemmas affect moral action. Granting the tentativeness of the findings, in discussion sessions higher average moral levels were observed when the contents of the dilemmas were well-known, were subtle, involved little damage to victims, and were close to students' experience. In contrast, the self-directed game groups were more effective when the contents of the issues were unfamiliar, were distant, and involved great damage to the imagined victims. Thus the objective contents of dilemmas had opposite effects on gaming and discussing (p. 344).

(4) The individual student's personal ways of handling and solving problems had the most important effect on moral-action levels, whether these were characteristic ways of dealing with problems or unique to the present problem. Effective moral action was almost always facilitated by coping strategies and thwarted by defensive adaptations. Haan et al. interpret this to mean that knowing the moral or just thing to do is not enough to be effective in moral interaction; there must also be an ability to interact effectively in the often stressful context of moral discourse.

The students' situation-specific adaptive strategies influenced their levels of moral action to a greater extent than their characteristic strategies by a ratio of about three to one. Two defensive strategies were especially maladaptive. The first was *isolation*, which was not social isolation, but an isolation which prevents related ideas from being integrated and ideas from being associated with appropriate feelings. The second was *displacement*, which allows people to negate their frustrations by taking it out on others. Displacement prevents disputants from considering the possibility that their self-interest may not have priority and this prevents truth-identifying dialogue (p. 345).

Failures in moral dialogue. Why do people fail in moral dialogue? Failures abound, and an adequate theory must recognize why, as well as account for successes.

Moral action requires motivation to act sincerely (by entering, remaining in, and concluding dialogue), instead of defaulting (by "stonewalling," deserting, or refusing to give up any part of one's self-interest). During dialogues, ineffective moral action occurs when people violate the stipulations that all can speak, none must dominate, and all may veto. Also ineffective action occurs when people proclaim their intentions of carrying out an agreement and then do not, or do so only half-heartedly. When discussants deliberately dissemble or, less consciously, deceive both themselves and others with superficially compliant but defensive maneuvers, then their action is ineffective whatever their level or stage of moral skill. In either event, ineffective balances are the end result. Morally adequate processes tend to insure morally adequate conclusions; the latter can be attained only accidentally when processes are inadequate (p. 350).

Ineffective action in this study was not due to students being at a lower stage of moral development or lower levels of reasoning skill. Instead it resulted from incomplete or warped consideration of the issues, failure to consider all participants' needs and contributions, obliviousness to the group's processes, fantastic formulations and resolutions, impractical solutions, and false balances that swept disagreement under the rug (p. 350).

Sincerity during dialogue and sincere effort to reach agreement enhances human relations and the group's effectiveness. Everyone then has a "good conscience" when a dialogue is successfully concluded, and the group builds a sense of its own good faith, which in turn increases its potential for later accomplishment. When groups and societies are morally sensible, people are reassured (p. 349).

Values as Adaptations

Besides their major role in supplying evaluations, choices, ideals, goals, and meaning in lives, values may have other functions of a broadly "useful" or adaptive sort, such as facilitating acceptance by selected persons and groups through adoption of compatible values, creating a favorable self-image, asserting self and expressing independence, or as part of the total way of life or adaptive strategy of the maladjusted person. Several of these latter are briefly described below.

(a) *Values may facilitate interpersonal relationships.* We have seen above that values may dictate choice of mates, friends, and associates. Now, shifting the emphasis a bit, it may be said that shared values can be the ticket of entry into a personal relationship or group and can produce compatibility once in the relationship or group, and thus can help satisfy important needs for affiliation and approval.

If the compatible value is already possessed by our person then the process is straightforward. If not, then he may feel a need, conscious or subtle, to hold the "right" value, and the intellect may go to work to create it. He wakes one morning with the compatible conviction. In general, needs may create values. See, in next chapter, the review of Newcomb's research on the attitudes and values of Bennington College students for examples of this sometimes strong need.

(b) *Values may be adopted to create a pleasing self-image.* One function that values may serve is fulfillment of a need for a pleasing self-image -- to satisfy the need to be satisfied with self! The neurotic person (described below) may represent the extreme of this, for his feelings of inadequacy may lead him consciously to adopt a set of values to give legitimacy and nobility to an enforced (crippled) way of life. Some of the rest of us are free of any need to create a noble self and give the matter little thought, but apparently many have at least a need to feel good about self. Because many values carry the connotation of goodness -- examples, kindliness, cleanliness, bravery, honesty, self-sacrificingness, reverence -- and can be seen as personal traits (kindly, clean, brave, etc.), it is natural for a person to adopt some of them. Also, opportunities arise to describe self to others, so again these values may serve a useful purpose of perhaps winning approval and admiration.

Such values as these may be mere conscious "put-ons," but it is more likely they were innocently and automatically (unconsciously) adopted. Their weakness may be that lacking any basis in conviction and feeling, they will be violated with some frequency as other stronger motivations arise. But there is always the possibility that a shallow value will deepen as the person himself matures and becomes a more "real" person.

(c) *Values adopted as assertions of independence and importance.* As will be elaborated in next chapter, it is normal for the young person, as she/he approaches maturity, to become aware of the larger world around, become involved, and adopt some values. But often an additional need is felt by the young person (and often by the not-so-young as well) to "take a stand" -- adopt attitudes and values as an act of self-assertion and independence. It is a logical action at this point in life as the young person's ideas may not receive much respect from elders; he/she may still be under parental domination, feeling resentful, and finding it difficult to make the transition to independent adulthood; and his self-esteem may be unstable just at this point and a psychodynamic process be at work to try to gain attention, respect, and esteem.

Exemplification of this assertion process will be found in the review of the Newcomb research and in the biographical report on Vera Brittain (specifically her early involvement in the women's rights movement), at end of next chapter.

(d) *Adaptive role of certain values in maladjusted persons.* Certain values may be manifested by a troubled, neurotic person that are part of the psychodynamics of the neurosis itself, rather than the result of a rational, conscious process of selection. The clinical insights of Karen Horney (1945) may be used to outline their role, though it should be noted that other therapists might formulate the process somewhat differently.

In the next chapter we attempt to fill in some of the details on the origins and psychodynamics of the troubled-neurotic personality. Let it suffice here to say that various adverse childhood experiences, if long continued, can have the effect of making a child feel anxious, resentful, helpless, and isolated in what he experiences as a potentially hostile world. This amounts to being a grave psychological crippledness. Just as a physically crippled person must go through life dealing with the same problems as a sound-bodied person, so too the psychologically crippled person must go on through life dealing with the usual daily problems as best he can. But because of his anxiety and helplessness, he must discover special strategies for dealing with others and the world generally. Where a normal person remains reasonably open and flexible and hence is able to deal with a great variety of specific situations as they arise, the anxious-resentful-helpless person find himself driven into use and overuse of a narrow array of adaptive strategies.

Horney observed three patterns of such rigid adaptive strategies: moving *toward* people (the compliant type); moving *against* people (the aggressive type); and moving *away* from people (the detached type).

In the *moving toward* strategy the compliant person's felt helplessness stands out, and in spite of his estrangement and fears of others tries to win their affection and lean on them. Only in this way can he feel safe with them (p. 42). Specifically, this type has an insatiable need to be liked, wanted, desired, loved; to feel accepted, welcomed, approved of, appreciated; to be needed, to be of importance to others, especially to one particular person; to be helped, protected, taken care of, guided (p. 51). In his desperate need to feel safe he may carry the need to please to extremes, trying too hard to live up to other's expectations; become over-self-sacrificing, undemanding, overappreciative, overgrateful and generous; subordinates self to others and is appeasing and conciliatory;

automatically shoulders blame and tends to scrutinize self or be apologetic in the face of obviously unwarranted criticism or anticipated attack (p. 52).

In the *moving against* strategy the aggressive person's resentment and hostility predominate, he takes for granted the hostility of the world around him, and attempts, consciously or unconsciously, to fight. He implicitly distrusts the feelings and intentions of others toward himself. He rebels in whatever ways are open to him. He wants to be the stronger and defeat them, partly for his own protection, partly for revenge (p. 43).

In the *moving away* strategy the detached person's feelings of isolation and fear of rejection predominate and he wants neither to belong nor to fight, but to keep apart. He feels he hasn't much in common with them, they do not understand him anyhow. He builds up a world of his own (p. 43).

Now turning to his values, Horney suggests some of the values often seen in each of the three adjustive patterns.

Following a detailed presentation of the moving toward people strategy of the compliant person she continues:

> All of this contributes to his special set of values. Naturally, the values themselves are more or less lucid and confirmed according to his general maturity. They lie in the direction of goodness, sympathy, love, generosity, unselfishness, humility, while egotism, ambition, callousness, unscrupulousness, wielding of power are abhorred -- though these attributes may at the same time be secretly admired because they represent "strength."
>
> These, then, are the elements involved in a neurotic "moving toward" people. It must be apparent now how inadequate it would be to describe them by any *one* term like submissive or dependent, for a whole way of thinking, feeling, acting -- a whole way of life -- is implicit in them. (p. 54-55)

Similarly, the aggressive person's values and ideology will be in the direction of such qualities as cleverness (outwitting), toughness, aggressiveness, excellence, control or power, realism (unsentimental), self-interest. He could be expected to be equally emphatic in his rejection of such qualities as weakness, softness, sentimentality, fear, love, friendship, pity, sympathy, impartiality (self-disinterest).

Lastly, the detached person's values and ideology will be in the direction of self-sufficiency, detachment, uniqueness, resourcefulness (in the Robinson Crusoe sense), self-denial or asceticism, independence and freedom, privacy, aloofness. Perhaps more than with the other two personality patterns, in this pattern there is need to see self as superior, so the values might better be worded as detached superiority, self-sufficient superiority, aloof superiority, etc.. He could be expected to be averse to such things as gregariousness, self-indulgence, effusiveness, obligation (as in marriage), competition, communal living, sentimentality.

But why such philosophies of life? One could be compliant or aggressive without making a virtue of it. But that is just the point, one does need to convert an enforced way of life into a chosen *enviable* way of life.

Again, why? This person has a desperate need to feel good toward himself, to have an adequate self-image. More, his need has the quality of a hungering for superiority (Horney calls it "the search for glory"), of seeing self as well above the average. Why the hunger? Beneath all facades and "solutions" is a threatened, vulnerable self-esteem resulting from the feelings of anxiety, resentment, helplessness and isolation. So, reversing the sequence, the vulnerable, low self-esteem drives him to try to feel competent and superior; a glorification of his way of life adds to his sense of superiority.

Interaction of the Person's Values

Since any person possesses a number of values there is always the possibility of interaction among them -- two or more in conflict, perhaps two combining with an increase of strength of both, or a number forming a hierarchical ranking, or other, together with various psychodynamic reactions, such as solving a conflict between two by choosing and highlighting ("overvaluing") the one while diminishing the other. The most striking form of interaction is value conflict and a special section is devoted to it below.

For interaction to occur at all the two or more values must have some relationship, and in most obvious cases would be held toward the same object.

A familiar example of interplay would be that occurring at time of selecting a career. Assuming the person to be mature enough to have clarified values at all (many have not), typically she/he will hold at least several values as to what he wishes to have happen during the working years -- perhaps attain job security, experience variety and challenge, form enduring friendships, and rise in status to a position of authority and prestige. But often not all can be had in the positions available -- indeed, often only one can be had -- so some sort of ranking in importance must be made, however difficult.

Other possible situations where comparable value interactions might occur would be in choice of a mate, choice of groups to which to belong (club, lodge, recreational, political), organizations to support, public issues to actively support (possibilities: environmental protection, women's rights, civil rights, right-to-life, animal rights).

Among theorists who have proposed that values form systems or hierarchies, Rokeach's work is best know. He writes that what is still missing from many discussions of values is the notion of value systems or hierarchies, the idea that societies and individuals can accurately be compared with other societies and individuals not only in terms of specific values but also in terms of value priorities (Rokeach & Ball Rokeach, 1989, p. 775). It was natural for him to propose systems since his *Values Survey* is answered by having the person rank, from most important (strongest) to least, each of the two sets of 18 values of the questionnaire (though there is nothing to prevent its being answered in another way). In effect, the respondent is indicating the relative importance to him of each of the values. When respondents are later asked to repeat the ranking it is found that any one value tends to keep its relative position among the others -- in other words, the whole forms an enduring value system.

Though Rokeach was convinced of the reality of individual systems, it would be desirable to have additional evidence from other methods. This method of answering the questionnaire may have artificially created the appearance of a system. That is, everyone performed a ranking of the 18 value concepts whether or not he actually possessed a set of values of different strengths. By some manner of follow-up interviewing it could be learned whether a system actually existed in each person and its nature.

Rokeach has focused on two of the 18 terminal values, *freedom* and *equality*, and published a variety of findings showing that these two form ideological systems, depending upon the relative importance of each to the person or group.

He began by proposing that the traditional single scale of political ideologies varying from leftist-liberal to conservative-rightist be abandoned in favor of two scales -- high-to-low freedom values and high-to-low equality values. As he says, "freedom cannot mean the same thing to socialists and capitalists even though both may insist that they value it highly. It is one thing to value *freedom* highly and ignore or be silent about *equality*, and it is quite another thing to insist that *freedom* is not truly possible unless it goes hand in hand with *equality*. To American conservatives, *freedom* probably means lack of restraint on individual initiative and the *freedom* to achieve superior status, wealth, and power; to socialists *freedom* probably means sufficient restraint on individual initiative to ensure greater equality for all. To American conservatives, social *equality* is perhaps seen as a threat to individual *freedom*; to socialists, there can be no *freedom* for the citizenry without social *equality*. Similarly, both communism and fascism place a low value on *freedom* and advocate instead the supremacy and power of the state. But to fascism, the power of the state is seen to be a weapon to coerce inequality, whereas to communism it is a weapon to coerce *equality*.

Our results clearly show that the traditional left-right dimension turns out to be a two-dimensional one." (1973, p. 183-85)

His main supporting evidence was findings from a content analysis of the writings of Lenin, representing communism, Hitler, representing fascism, Barry Goldwater, representing American capitalism, and chapters by five writers in a book edited by Eric Fromm, representing socialism. The socialist writing yielded ranks for *freedom* and *equality* of first and second among the eighteen terminal values; Hitler's yielded sixteenth and seventeenth; Goldwater's yielded first and sixteenth; and Lenin's seventeenth and first (1973, p. 174).

Studies of supporters of Republican and Democratic presidential candidates in the 1968 campaign generally supported Rokeach's theory -- that is, all supporters gave high ranking to *freedom* but supporters of Democratic candidates also gave *equality* a relatively high ranking while supporters of the Republicans gave *equality* a much lower average ranking (middle to lower).

Americans generally, as revealed by national samplings in 1968, 1971, 1974, 1981, gave *freedom* a high ranking (third in 18) and it retained this position throughout. But *equality* received a lower average ranking and its position was variable -- seventh in 1968, fourth in 1971, twelfth in 1974 and 1981 (Rokeach and Ball-Rokeach, 1989, p. 778). Freedom is one of the great American ideals and has been stressed throughout American history ("Let freedom ring!") and also has an inherent personal appeal in the form of personal independence and freedom of choice. Equality (brotherhood, equal opportunity for all) is another American ideal but evidently has never been as strong and its salience waxes and wanes with the times. Of course, it would be expected to be more important with groups of Americans who lack equality. In the 1968 sampling, when results from the two races were separated, black Americans ranked *equality* second, white *eleventh*. At about the same time a group of unemployed black job applicants ranked *equality* first, *freedom* tenth; at the same employment office a group of white applicants ranked *freedom* third and *equality* ninth (Rokeach, 1968, p. 170).

Values conflict. In a society where there is little diversity and most of its member's behavior is patterned by custom and rule few values will be articulated and little value conflict experienced. But in complex modern societies where individuals are expected to be self-directed in considerable measure, there will be diversity of value, with conflict within persons not uncommon.

The perfect contemporary example of a conflict facing many of us is the one relating to abortion and other birth-control activities. On the one side is the deeply-held valuing of human life (the right to life); on the other a valuing of the woman's right to control her own life (freedom), hence the right to choose whether to terminate or complete a pregnancy. This second value position may acquire additional support from a knowledge that unless humanity stops its own multiplication the carrying capacity of the earth soon will be exceeded, with catastrophic consequence, and a knowledge that many poorer women's pregnancies occur because they have no control over husband's lust, cannot practice birth control, and do not want additional children.

Other timely current examples are the conflict and soul-searching felt in deciding between protecting the forest habitats of endangered species versus providing jobs for lumbermen in forest areas; between protecting the constitutionally guaranteed right of free expression, including dissemination of pornography, versus protection of children and women from the consequences of uncontrolled pornography; between belief in the sanctity of life, even of the murderer, versus the ethic that brutal murderers don't deserve to live.

Another type of value conflict involves a value in opposition to some other motivating disposition. Most of these seem to involve moral values in opposition to strong motives, such as the needlings of conscience to behave honestly versus the greed for wealth, or the sense of loyalty and fidelity to one's mate versus the drive of sexual lust to have other bed mates. Since moral values are discussed above no more need be said here, but a special sort of conflict is that experienced by the soldier who on the one side is strongly motivated to obey orders to kill (perhaps out of both an inner urging of duty and fear of punishment) and on the other feels a deep valuing of human life. The conflict may be so deep and so personal that conscience, that inner absolute sense of right and wrong, becomes involved. The annals of war tell us little of such conflicts but there is no doubt that many a soldier experiences it and some deal with it simply by pointing their guns at the ground or sky when firing. (Somewhere in print is an estimate of the frequency of this type of firing and it is significant.)

Here are two good examples of this type of conflict. These date from the Vietnam War, which probably produced many of the sort because the young American draftee soldiers lacked the usual justification for killing, that of defense of homeland and loved ones. These reports were written by young persons in response to a contest titled, *Interview a Vet Contest,* sponsored by the Central Committee for Conscientious Objectors. Both are shortened versions of longer reports, but otherwise are unedited.

> On patrol over rice fields, my father sighted an aged, Vietnamese farmer and his one ox. He was standing alone, washing his ox amid the vast chain of fields. Diligently he poured water and scrubbed the ox. But in a Free Fire Zone or "Free Kill Zone" as called by the crew, even the act of cleansing became a target. Others had divided this rice field and judged that no one belonged. Anything in this zone was considered the enemy. Obeying this, the pilot ordered the gunners to lock and load. Ignorantly the choppers whizzed past the farmer, and then they whipped around and converged. The conflict between the soldier's duty to obey and the human conscience emerged within my father. In confusion, he aroused the might

to avert his fire harmlessly away. However, the fixed guns of the helicopter remained. Back into its lazy course, the helicopter eased. The farmer and his charge lay helplessly riddled, forming the last picture.

Though he did not kill him, the wish to have cried out remained. Confusion and conflict had blocked him, yet he courageously freed himself in time to control his fire. He, the soldier and the human being, faced his imperfections and his humanity. His actions were not perfect, only human and conscientious in an imperfect and devouring situation. (by Richard N. Hoover)

You went to Vietnam feeling "Sober, pensive . . . trying to form an opinion." You did not want to be "violent or aggressive . . . a warrior who would take lives."

But you did, just before Thanksgiving, November 1969. In your own words, "Once there were three North Vietnamese that did walk out in front of me . . . I still have to regain composure and live with that . . . and I opened up and they stopped and were startled because they heard the guys in back of me . . . and that's my terrible sense of pain and loss; I live with that daily . . . some people will say, well, you had to do it . . . the government sanctioned it . . . but my conscience was so violated that I had taken lives, killed two other human beings and the third one got away . . . and another pain and hurt: There were people, men in my company that were jealous that they didn't get to shoot them, and I always thought that was so sick . . . I gladly would have let them do it, but it was like Fate -- I had to be the one to do it . . . I was ordered to go down the trail . . . but I really thought they would turn into Americans -- this is truly the way I thought -- I thought they would turn into Americans . . . and I even got on the radio and asked if there were any Americans out . . . even to this day I still have this wishful thinking that they'd turn into Americans . . . and I still wonder about their families, their friends, their lovers, and I still have the sense that if America . . . felt my pain they would have stopped the war -- and I'm not trying to make it sound too sensational or melodramatic, but I did have to embrace an awful hurt. I'll carry it with me the rest of my life . . . and it seems to get worse as I get older." (by Megg Magee and Meg Ridgely)

Saliency and Relativity of Values

Values differ greatly in saliency -- in how important they are at the moment. Perhaps more than most dispositions they are subject to a principle of relativity, their momentary strength being relative to how well they are being realized. Suppose I am a person who often does not know where my next meal will come from, hence I value material security. I also value freedom of speech and democratic participation; but because I have ample opportunity to express my opinions and vote I take this value for granted. It has low saliency, and it would take much mind-digging on my part to realize I had it. But if I were well-fed and deprived of freedom of expression, then the values would reverse in saliency. To the extent that the life situation is changing, values are shifting in saliency.

The relativity is especially prominent here because we adopt and carry for a lifetime many of our values, but any number of them may be lying there on the back shelf of the mind, seldom noticed for years at a time, because nothing is giving them saliency, yet overnight can become important.

Saliency and relatively have special significance at the point of assessing values. Usually when we assess people's values, by questionnaire or otherwise, we like to assume that what has been revealed is semi-permanent -- that these *are* the person's values and will be the same far into the future. The values may be long term but not their importance or saliency.

This matter of saliency obviously is important and deserves empirical support by way of spelling out its specifics, but no study is known to me. The above comment is just broad common-sense inference and research is bound to qualify it. The ideal study would assess the values of persons in one life-circumstance and then assess later in a different life-circumstance, such as securely employed the one time, unemployed and in want the next; healthy the one time, ailing the next; free the one time, imprisoned the next, etc..

Indirect support for the general phenomenon of saliency is found in some of Rokeach's data (1973). He found that of all 36 values of the *Value Survey*, *clean* best distinguishes the poor from the rich. *Clean* decreases in strength of ranking as income increases, moving from second highest for the lowest income group of Americans to second lowest for those of the highest income group. Rokeach comments, "The low ranking of *clean* by the rich may be interpreted to mean that the affluent take cleanliness for granted, rather than that they do not care about it. Its high ranking by the poor suggests that they are far from indifferent to it, that those who must live under squalid conditions regard cleanliness as a very salient issue indeed." (p. 62) *A comfortable life* is another that distinguishes rich and poor, having an average rank of sixth with the poor and fifteenth with the rich. Rokeach comments that, as with *clean*, the poor may value *a comfortable life* highly because they lack it and the affluent considerably less because they already possess it (p. 62).

Of all 36 values, *equality* shows greatest difference between black and white Americans, its average rank is second for blacks and eleventh for whites (p. 69). These findings, too, are interpreted as showing that white Americans are able to take equality largely for granted since most enjoy it, whereas many blacks are daily aware of their inequality and yearn for better. We can imagine how terribly important equality would become for many white Americans if suddenly all were deprived of it. (Once in India I was denied entry to a temple because I was not "twice-born" and lacked upper-caste status. For the first time ever I knew how it felt to be discriminated against and felt resentment, briefly.)

Salvation showed an interesting age difference in importance, with adolescents giving it lowest ranking and oldsters beyond age seventy giving it its highest (third overall) (p. 80). Surely we are safe in concluding that as we grow old and anticipate death what lies beyond becomes increasingly important, whereas all young people know they will live forever!

Israelis showed a markedly different value pattern from those of Canadians, Australians, and Americans, ranking *a world at peace* and *national security* first and second. These valuations are reasonable when it is recalled that Israel has been involved in several wars with its neighbors during its brief existence, continues to be involved in violent confrontation with the Palestinians with whom they share Palestine, and has tried to assure its existence by military means. No wonder peace and security have such salience for the Israeli citizen!

Do We Always Practice Our Values?

This is the question of the relation of expression of a value to carrying it out in action. A very important question.

Values are by definition *conceptions* -- that is, mental constructs, rather than action tendencies, so it should not be assumed automatically that they will or should produce action. Nevertheless, that many do is not to be doubted, else they would not have warranted the respect that they have enjoyed over the centuries. However, there will always be some persons who profess noble values but do nothing to practice them, which has led critics to charge that neither attitudes nor values are of much significance because so many persons profess admirable convictions but in the action situation more powerful determinants, motives especially, lead them to behave otherwise.

The question of extent of practice is a pertinent one, and was especially so earlier in the century with respect to attitudes because so many people would declare themselves free of racial or religious prejudice (and of comparable negative attitudes) but by their behavior would show they were practicing prejudice. There is a body of research literature on the subject going back many decades, but it has proved very difficult to investigate people's real-life attitudes and practices and nothing definitive has emerged. And we are unable here to give any sort of estimate of the percentage of persons who fail to practice given ones of their values. We can only suggest possible general causes.

In light of the definition it seems best to regard a person's *expression* of a value as the evidence of the value's existence or reality, and then separately raise questions about its possible behavioral effect in that person.

The above topic on people in value interaction nicely sets the stage for examining our question for it tells us that in daily social interaction people's moral values will show considerable variability depending upon such things as the nature of the problem or issue, the moral behavior shown by interactors, the interaction skills of the person, and his personal idiosyncrasies. It is a reasonable assumption that the same variability will be found with respect to other types of values in interaction situations. Generalizing still more broadly, it is safe to assume that a person's values are but one element in the mix of external and internal factors that determine his ongoing behavior, so could not be expected to be experienced the same or to motivate the same all of the time. A student might, for example, value honesty, yet being unprepared for a given examination and under great pressure to pass, might cheat the one time (or again at later times, under comparable conditions).

A glance through the list of types of values in Chapter 1 will show that only certain of the types could be expected to have behavioral effects, while others remain "in the mind" solely, or only indirectly manifest themselves in behavior. We would most certainly hope that all of one's moral values would lead to their daily practice -- to behave honestly, fairly, avoiding hurting, etc.. Similarly, major ones of the self-concepts are at once declarations of one's ideal behavior and actual behavior, as when one describes self to oneself, "I am persevering, friendly, cautious, etc.." Valued life goals, such as for wealth, service, or security, are by definition motivators toward their attainment, their practice, so are another type that would be expected to have a behavioral effect.

Some other types should be influencing one's behavior, but by their nature can be expressed only broadly or indirectly. One can value a socialistic society but could not straightforwardly "behave it"; rather, it would be a gradual group attainment marked by many small individual actions. Similar examples of such diffuse values would be a world of beauty, justice, an orderly world, national security, salvation, freedom, and wisdom.

Then examples of values that by their nature *cannot* be carried into behavior at all are moral values held toward the behavior of *others* ("*They* should be god-fearing, modest, and truthful.") and the daily behaviors (traits) of *others* ("*People* should be ambitious, compassionate, and conservative in dress.").

Though it is the personal moral values and the self-concepts that most certainly provoke the question of correspondence, and fuel the cynics' charge of hypocrisy, the values that create the greatest uncertainty as to behavioral effect are the above broad, general values that do not permit direct practice, such as justice and freedom. With respect to any person the question has to be asked, how does he express the given value in action, if at all. Is it just a broad ideal with him, or does he particularize it to the extent of perceiving specific violations of it in the world around him and specific things that need to be done to further it, such as vote a certain way, support a movement, give of one's wealth or labors, etc.. Most of us are notorious for not seeing the connection between what we believe in the abstract and the concrete situation at hand. One may value equality among men, but in a given situation of interaction with another person, a younger person or a laborer, say, fail to perceive that he is not being equalitarian. In general, the more concretely and sharply formulated the value, the more likely it is to be applied.

Rokeach (1973, ch. 5) has published findings on the relation between rankings of value concepts on his *Values Survey* and various behaviors of a number of groups of persons. Though this is evidence of a relation between professed values and actions, the nature of the findings do not permit our saying that the values caused the behavior, only that there was a correlation. University students who joined a civil-rights organization ranked *equality* relatively higher then did other students (date 1968-69). Another sample of students were asked about their participation in civil-rights demonstrations; those who demonstrated ranked *equality* considerably higher than non-participating students (1967). Several studies have shown that the amount of eye-contact is an unobtrusive measure of one's liking for someone. This measure was used in 10-minute discussions between pairs of persons. Amount of eye-contact between black and white discussants was most strongly correlated with *equality*. Both adult Americans and college students who are regular church attenders gave *salvation* a far higher ranking than non-attenders. Prison inmates ranked several values higher than non-inmates but the one showing greatest difference between the two groups was *wisdom*. But this finding leaves one groping for an explanation -- are the prisoners saying that they value the wisdom of a Confucius or are they thinking, "If only I had been wiser, I wouldn't be here now!" *A sense of accomplishment* received a significantly higher ranking by two groups of college professors, as compared to adult Americans generally, a clear value of persons in the academic field and perhaps the motivator of some to enter the profession. *Equality* again enters the picture as differentiating active supporters of the different presidential candidates in 1968. Supporters of Eugene McCarthy (liberal Democrat and opponent of the Vietnam War) gave it highest possible rank; supporters of Ronald Reagan and George Wallace gave it lowest possible (18th and 17th); supporters of Nixon, the winner, gave it a middling rank.

Closely related to the above degree of generality versus concreteness of the value will be degree of clear or conscious conceptualization. It is a safe assumption that people's values vary in clarity of conceptualization and individual case-reports tend to exemplify this, for first statements of the person's values or philosophy of life usually are quite nebulous and brief; only after further discussion do specific values begin to acquire names. We lack the desirable empirical evidence for the point but may generalize from clinical experience and say that the more any feeling or concept can be brought to awareness and fully grasped, the greater is the self-insight and self-direction and the more likely it can be used in pertinent situations. As one researcher has pointed out, a vague valuing of "social betterment" is much less likely to result in social betterment behavior than a clarified one of wanting to build schools and clinics in backward villages (Danziger, 1958).

A fairly obvious additional influence on whether a value concept produces action is strength or conviction of the value. Strongly held values tend to move one to express them in action; weakly held are easily cancelled or overwhelmed by other influences. We have already suggested that values adopted to create a pleasing self-image often lack depth, and that values composing the three neurotic strategies (Horney, 1945) are there because of a need for self-aggrandizement rather than from strong conviction, hence easily would be violated. In addition, common sense suggests that all of us hold values in varying degrees of strength, with some having the quality of just "slightly" or "mildly" positive and producing little action.

But even when there is a strongly held value still there is the possibility of violation, for of course values do not operate in a behavioral vacuum. The folk-saying "every man has his price" states a psychological reality, though it is usually uttered by the unthinking cynic. In the given situation the interplay of the value with motives, opportunities, rewards and punishments, and encouragements or inhibitions from significant others is what determines one's actual behavior. I might be able to hold out against torture day after day rather than betray fellow freedom fighters, but be unable to resist the inducement of a million dollars as reward for "selling" the manufacturing secrets of my employer.

A final possible factor which produces, not a failure to act, but inconsistent action is value contradiction. One may hold two values which are contradictory, but each experienced at a different time and setting and the contradiction not recognized, with the result that one value determines behavior at one time, the other at another. The point is suggested by the finding of Lambert and Bressler (1958) that Indian university students who were studying in the United States would react both negatively and positively toward the same thing -- the American family structure and the role of women -- depending upon which of two opposed value orientations were evoked.

CHAPTER 4

ORIGINS OF VALUES

Insights from various directions permit our pointing to a number of influences in shaping people's values -- family, peers, school and college, religion and church, folk story, personal experience, and other.

Society-Wide or Group-Wide Influences

Society-wide values of the sort we saw in the previous chapter in the examples of the Sioux, Hopi, Tongans, and Chinese ordinarily are being shaped by the full array of cultural influences -- early by family, later by peers, school, church, and other groups or institutions, and within these by direct instruction, modeling and imitation, folk stories, epics and myths, story and lesson books, drama, and other cultural avenues of influence. Various of these are amplified below.

Early Family Influences: The Conscience Development of the Child

The teaching of morals and other important values begins in childhood, but because of the child's intellectual immaturity he will be able to assimilate only a limited part of the value environment to which he is exposed. It will not be until the adolescent years that he has matured enough to be wide-open to ideas and alternatives and begins to acquire the array of values seen in the adult.

Thus far research has focused primarily on the moral development of the child. Of course the nature of the child's morals is quite different from that of adults and research on the child has had to concern itself with such child-life things as resistance to temptation, sense of fairness, learning and obeying rules, and guilt over deviations. Questions naturally arise as to the connection between childhood morality and adult character but let us delay comment on this a bit.

We have seen in preceding chapters how necessary it is for the members of any society to share common moral values if the group is to function at all. All need voluntarily to deal honestly with each other, for example, else there is no basis for trust in one another and without trust social interaction (cooperating, planning, marrying, etc.) and commercial interaction and livelihood gaining (contracting, buying, selling, borrowing-lending, hiring, etc.) cannot occur.

So children must be shaped in such a way that they carry within themselves the impulsion to behave morally. They must develop conscience, that inner feeling-certainty of the right-wrong of something with its powerful motivation to do right and avoid wrong and associated feelings of troubledness and guilt at violations of one's code.

Freud left us with a conception of conscience (superego) as powerful in its dictation to the person and largely unconscious, its working but faintly grasped, unrealistic and irrational, demanding perfection of a imperfect creature, and source of much distress and guilt, together with reactions such as self-deception and repression. He really had the adult in mind when he wrote but felt that the origins went back to childhood. Skipping his explanation of the origin of the superego itself, he reasoned that the child takes on parental "do's" and "don'ts" in fairly unmodified form, by a process of "internalization," and afterward the now-internalized rules motivate as parents formerly did. He writes (1933, p. 89):

> Small children are notoriously amoral. They have no internal inhibitions against their pleasure-seeking impulses. The role which the superego undertakes later in life is first played by an external power, by parental authority. The influence of the parents dominates the child by granting proofs of affection and by threats of punishment which to the child mean loss of love and which must also be feared on their own account. . . . It is only later that the secondary situation arises, which we are far too ready to regard as the normal state of affairs; the external restrictions are introjected, so that the superego takes the place of the parental function, and thenceforward observes, guides, and threatens the ego in just the same way as the parents acted to the child before.

In light of later research, Freud's formulation appears too simple in its explanation of the origin of conscience. The development of moral behavior and values in children, and individual differences in their nature, is determined by the nature of the socialization practices of the parents.

The key essential for producing a mentally healthy child with well-developed conscience is interest and warmth (acceptance, love) by parents. This needs to be combined with a stable structuring of the child's world, with definite but reasonable demands and rules and consistency in treatment. Usually in this home there is also discussion with the child about moral matters, explanation, urging to behave in given ways, and appeal to conscience ("How would you feel if he treated you that way?"); all of this contributes to his moral development. Very important, too, is parent's observing their own rules and being consistent models of their own values, thus providing good models for the child to copy.

An excellent example of these influences, especially of the parents providing good models, is given by White (1975). One of the several adults who he studied in depth reported that as a child she felt much loved and secure, and was strongly motivated not to hurt or disappoint her parents. Later, admiring her parents, she copied them and thus absorbed their moral values. When interviewed and asked to recall childhood moral instruction and chidings, she could recall little and concluded that her "moral training seems to be in what Mother and Daddy have lived." She described her parents as "always consistent in living their religious principles," and she considered this "a far more effective teacher than all the spoken words could ever have been." (p. 321)

Hoffman (1983) has attempted to supply some of the details as to how the initially external moral values of parents and society become internalized and experienced as one's own. One idea is that parental pressures of "low saliency" lead the child to adopt the value and forget its source, so later experiences it as his own. A related meaningful idea is that motivation must be produced in the child to assimilate the moral teaching and behave accordingly. A good relationship permits an approach of low saliency -- a quiet manner -- by parents and a good chance of child's really hearing, whereas too strong an approach, with irritation, love-withdrawal, and power assertion, may provoke such emotions as anxiety and resentment, which interfere with assimilation of the teaching and may block it entirely. (Incidentally, it has been found that the common parental reaction of brief love-withdrawal as punishment is effective in a warmth relationship but ineffective where it is lacking.) Hoffman also feels that the discipline technique of pointing up the effects of the child's behavior on others (termed "inductions"), in a context of warmth, is especially effective and tends to produce a moral orientation characterized by independence of external sanctions and by high guilt ("high guilt" here means a normal self-discipline, not a crippling high guilt).

Another likely influence on the child's adoption of parental morals and values is his identification with parents. Identification involves an extension of self to other persons and groups, such that they are experienced as part of self. A familiar example is the sports fan's identification with a favorite team and personally living the team's ups and downs and feeling especially elated when "we" win the championship. In the child's case, as part of that experiencing of parents or family as part of "me," there would be the experiencing of their standards as "me" (mine) as well.

In her thorough survey of influences on the moral shaping of the child Maccoby (1980) does not include identification and explains that it is difficult to study because it is a wholly subjective thing (and a child could not be expected to describe it). She also mentions that psychologists have been preoccupied with the concept of identification employed by Freud, which is a convoluted thing and has been both difficult to study and fruitless.

Though difficult to study in children, the commonness of identification in human affairs makes it a logical possibility. That is, identification occurs not only with sports teams, but with schools, churches and religions, gangs, cliques, and clubs, and a variety of other groups. Identity with one's nation is encouraged and manipulated in wartime to get soldiers to risk lives for something experienced as part of self. And one of the closest identifications beyond childhood is with own family. Note especially in the above example from White that the young woman reported *admiring her parents*, so copied them and thus absorbed their moral values. "Admiring" and "identifying with" seem much the same. Be that as it may, both Hoffman above and Maccoby below seem to be pointing to something that, if not identification, is very close to it.

> A common theme in these various findings seems to be that parental warmth binds children to their parents in a positive way -- it makes children responsive and more willing to accept guidance. If the parent-child relationship is close and affectionate, parents can exercise what control is needed without having to apply heavy disciplinary pressure. It is as if parents' responsiveness, affection, and obvious commitment to their children's welfare have earned them the right to make demands and exercise control. (p. 394)

Prothro (1961, 1970, p. 247-260) studied the childrearing practices of three distinct ethnic groups in Lebanon -- Sunni Moslem, Greek Orthodox Christian, and Gregorian (Armenian) Christian -- and found good support for the American findings as to the importance of warmth and structuring. As he summarizes:

> The Lebanese child was more likely to exhibit behavior considered to show a strong degree of conscience if he had a warm mother who used explanations and reasoning when he did wrong, who did not use a great deal of physical punishment, and who did not ignore his positive achievements. In this sense the Lebanese child was similar to the American child. Conscience was not a product of sex, class, sect, or place of residence. (p. 255-56)

The last sentence was included because some difference was found between the three ethnic groups in certain child-rearing practices and consequent behavior. Specifically, it is thought that parents' manner of reacting to good behavior influences the child's motivation to achieve (which ordinarily would carry over to adulthood and often become a value as well). A majority of both Gregorian and Orthodox mothers said they systematically rewarded good behavior, and a majority of the Sunni mothers said they did not. The Sunni mothers, on the other hand, described themselves more often than did the other mothers as depending upon threats -- which they often failed to carry out. Prothro comments, "If the assumption that middle-class Beirut Christians are the 'high achievers' among the groups we studied be granted, then our data confirm the American finding that the frequent use of rewards for accomplishing approved tasks characterizes the child-rearing practices of mothers in high-achieving groups." (p. 257)

Not only does parental warmth influence moral development, studies have shown that it influences such things as intellectual development, grasp of reality, self-esteem, initiative, self-direction and self-control, openness to learn, and more -- in other words, nearly every aspect of the developing child is favorably influenced. So while producing a moral person, warmth is producing an effectively-functioning person with good potential for coping effectively with all situations of life. Too, the same childhood strengths should produce an effective adult, including an adult with a good moral sense. (As one reviews the various studies on the effect of warmth and as the above findings one by one come to light the insight begins to dawn that humans evolved needing warmth as a basic essential for humanness, not merely as a desirable extra. The human situation might be likened to the need of the monkey for social-physical contact, particularly the infant's need to cling to its mother -- both becoming dramatically disturbed if separated. In comparable sense the human infant and child needs warmth -- attention, affection, acceptance, interest -- and if it is missing for any length of time begins to show disturbed human functioning. It takes no special effort to be warm, and lavish shows of affection are not needed; one need only be naturally human.)

The consequence for conscience of other patterns of parent-child relationships is not nearly as clear as for the warmth relationship, in part because findings have differed but also because many fewer cases are found and we have to do some inferring from absence of desirable conditions to consequences. Thus parents who show low or no warmth are assumed by inference to produce a child somewhat opposite his loved counterpart -- defective socialization, poor sense of identity with parents, and defect in self-direction and feelings of guilt. A specific form of this pattern might be a parent who nags and scolds often, uses physical punishment, seldom shows interest or gives rewards, and produces a child who has little sense of right and wrong, yields to impulse, and will lie and steal if he can get away with it. Bandura and Walters (1963) say of the use of punishment that it is more likely to cause the child to learn to avoid the source of the punishment than to produce an inner motivation to behave properly. They cite evidence that a regime of punishment, especially if there is a shortage of warm affection, leads a child to be smart about avoiding punishments but otherwise to get away with everything he can. Maccoby (1980) comments that ultra-permissiveness does not produce a well-socialized child, and an ultra-permissive rejecting parent is perhaps better described as neglecting and his child tends to become antisocial. Even where parent is warm, an absence of at least moderate parental control is likely to be associated with low impulse control. High degrees of restrictiveness by warm parents, on the other hand, may mean that the child is over-controlled and inflexible, remaining dependent upon external authority for control of his actions instead of developing ability to make his own judgements and discipline himself. Common sense tells us that an inconsistent parent makes a poor model, a dictatorial arbitrary parent breeds resentment, and one who scolds and punishes without ever talking things over and posing moral choices will implant nothing in the way of a moral concept. Hoffman (1983) writes that a child's moral orientation based on fear of external detection and punishment is associated with the frequent use of power-assertive discipline (that is, physical force, deprivation of possessions or privileges, direct commands, or threats). And there appears to be no relationship between internalization of morals and love-withdrawal techniques in which the parent simply gives direct, but non-physical, expression of anger or disapproval of the child for engaging in some undesirable behavior (p. 247).

So though the evidence is uneven on the negative side we are given a clear impression that differences in moral behavior and values in children are associated with differences in the socialization practices of their parents (Maccoby, 1968, p. 251).

Thus far little seems to have been done to learn what happens to either the morally strong or weak child as he matures to adulthood. The only way to really find out is to follow the lives of actual children through the growing years to adulthood by means of longitudinal studies. Only one longitudinal study was seen, that of Kohlberg (1976, 1969), but it was a study of development of moral reasoning, a different form of moral development from the one we are considering here. The adult outcome for the morally strong child might be safely predicted, considering that he/she is an effectively functioning person generally, but it would be especially valuable to follow the lives of morally weak children, for this child not only will be handicapped in the moral conscience sense but be a generally handicapped or ineffective person and a variety of less than ideal outcomes are to be expected.

Below we analyze the two extremes of adult moral or conscience behavior -- the person with too strong a conscience, and his opposite, the one with little or no conscience. Both appear to flow from notably faulty parent-child relationships; the faulty relationship can take a variety of forms and produce a variety of specific outcomes, including the extremes of too little and too much conscience.

Is too strong a conscience possible? Daily events make us aware of how frequently people have too little conscience, so we are quite aware of that possibility, but how about its opposite, is it possible to have so much conscience to the point of its being an unnatural burden? The clinical literature tells us that it is, and at several points in preceding chapters such a condition was briefly mentioned, though it always occurs in the context of a troubled personality. This will be a person who experiences a notable number of moral faults and failings, perhaps experiences self as insincere, dishonest, immoral, etc., is perfectionistic, hence often self-dissatisfied and self-condemning, and frequently has feelings of troubledness, guilt, and depression at experienced faults and shortcomings. As Horney (1939) says, "the individual seems to have no say in the matter of self-imposed rules; whether he likes them, whether he believes in their value, enters as little into the picture as his capacity to apply them with discrimination." (p. 208)

This personality handicap is assumed to begin in childhood as a result of faulty parental treatment. (Though theorists of an earlier day, such as Horney, never mention a genetic-constitutional contribution in these cases, there is always that possibility, such as a marked timidity from birth that would make the child unusually sensitive to certain treatments, treatments that might have but slight effect on another child. See Kagan and Snidman, 1991, for a recent discussion of genetic-constitutional differences in temperament in young children, together with a summary of their findings on the specific subject of inhibition and uninhibition to the unfamiliar in children.) Horney (1945) lists a variety of adverse conditions that can be having a harmful effect:

> A wide range of adverse factors in the environment can produce this insecurity in a child: direct or indirect domination, indifference, erratic behavior, lack of respect for the child's individual needs, lack of real guidance, disparaging attitudes, too much admiration or the absence of it, lack of reliable warmth, having to take sides in parental disagreements, too much or too little responsibility, over-protection, isolation from other children, injustice, discrimination, unkept promises, hostile atmosphere, and so on and so on. (p. 41)

Clinical writers stress that children can live through amazingly severe experiences, such as terrible accidents or wartime bombing, or even physical beating, without harmful after-effects as long as the child's world returns to a state of reasonable security and stability, but long continued insult, as is the usual case with these rejected-threatened (etc.) children, is overwhelming.

From her clinical work Horney (1937) concluded that such long-continued adverse treatments as the above can have the effect of making a child feel resentful, anxious, helpless, and isolated in what he experiences as a potentially hostile world. The specifics of each case will dictate the specific patterning of these, but all four emotions typically are present together and constitute the very heart or essence of neurosis. She termed this "basic anxiety" and has defined it as "the feeling the child has of being isolated and helpless in a potentially hostile world."

The emergence of these feelings might follow some such course as this: The rejection or other mistreatment spontaneously arouses feelings of resentment (irritation, hostility). But any show of resentment, anger, or fighting back usually brings actual or feared retaliation, including possible further rejection. So the next spontaneous reaction is fear or anxiety. This leads to a "bottling-up" of the hostility (though it will still be there and continue on into adulthood, manifesting itself from time to time, since it will be a deep feeling). The anxiety will continue and be the key to everything. Anxiety is fear and a person continuously anxious (fearful) is of course insecure. The insecurity itself will be a cluster of feelings with helplessness and isolation prominent among them.

The cluster of feelings -- resentment, anxiety, helplessness, and isolation -- drive the person to do various things by way of trying to handle the normal problems of daily life, especially relationship and interactions with other people, so he might become overly compliant (out of fear of rejection), overly dependent (to gain security), unable to stand up for self (but inwardly resentful and hostile toward the other), overly-possessive and jealous (more insecurity), over-demanding (needs much evidence of acceptance), and sometimes driven to seek power, prestige, and possessions (all evidence of acceptance and security).

In her final book, *Our Inner Conflicts* (1945), Horney concluded that these different sorts of reaction fall into three general clusters, representing three different adaptive strategies. These are the moving *toward* people (the compliant pattern or type); moving *against* people (the aggressive type); and moving *away* from people (the detached type), mentioned above in Chapter 3 (p. 97-99). Possibly some sort of success in gaining protection in childhood moved the person toward a compliant personality and way of life. Similarly, possibly much provocation of resentment and less punishment led to an aggressive nature and life style, and possibly the opportunity in childhood to the escape the nagging and harassment by isolation might have predisposed to the detached nature and pattern. But each pattern must be employed rigidly as the anxiety-insecurity permits no flexibility. Yet the rigidity makes them maladaptive, as all three need to be used fluidly to handle problems and human relationships of everyday life. Too, elements of the other two will be present semi-unconsciously and by their contradiction create conflict. So though the resentment-anxiety-helplessness-isolation is the core or foundation of the handicap, it is all of the forms of inconsistency, contradiction, compulsiveness, confusion, impoverishment (caused by all the alienation from real self), fears, and conflict generally that is the immediate neurosis, the part that must be slowly worked through if the person is ever to feel whole and at peace.

Turning now to conscience, Horney (1937) begins a chapter, "In the manifest picture of neurosis guilt feelings seem to play a prominent role." (p. 230) She assumes the anxiety-insecurity to be the underlying cause with fear of disapproval the immediate cause. She reports that nearly every neurotic is excessively afraid of being disapproved of, criticized, accused, found out. Inwardly he feels weak and helpless and in-effect "half a person," and despises himself. He reasons that if others find out all this weakness, they will despise him, too, which is dreaded. Thus more anxiety is generated, feeding on itself. Self-recrimination (self-blame and guilt) comes easily because of the self-hatred, hence all the moral faults. Further, and probably especially determinative, since there is no sense of being a real person with real strengths and weaknesses, *perfection* becomes the standard of self-judgement and the inevitable shortcomings condemned. Self-criticism (guilt) can also come from blaming self for other's faults and thus avoiding criticism and rejection from others. In childhood much fault-finding by a rejecting parent easily leads to the child's believing self inferior; any contrary assertion is likely to be punished. Resentments that should have been expressed toward others easily get directed toward self in the form of finding fault with self. Horney mentions as a example that a girl who is always subordinated to her sister and out of fear submits to unjust treatment, choking the accusations she really feels, may tell herself that the unequal treatment is warranted because she is inferior to her sister (less beautiful, less brilliant), or she may believe it justified because she is a bad girl. In both cases she takes the blame on herself instead of realizing that she has been wronged (p. 249). Were these causes not enough, self-criticism can also be an invitation to others to make reassuring remarks, for in spite of all the self-depreciation and guilt, there is an ego-defensiveness and a desperate hunger for admiration.

Horney says that when a neurotic accuses himself and indicates guilt feelings of some kind the first question should be *not* "What is he really feeling guilty about?" but "What may be the functions of this self-recriminating attitude?" We have just suggested some of those functions.

Fortunately not many persons show such an extreme of insecurity, self-depreciation and guilt, and all can be helped. For our purposes they exemplify the extreme of possible patterns of moral disposition and allow us to imagine the great variety of individual patterns to be seen between this and normal, typical patterns of conscience and guilt.

(As a technical note, the above ideas on the psychodynamics of guilt were formulated by Horney before she had conceived of the three adaptive strategies. They seem to suit the compliant-going-toward-people type especially well and we may wonder whether the aggressive or the detached types would be as prone to all these forms of self-criticism. Or, putting the question in another way, possibly not all maladjusted-neurotic persons are prone to self-criticism and guilt.)

Cases of too little conscience -- the antisocial (psychopathic, sociopathic) personality. Having noted cases of too much conscience and guilt we should go to the other extreme and note cases of too little. Some persons show a marked lack of moral development and adult conscience. They are variously labeled antisocial (DSM III R, p. 342), psychopathic, or sociopathic personality (Coleman et al., 1984, p. 248). The condition is of great importance for whereas the overly guilty person hurts only himself, the conscience-lacking person can do tremendous harm, often leaving a trail of misery, disappointment, and disillusionment behind. They tear at the fabric of trust that is so necessary if a community is to function, and exemplify what community life would be like if all lacked morals and conscience.

Psychopaths span the socio-economic scale, from unscrupulous business entrepreneur at the top to delinquents and criminals and some prostitutes at the bottom. Though some are violently dangerous, probably most dangerous to society are those that commit such crimes as dupe older people out of life-savings, pass themselves off as doctors or other specialists, and organize confidence rackets and mail frauds to steal from people by the thousands.

They manifest no outright mental symptoms so there is no basis for commitment to mental hospitals and rarely would one seek counseling assistance. They regularly come to the attention of law-enforcement officials, though most are clever enough to avoid arrest. Because of these characteristics, it is not known how many there are in the country and the number likely is increasing as family and community disorganization increases. Apparently most of these that have been studied have been in prison. (Effort to help them by psychotherapy usually is ineffective as there is no motivation to change; but it has been suggested that behavior modification in a prison setting may be effective, where the leverage of eventual release may be used to reshape behavior along lines suggested by Bandura, 1969 (Coleman et al., 1984, p. 257-8).)

The DSM III R focuses on a pattern seen more often in persons of lower-class background and reports that lying, stealing, truancy, vandalism, initiating fights, running away from home, and physical cruelty are typical childhood signs. This antisocial pattern continues into adulthood and may include failure to honor financial obligations, function as a responsible parent, or stay at a job. They fail to conform to social norms and repeatedly commit antisocial or illegal acts, such as destroying property, attacking and harassing others, stealing and having illegal occupations. They tend to be irritable and aggressive and repeatedly get into physical fights and assaults, including spouse- and child-beating. Generally they have no remorse about the hurtful effect of their behavior on others and may even feel justified in what they have done (p. 342).

Textbook writers such as Coleman (now Carson, Butcher, Coleman, 1988) typically focus on a pattern seen more often in persons of higher socio-economic status and describe them as often intelligent, spontaneous, and likeable at first acquaintance. Indeed, having actual cases in mind, it would not be unusual for a man to fabricate a whole successful personality, seek out a well-to-do woman, sweep her off her feet with flattery and declarations of love, capture her heart, propose marriage, and then before or after the wedding disappear with her wealth. Coleman (1964, p. 364) reprints a letter written by a man who declares, "June, my darling, I love you. I love you with all my heart and soul." It was written to a girl who he had never met, proposed marriage to her, described himself as a successful businessman with luxury apartment and vacations in Florida -- all this written from prison.

Of course the one outstanding characteristic is absence of a sense of moral rightness or any feeling of remorse or guilt at unethical-immoral behavior. But ordinarily there is knowledge of ethical rules, as shown by their profession of high standards. Additionally, they often are egocentric, impulsive, and irresponsible; unable to forego immediate pleasure for future gain; unable to profit from mistakes; have a powerful need to "be somebody"; are often hostile and aggressive, but often charming and likeable with a disarming manner, good sense of humor, and optimistic outlook; can put up a good front to impress and exploit; are usually cynical, unsympathetic, ungrateful, and remorseless; have no close friends or loyalties; are unable to understand love from others or to give it in return; and have quick ability to rationalize and project blame on others.

There has been much curiosity and speculation as to the origins of this remarkable disorder and its psychodynamics, but so far all we have are interesting lines of research and theory.

One line of thinking has been that there is some defect in constitutional makeup. A specific assumption has been that there is malfunction in the inhibitory mechanism of the brain, since impulsiveness is a common characteristic. Another has been that there is a deficiency in emotional arousal since they seem to lack normal fear and anxiety reactions and fail to learn from punishment. Closely related has been the assumption that because they operate at a low level of arousal, they suffer a stimulation deficit and have an insatiable drive to find excitement and stimulation, as by drugs, dramatic crime, constant activity, and dangerous recreations. However, all of these could be due to personality malfunction rather than organic malfunction. With the advent of newer techniques and discoveries, such as analysis of genes for missing parts (and consequent lack of key metabolic sequences in brain or gland) and analysis of brain neurotransmitters for aberrations, it may be possible to identify something. (Too, we need keep reminding ourselves that always there is a young person of given unique constitutional makeup in interaction with a unique pattern of parental treatment, so even if general organic causes are ruled out there still will be individual constitutional determinants playing their part.)

So far, the strongest causal possibility has been disturbed parent-child relationships, but because of the rather long list of characteristics, above, there is much to be explained and even this possibility leaves us with unanswered questions.

It will be recalled that studies of children found that the two key ingredients for good conscience development are warmth (acceptance, interest) and firm structuring. Given the two basics, discussing reasons for conforming to moral rules with the child increases considerateness toward others and strength of internal moral standard (Hoffman and Saltzstein, 1987, Ch. 9). So any pattern of parent-child relationship that is significantly different has the possibility of producing a defective conscience.

In a review paper published in the mid-1960s Becker (1964) summarized the child-rearing research that had been done up to that time. His interest was in learning the effects of restrictive versus permissive parenting, and he seemed to find a number of contradictory results. But when allowance was made for amount of parental warmth, the contradictions disappeared (Maccoby, p. 393). Restrictiveness in a context of parental warmth was associated with politeness, neatness, obedience, and nonaggressiveness in children. Restrictiveness, when imposed by hostile parents, was associated with a variety of neurotic symptoms, including withdrawal from social interaction with peers. Similarly, as to the effect of permissiveness, children whose parents were both warm and permissive tended to be socially outgoing, independent, active, creative, and domineering, while children whose parents were hostile and permissive tended to be aggressive or delinquent and noncompliant with adult demands. More recent work by Baumrind (1967, 1971) supports Becker's analysis. Her permissive parents were relatively warm, but they did not exercise firm control. Their children tended to be impulsive and immature. When parents were authoritative -- combining warmth with firm control and open communication -- the children were self-controlled and unusually competent for their age at activities (Maccoby, p. 393). Note the likenesses of several of these reactions to symptoms of the psychopath.

Impulsiveness and want of foresight are especially prominent features of psychopaths (though some have to be good planners in order to carry out their crimes). All young children are impulsive and must learn slowly to control themselves. Block, in collaboration with Haan (1971), studied a group of teenagers who were impulsive. As compared with age-mates, they were less able to wait for what they wanted and demanded immediate gratification, expression of emotion often was explosive, they had poor ability to maintain attention at tasks, and changed minds and enthusiasms frequently. The parents of these impulsive children showed these characteristics: a) considerable conflict between them, b) tended to disagree with each other about child-rearing values; c) neglected their teaching functions -- did not take time or trouble to teach age-appropriate skills to the children; d) seldom assigned chores or required the children to assume responsibilities for own needs or those of others in family; e) placed few demands for achievement on the children. None of these parental weaknesses in itself is grave and of the magnitude of, say, rejection, but as the researchers point out, these parents, by virtue of their own impulsivity and self-absorption, simply did not invest the time nor exhibit the constancy needed to deliver the precepts of self-regulation to the child (p. 263-64). This neglect in a context of rejection or ignoring-insensitivity can be devastating.

Redl and Wineman (1951, 1952) worked with a group of boys who suit the condition. They established a residential treatment center housing six to eight boys between the ages of eight to ten years who were "out of control." That is, the boys' parents were missing or had stopped trying to supervise or care for them. Most of the boys had lived in a series of foster homes, where they had proved too aggressive or too impulsive for a family-living situation. Their core problem was a profound deficiency in every aspect of impulse control. Here is an example of their low patience and impulse control at the beginning of treatment:

> One of the most regularly occurring frustration reactions, during the early phase of treatment, would be produced when, on our numerous station wagon trips, we had to stop and wait for traffic signal lights. This was intolerable to the children. Even though they knew this delay would be automatically terminated in thirty to forty-five seconds, though they could so to speak *see* it right out there in front of their noses, still they were unable to handle their tension. Aggressive behavior would break out: throwing things at the counselor who was driving, cursing and hitting each other, etc.. Shouts of "Goddamit, let's go, hit the bastard up there, what the hell are we waiting for," would fill the air. (Redl and Wineman, 1951, p. 78)

When Redl and Wineman investigated the early histories of these aggressive, out-of-control boys they found that they had never experienced continuing affection from a trustworthy adult. When the boys had tried to form attachments, they were repeatedly let down by adults who abandoned them. As a result, they had developed strong defenses against forming new ties. They were shocked when the adults of the residence offered them continuing affection and acceptance (along with control) and when the adults made a special point of keeping the bargains they had made. If the boys felt themselves developing affection and trust they fought against it. A favorite device was to try to goad the adults into violence -- if they succeeded, the children could then justify their anger against the world and would not have to feel guilty about their own violence. David Wineman describes as an example the case of Danny, who was especially violent during his first month at Pioneer House. The boy would begin each incident by teasing and insulting various members of the staff. When this did not provoke them into punishment, he would attack physically or smash up furniture or equipment. In order to prevent physical injury or unacceptable destruction, a staff member would have to restrain him physically (by holding, not punishment) until he calmed down sufficiently so that he could rejoin the other residents of the house. Incidents of this kind occurred at least twenty-five times during his first month at the House.

When faced with nonviolent control, one of the boys shouted "Why the hell don't you hit us?" Clearly, the boys were trying to prove that these adults were as abusive as their previous caretakers had been. Their provocations were extreme, and the staff members must have had to exercise enormous self-control to keep themselves from falling into the boys' traps. However they did continue with their control-plus-affection-plus-trustworthiness regime, and when the boys finally were able to reciprocate affection, the treatment program turned a corner -- the boys began to exercise self-control. Their work graphically illustrates the importance of affectional ties in the socialization of children. (The above description essentially quoted from Maccoby, p. 394-95).

Several things are to be noted especially here -- first, the hostility of the boys toward the world generally for the way they had been treated, a predictable reaction in rejected, neglected children; second, the utter illogic of their aggression in order to justify their anger -- only a perceptive therapist could give it any meaning; third, when a relationship of affection and trust finally was established the boys began to exercise self-control -- another remarkably illogical connection.

Turning to the several specific studies on psychopathic persons, McCord and McCord (1964) concluded that severe parental rejection and lack of parental affection were the primary causes. Buss (1966) concluded that two types of parental behavior cause psychopathology. In the first, the parents are cold and distant toward the child and allow no warm or close relationship to develop. A child who imitates this model will become cold and distant in later relationships and does not develop empathy for others or become emotionally involved with them. The other type of parental behavior involves inconsistency in supplying affection, rewards, and punishments. Usually these parents are inconsistent in their own role behavior so the child lacks stable models to imitate and fails to develop a clear sense of self-identity. When parents are both arbitrary and inconsistent in punishing the child, avoiding punishment becomes all-important. Instead of learning to see behavior in terms of right and wrong, the child learns how to avoid blame and punishment by lying and other manipulations. Heaver (1943) emphasized the influence of faulty parental models -- typically a mother who overindulged her son and a father who was highly successful, hard-driving, critical and distant. Greenacre (1945) generally supported this view, finding psychopaths from middle-class families often to have fathers who were successful and respected but distant and fear-inspiring to his children. But the mother would be indulgent, pleasure-loving, frivolous, and often tacitly contemptuous of her husband's importance. The family would find it necessary to maintain an illusion of a happy family by concealing and denying any evidence of discord. Thus the children would learn to play a part and never acquire a sense of reality, always putting on charm and trying to impress others. Coleman et al. (1984) remark that if we add one additional factor -- the contradictory influence of a father who tells his son of the necessity for responsibility, honesty, and respect for others, but who himself is deceitful and manipulative -- we appear to have a family background capable of producing a middle-class psychopathic personality. Incidentally, possibly all of the above-suggested causes operate in given cases, as all are but variants on the general theme of faulty parent-child relationships.

While it is the middle-class psychopathic person who leaves us most mystified as to the psychodynamics of his condition, it is the lower-class antisocial person who tends to reveal most obviously the origin of his condition, for often these young men who now get themselves into trouble by fighting, cruelty, destruction, and theft suffered years of harsh treatment with frequent beatings and physical deprivation with no ameliorating warmth or affection. Some proportion of working-class men (and women) are hard, feelingless, morose individuals, in part because they were treated harshly and without affection themselves in childhood, and in part because life itself is hard for them, toiling as they must, year after year, in heat and cold for a meagre uncertain living. In turn, they treat their own children harshly and without feeling.

The case of "J.O." (Linder, 1955, p. 290-306) nicely exemplifies this type of psychopathology and its causes. J. O.s mother died in childbirth so he was given to his grandmother to bring up. She treated him with love and kindness, but died when he was 5. He was returned to his father, who was a cold cruel man who expected the tiny boy to do an adult's work -- care for livestock, milk cows, shovel manure, work in the fields all day -- and would beat him for minor childish mistakes. J.O. came to hate the father and would do small things to try to get revenge. At age six he accidentally overturned a lantern and set fire to the barn; for this the father gave him a terrible beating. Crying, afraid, and hating he ran away. He was soon caught and returned, but a relative interceded and he was given foster-home placement. This couple were not cruel to him, but were on the severe side, with no affection, and required Bible study as punishment. At 8 he ran away again and this time was caught riding a freight train, a crime, and sent to a state training school. Again more physical punishment, hard work, and religious training, plus frightening hazing by the other boys. He stayed here for four years and as he grew he became more hostile and more of a trouble-maker. His hate became so great that he would fly into rages and attack guards, furniture, plumbing -- anything. He escaped and returned home but received no welcome or warmth from his father and was rejected by everyone else in the small rural community, so soon left and sought out the criminal elements in a nearby city and began a life of crime -- larceny, armed robbery, mugging, etc.. Upon arrest he was sent to a state reformatory for three years. Upon his release he went back to his life of crime, was arrested within a year for armed robbery, and this time sent to prison. There he was in trouble from the outset, his powerful hate driving him to seek opportunities for aggression. He took part in a major prison riot and as a ringleader was severely punished and his sentence extended with no possibility of parole and kept always in close confinement. He was only 22.

At this point he came to the attention of Linder, a clinical psychologist. A buddy had suggested to J.O. that he seek help and J.O. felt sufficiently desperate because of being locked up all of the time to try anything. He appeared surly and hostile at first interview and doubted that any one could help him. The psychiatric diagnosis was "psychopathic personality (character disturbance)." The report says nothing as to whether he was given psychotherapy or its outcome. Likely the reader will be curious as to what happened to him. I like to think he could have benefited from the counseling help because of the good start he had during the first five years.

Though J.O. was a product of rural America, the place where psychopaths are being created by the dozens or hundreds is big city ghettos. As Coleman et al. (1984) comment, "An environment characterized by the breakdown of social norms and regulations, disorganization, undesirable peer models, and pervasive alienation from and hostility toward the broader society appears to produce inadequate conscience development, lack of concern for others, and destructive, antisocial behavior. On the family level the picture is often aggravated by broken homes, parental rejection, and inconsistent discipline, leading to distrust, a confused sense of personal identity, self-devaluation, and feelings of hurt and hostility." (p. 257)

Though psychopathic personalities represent an extreme lack of morals and conscience, there must be millions of persons in this country today who fall but little short of having no morals and conscience and regularly commit crime whenever they think they can get away with it. Fear of apprehension, not an inner restraint, is the only deterrent, and whenever law enforcement becomes lax they have an ability to "smell out" the possibilities, much like animals drawn to carrion, and soon are exploiting the situation. When the Reagan Administration reduced the number of agents that enforce banking laws in savings and loan institutions the white collar crooks moved in. The director of the FBI has testified that fraud was pervasive in the institutions, criminal fraud was discovered in 60 percent of savings institutions seized by the government in 1989, and the number of fraud cases likely to increase steadily (*San Jose Mercury News*, 12 April, 1990).

Theories of the Development of Moral Reasoning

A relationship of warmth and firm structuring creates a conscientious child -- one who is impelled from within to behave in a moral manner. But our description of conscience development took for granted the child's ability to comprehend the moral teaching, whereas his actual moral behavior will depend upon his age and stage of intellectual development. Two-year olds, who are just beginning to talk and who have only the dimmest understandings of the causal sequence of events, are incapable of being moral or immoral. Even when they reach the age of "getting into everything," handling dangerous objects, and perhaps pulling the hair or taking the toy of another, they are still unable to comprehend very much, and it is common for mother to take away the scissors or restore the toy to its wailing owner, with hardly a word of admonition, because of her knowledge that admonition or explanation will not be comprehended. Question naturally arises as to when the child is mentally mature enough to acquire the different sorts of moral values. How often have you heard a child exclaim, in outrage or in tears, to playmates or to parent, "That's not fair!" At what age does a child begin to have a sense of the right and fair?

Modern thinking on moral development began with Piaget's study of children's thinking (1965; first published 1932). He had been analyzing children's logical reasoning about the physical world so it was natural for him to extend the analysis to their understanding of moral rules. He saw moral development as but an aspect of the child's general intellectual development. From talking with the child about the rules of games and discussing incidents that contain moral dilemmas he concluded that the child passes through stages of intellectual moral growth. It might be noted that it was not the child's actual moral behavior he was studying; rather, the intellectual aspect of moral growth.

To illustrate his approach, let us consider his method of assessing children's thinking about the role of *intent* in moral judgements (Maccoby, 1980, p. 302). Piaget worked with a substantial number of Swiss children in the age range six to twelve. He told them stories about childish transgressions, in each case asking the child to tell him which action was naughtier and why. He was more interested in the reasons his subjects gave for their choices than in the choices themselves. One set of stories follows:

A. There was once a little girl who was called Marie. She wanted to give her mother a nice surprise, and cut out a piece of sewing for her. But she didn't know how to use the scissors properly, and cut a big hole in her dress.

B. A little girl called Margaret went and took her mother's scissors one day that her her mother was out. She played with them for a bit.

Then, as she didn't know how to use them properly, she made a little hole in her dress. (1965, p. 122)

Younger children usually insisted that the girl in Story A was naughtier because she made a bigger hole in her dress. Did they conclude this because they did not understand that she was trying to be helpful? Piaget found that even when they did understand this, the younger children still based their decision on the amount of damage that had been done. In general, at this stage it is the material outcome, not intent, that determines the judgement. Armsby (1971) followed up on this, asking children to compare a small amount of deliberate damage with larger amounts of accidental damage, and found that even children as young as six usually say that the deliberate damage is naughtier. Armsby's work suggests that young children can understand intent in the sense of recognizing deliberate naughtiness. They also are aware that damage to valued objects is something to be avoided. Children do have difficulty, however, weighing the relative importance of these factors, and they sometimes have trouble inferring other people's intent (Maccoby, p. 303).

One of Piaget's general insights was that children pass through a stage of moral realism and later enter a stage of moral relativism. The realism stage is typified by reasoning that a rule is something that simply exists, much like a physical object, and that wrongness is whatever adults forbid or punish. Piaget assumed that this outlook results from the child's subordination to adults and their stating rules as absolute. Later, when children begin to free themselves from adult authority and interact with age-mates, they enter the stage of moral relativism where precepts are perceived in relation to the intentions behind them and the social purpose they are designed to serve.

Piaget's work is useful not only in telling about children's moral development but also in spelling out specific aspects of general moral development in anyone. Such development will include: learning to use truth-telling in a relative way, perceiving the perspective and rights of the other person, developing empathy for the other, developing a sense of justice, perceiving the greater good beyond immediate concerns, and learning the importance of trust and promises.

Kohlberg picked up on Piaget's work and extended it, using the same methods of having the child or teenager play moral games and discuss moral dilemmas. His purpose, too, was to discover the intellectual stages the child goes through in his moral maturing. He accepted much of Piaget's findings but formulated the stages somewhat differently.

Kohlberg (1969, 1976, 1983) labels his system "six stages of moral judgement," and it may help one understand what he is doing if we imagine his sitting talking to a child (or teenager or adult) and posing an ethical dilemma to him, and then asking, what is the right (fair, just) thing to do? Since this is his purpose he is not concerned at any point with accumulating lists of people's morals or with describing the psychodynamics of morals in lives, but only with how they understand and justify ethical judgements.

The most famous of Kohlberg's moral dilemmas was concerned with a hypothetical person, Heinz, and a brief description of it, followed by actual comments of a young person named Joe will exemplify his research method and people's reactions:

> Heinz's wife is fatally ill with cancer. A drug that may save her is invented by a local druggist. The price is very high. Heinz does not have enough money to buy it. He borrows part of what is needed and offers to pay what he has and try to pay off the rest later. The druggist refuses to sell, saying that he put many years of work into his invention and deserves to be adequately compensated. Heinz, in desperation, breaks into the drugstore to steal the drug for his wife. The question is: Should Heinz have done this?

Though the story presents issues that do not arise in the lives of children, still most children understand the problem well enough to discuss it, and as they grow older the nature of their reasoning clearly changes. Note the changing reasoning of Joe as his age changes:

> At age 10. (Why shouldn't you steal from a store?) It's not good to steal from a store. It's against the law. Someone could see you and call the police. (1976, p. 36)

> At age 17. (Why shouldn't you steal from a store?) It is a matter of law. It's one of our rules that we're trying to help protect everyone, protect property, not just to protect a store. It's something that's needed in our society. If we didn't have these laws, people would steal, they wouldn't have to work for a living, and our whole society would get out of kilter. (p. 36)

> At age 24. (Why shouldn't someone steal from a store?) It's violating another person's rights, in this case, to property. (Does the law enter in?) Well, the law in most cases is based on what is morally right, so it's not a separate subject, it's a consideration. . . . (What does "morality," or "morally right" mean to you?) Recognizing the rights of other individuals, first to life, and then to do as he pleases as long as it doesn't interfere with somebody else's rights. . . . (returning to Heinz) It is the husband's duty to save his wife. The fact that her life is in danger transcends every other standard you might use to judge his action. Life is more important than

property. (Suppose it were a friend, not his wife?) I don't think that would be much different from a moral point of view. It's still a human being in danger. . . . (Should the judge punish the husband?) Usually the moral and legal standpoints coincide. Here they conflict. The judge should weigh the moral standpoint more heavily but preserve the legal law in punishing Heinz lightly. (pp. 37-38)

Kohlberg (1981, 1983) identified six stages of development of moral judgement, divided into three levels. These may be outlined as follows:

Level A. Preconventional Level (The level of most children under nine, many adolescents, and many adult criminal offenders)

Stage 1. The Stage of Punishment and Obedience

Right is literal obedience to rules and authority, avoiding punishment, and not doing physical harm.

Motivation to conform is evoked by external punishments and rewards. No awareness of psychological interests of others. No awareness that parents' perspective not one's own.

Stage 2. The Stage of Individual Instrumental Purpose and Exchange (self-interested exchanges)

Right is serving one's own and other's needs and making fair deals in terms of concrete exchange -- in brief, conform to obtain rewards and have favors returned.

Now separates own interests and points of view from those of parents and others; aware that everyone has individual interests, so that right is relative (in a concrete sense). Can integrate or relate conflicting individual interests to one another, such as in fairness giving each person the same amount.

Level B. Conventional Level (The level of most adolescents and adults)

Stage 3. The stage of Mutual Interpersonal Expectations, Relationships, and Conformity (maintaining good interpersonal relationships)

The right is playing a good (nice) role, being concerned about other people and their feelings, keeping loyalty and trust with partners, and being motivated to follow rules and expectations.

Wants to be seen by others as good and also wants to feel that way about her/himself. The rules are internalized as one's own and felt to be right; experiences guilt and shame at transgressions.

The person is aware of shared feelings, agreements, and expectations and these take primacy over individual interests. Relates points of view through the "concrete Golden Rule," putting oneself in the other person's shoes. Does not yet consider the perspective of the larger society (the generalized system).

Stage 4. The Stage of Social System and Conscience Maintenance (doing one's duty and obeying one's conscience)

The right is doing one's duty in society, upholding the social order, and maintaining the welfare of society or the group.

Now one can differentiate the point of view of the larger society from interpersonal agreement or motives. Now takes the viewpoint of the system (society) which defines roles and rules. Considers individual relations in terms of place in society.

This stage has sometimes been called the law and order morality. Persons at this stage feel that people have a duty to live up to accepted obligations and feel guilty at own failures to do so.

It may be noted that a person at this stage is a fully socialized, ethical person who uses the community good as standard of judgement. Kohlberg (1976) says that only about 5 percent of persons go on to Stage 5, which means that the great majority of adults will be at Stages 3 or 4. Note the special nature of the next two stages.

Level C. Postconventional and Principled Level

Moral decisions are generated from rights, values, or principles that are (or could be) agreeable to all individual composing or creating a society designed to have fair and beneficial practices. Society's rules are accepted but these persons go beyond and experience their own understanding of the basic moral principles that underlie the rules.

Stage 5. The Stage of Prior Rights and Social Contract or Utility

The right is upholding the basic rights, values, and legal contracts of a society, even when they conflict with the concrete rules and laws of the group.

Here a person is able to see the greater good beyond the specific attachments and contracts of the group.

Stage 6. The Stage of Universal Ethical Principles

This stage assumes guidance by universal ethical principles that all humanity should follow.

Here a person is able to take the perspective of a moral point of view from which social arrangements derive or on which they are grounded. The perspective is that of any rational individual recognizing the nature of morality or the basic moral premise of respect for the other persons as ends, not means.

This final stage seems almost a description of the hypothetical ideal moral person who is able to know the universal ethical principles. In fact, it is attained so seldom that provisions for scoring it have been dropped in the most recent manual (Colby and Kohlberg, 1987).

What is causing the person to move up through the stages? Kohlberg concluded that it is primarily intellectual maturing itself, which means that every mentally normal person should reach stage 3 or 4, at least.

As always happens when a new discovery is made, these findings provoked new questions. A major question was the relationships between the moral reasoning and moral behavior. A person might show a high level of moral reasoning but leave us uncertain as to his moral behavior. A good example might be the case of Joe above. At age 24 Joe is showing a mature level of moral reasoning and it would be reasonable to expect a comparable level of moral behavior from him. But this is a high level of reasoning in the abstract and it is always possible that a person may show such reasoning yet in various concrete ways behave immorally, much as an attorney will know the law in principle yet violate it. Another question was the relation of development of moral reasoning to the child's social environment, since the only influence formally recognized is that of mental maturing. And inevitably questions arose as to the specific nature of the moral disposition -- is moral reasoning a pure act of logic with no feeling involvement, or is there some amount of feeling also, perhaps sympathy or empathy, as when out of sympathy we reason that Heinz should have stolen the medicine to save his wife's life. And if we assume that feeling-emotion has a role, then it is possible that a person will show considerable variability in his moral judgements depending upon the feelings being roused by each particular moral problem.

Kohlberg has always been open to new insights and he and students and associates have followed up different ones of the questions. Early he concluded that the social environment does influence the development of moral reasoning, accelerating it in some cases and inhibiting in others. Though the theory proper says nothing of influences in addition to the one of intellectual (cognitive) development, Kohlberg did assume the whole to be taking place in a social context. In one place he has written that the self is born out of the social or sharing process (1969, p. 416). "It appears that participation in various groups converges in stimulating the development of basic moral values." (1969, p. 399-402) And again that moral development is fundamentally a process of the restructuring of modes of role-taking; and the fundamental social inputs from family, peer group, and workplace may be termed "role-taking opportunities." The term "role-taking opportunities" is meant to suggest that the person is having opportunities of putting self in the other person's shoes and experiencing that person's feelings. Such empathic experiences appear to be an important part of moral development and Kohlberg seems to be recognizing the role of feeling-emotion in at least certain moral values. In recent years Kohlberg (1984) has made clear his view that moral decision-making and action almost always take place in a social context; indeed that "moral atmosphere in the form of collective norms and a sense of community can be very strong factors in determining moral behavior." (p. 267; cf. Gibbs and Schell, 1985, pp. 1070-80)

Kohlberg has not wanted to involve himself in the frustrating problem of relating expression of moral judgement to moral action, reasoning variously that moral reasoning is a sufficient concern unto itself and is its own validation (its reality does not need to be proved by additional means); that it is a reasonable expectation that people will behave as they reason; and that specific actions result from the specifics of personal makeup and situation so lie outside a general theory. Nevertheless, a number of studies have been done by various researchers and much of his latest work has been concerned with moral behavior, as in his "just community" work in several schools and prisons. To give but one example, Kohlberg states that one can reason in terms of principles but not live up to principles (in Purpel and Ryan, p. 181). In support, he and Krebs found that only 15 percent of students showing some principled thinking cheated as compared to 55 percent of conventional thinking subjects and 70 percent of preconventional subjects. Nevertheless, 15 percent of the principled subjects did cheat, suggesting that factors additional to moral judgement are necessary for principled moral reasoning to be translated into "moral action." Some of those factors are situational pressures, individual motives and emotions, and the person's general sense of will, purpose, or "ego strength." This last amounts to saying that in addition to knowing what is the right or just thing to do one must also have the courage of his convictions to do the moral thing.

One whose thinking was especially provoked by Kohlberg's theorizing has been Norma Haan, who has proposed a somewhat different formulation. Part of this theory was reviewed above in Chapter 3, under "People in value interaction." Her concern is with practical morality, which must mean the everyday morality of you and me. She assumes this morality always to be social, involving interaction with actual or imaginary other persons. So it is termed a *social interaction* theory. She assumes that the ideal moral state of affairs is not attainment of justice (fairness, democracy), as does Kohlberg, but equalization among interactors in the solving of problems. This turns out not to be very different from justice, for in effect equalization is just and fair, but it directs our attention away from the attainment of justice in the abstract to people in interaction and to what must be happening between them to achieve morality. Unlike Kohlberg, her emphasis is not primarily upon intellectual growth producing morality but upon the social experiences of childhood and youth that are producing interactional strengths and weaknesses (some of which we saw in Chapter 3).

Social interaction begins at birth, between child and adults, and because each has his own needs and purposes there will be some conflict of interest, necessitating a resolution of the conflict: child may want food now and begin to fuss; parent may want to sleep. One time, parent may have to yield in order to sleep; another time, child has to yield. Daily life will be full of situations of interaction and conflict of self-interest. Even when parental self-interest prevails, as usually happens, still there has been the interplay of self-interest. From innumerable daily situations of needing, asserting, yielding, compromising, etc., child is developing techniques of interacting ("negotiating" in the broadest sense) together with a sense of the ought and right. Early-on self-interest is the automatic "right" (if it could be worded by the child) with no sense of other's interests or of mutual interests. But with further interactions and intellectual development a sense of other's interests emerges. As Haan et al. put it, "pressing the legitimacy of one's own claims is soon understood by the very young to be an admission, in itself, that others also have legitimate claims." (p. 65)

The theory assumes that with continued interaction throughout childhood the child is acquiring increasing skill in interacting and dealing with moral problems, so moral development is gradual rather than in stages. But the progression is not smooth because moral interaction situations are never repeated exactly -- interacting with different persons, facing different problems in different states of mind, etc.. Nor are moral conclusions ever final. New interactions produce new insights and nuances of conviction. So what develops in this theory is increasingly reliable skills in resolving moral conflict, no moral concern itself (p. 240).

The theory invites observing children and adults in interaction as they deal with ethical problems. We have already reviewed their study of college students in moral interaction (pp. 83-95) and now may review their study of four-year olds.

Moral action of four-year-olds. Since both Piaget and Kohlberg reasoned that young children could not consider the interests of others because they could not coordinate divergent points of view yet, and Kohlberg concluded that young children's moral judgements are based on threats of punishment (it is wrong to steal another child's toy because punishment results), a study was designed to test these assumptions and observe moral interactions using four-year-olds as subjects.

Packer, Haan, Theodorou, and Yabrov (in Haan et al., 1985, p. 280), the study authors, report that the behavior of preschoolers in natural settings suggest that four-year-olds manifest a variety of prosocial actions. They will assist one another, help or comfort each other in distress, punish the cause of another's distress, and ask an adult to help a peer. The authors add that after extensive review of the great number of studies now available, Radke-Yarrow, Zahn-Waxler, and Chapman (1983) concluded that preschool children "are not only egocentric, selfish and aggressive; they are also exquisitely perceptive, have attachments to a wide variety of others, and respond prosocially across a broad spectrum of interpersonal events in a wide variety of ways and with various motives." (p. 484)

Eighteen pairs of preschoolers, of average age four years six months, were had to play the game NeoPd (abbreviation for neo-prisoner's dilemma). The essence of the game is that each player has a card which is red on one side and blue on the other and which side is turned up determines the reward or loss. When played by adults the rules will be more complex but here if both children chose the red card each received a penny; if both chose blue neither received a penny; if one chose blue and the other red then the blue received two pennies and the other none. The children were keen to win pennies (and in preliminary trials became so upset if pennies were taken away that the game was changed to avoid this).

Because of the immaturity of the children everything was well-structured -- pictures of everything were provided to supplement spoken instructions, clear glass containers put before each child for his/her pennies, and especially an adult leader was there throughout to explain and guide to next steps and question them. But as the researchers stress, *"Nonetheless the terms and nature of the moral issues remained basically the same as for the adolescents and young adults.* The main moral questions were still: Do I care about my friend having less? Is it all right to defend my self-interest? Can I trust my friend to keep an agreement?" (p. 282)

The following excerpt should give a good impression of the children's interaction. (p. 276)

> Two four-year-old girls have played the game NeoPd so that each has won an equal number of pennies. The staff leader is not certain that they understand this equalizing solution so she ask:
>
> STAFF LEADER: What would happen if you, Jackie, put down a blue card and Mary put down a red card?
>
> JACKIE: I would get pennies and she wouldn't.
>
> STAFF LEADER: Would that be fair?
>
> JACKIE: Nooooo. Because then I get pennies and she doesn't. (*Pause.*) It gets really kinda unhappy.
>
> STAFF LEADER: Mary, how would you feel if you got some pennies and Jackie didn't?
>
> MARY: (*biting her lip*) Sad.
>
> STAFF LEADER: How come?
>
> MARY: I don't like Jackie getting sad and we're friends and we always do the same thing.
>
> STAFF LEADER: When you both put down red, how does that make you feel?
>
> BOTH GIRLS: Happy!

JACKIE: 'Cause then it's more like it, 'cause we both get something.
(*Each will receive one penny.*)
As to results, five different kinds of moral interaction were possible:
  EQUALIZATIONS: Both children play cooperatively (play their red cards), enabling each to win one penny, or the two children agree that they will take turns. First one will play red (no payoff) the other plays blue to win two pennies; on the next play they will reverse their choices of play.
  REPARATIONS: They attempt to equalize previous imbalances in total number of pennies won. The winner agrees to play red for no gain so that the loser may play blue and win two pennies.
  STALEMATE: Both children deliberately play competitively (blue-blue), with the result that neither child obtains pennies.
  DEFAULT: Competitive play (blue) is continued by the winning child, while the loser continues to play red, apparently attempting to cooperate.
  BETRAYAL: A child breaks a proposed or assumed agreement to play cooperatively. (p. 283-284)

Though all these forms of morality were shown by these four-year-olds, clearly a majority were manifesting concern for the interests of the other and a sense of fairness, as shown by percentages of equalizations and reparations (p. 370-71).

Haan et al. offer the remarkable conclusion from this study that *the moral concerns of preschoolers and adults are basically the same.* They had essentially the same moral experience. They coordinated benefits, stalemated, made reparations, defaulted, and betrayed. They became angry or sullen during stalemates, defaults, and betrayals. They palpably experienced the glow of good conscience when they achieved mutually acceptable solutions. They worked for their self-interests but changed course when they became aware of their partner's plight. But some children were also inept -- as were some university students and adolescents -- in protecting their legitimate interests (p. 371).

Of course they add that there will be differences between the age groups because children must gradually develop the skills that enable them to act in a wide variety of complex situations. Too, they are tiny persons in an adult world, lacking knowledge, reasoning skills, power and authority, and readily become upset at the unusual and threatening, so in a practical sense the difference will be great.

As mentioned, in the interactional theory development is thought to be tied to the child's interdependency with others and the need to make adjustments to the self-interest of each other. As Haan et al. (1985) elaborate, the pervasive motive for moral development is the desire of all people, whatever their age, in maintaining and enhancing social bonds. The motive arises from social living itself, the nuances of which children increasingly come to understand. As they seek to protect their own interests they discover that their interests are protected only by recognizing and protecting the interests of others. "The interactional theory takes this dialectic -- an immutable feature of social life -- as the necessary condition of development." (p. 241)

The course of moral development in children is marked by gradual improvement in practical reasoning, rational consideration of factual details, and the ability to "read" the emotions aroused during interchanges; thus they acquire a repertoire of successful, adaptable ways to solve moral problems.

Another necessary development is learning about the risks and futility of trying to deal with insincere protagonists. In their innocence children often assume that others are as sincere as they, until experience teaches otherwise.

Since the theory assumes that equality between interactors is a necessary condition for morality, inequality between them can be a problem, especially for children as they are physically and experientially inferior, but Haan et al. point out that discussants of any age can achieve equalization if they make allowance for each others' peculiar needs, contributions, and status. Too, equalization of relations between persons of unequal power and skill, as between parent and young child, is seldom literal. From the interactional perspective these are allowable and socially necessary imbalances and need not prevent productive interaction as long as the person of greater resource makes allowance for the needs of the lesser (p. 241).

The course of development is not always positive, toward increased social skills. The theory recognizes that *regressive* changes may also occur, as when people find themselves inescapably immersed in relationships of bad faith and their attempts to correct these relationships consistently fail. Even then, the person may not abandon his moral concern but instead become selective in his commitment to good faith (p. 242).

But continual betrayal is traumatic; it threatens existence, for people rely on interpersonal accountability as the underpinning of their interaction with others. Betrayal forces them to employ defensive negations and distortions, in the end sacrificing social sensibility and interactional effectiveness in order to protect their private sensibility (p. 242).

Regressed development can be reversed if old conditions are replaced, but trust is not easily reconstructed. Clinicians who work with juvenile delinquents and abused children will know the difficulties. Socially deviant persons are wary about taking the risk that proffered good faith might be authentic (see above in the Redl & Wineman report, page 121-2, for good exemplification of this wariness). Not only do they require social conditions that consistently deliver good faith, but they also need support so that they themselves can personally invent new solutions (p. 242).

It may be recalled from their analysis of moral effectiveness (Ch. 3, above) that Haan et al. (1985) found that the main determinant was whether the person was able to use coping rather than defensive techniques in moral interactions. Defensiveness means there have been less than ideal personality shaping influences.

The following nicely describes the mature or effectively functioning person as seen by the interactional theory:

> [T]he moral agent in the interactional theory is envisioned as an actor in a social setting, engaged in a real or imagined dialogue with others or "society." By necessity, the actor takes into account all sociopsychological aspects of participants and extenuating circumstances, including moral understandings, emotions, motivations, and cognitions, as well as the social meanings and the outward characteristics of the situation. The moral person need not be educationally sophisticated nor necessarily chronologically mature. Instead he or she skillfully deals with conflict, and tolerates tension to achieve and sustain mutually sensitive moral balances that equalize relationships. Reasoning is applied and practical; it deals with the immediacies of the conflict. It may not always be strictly logical, and participants' emotions are always critical communications. *Resolutions should fit the particular situation, not rise above it.* (p. 55)

A study of moral development among college students. Apparently there has been but one comparative study of moral development, that of Haan, Aerts, and Cooper (1985), which was identified above in Chapter 3 in connection with their study of moral interaction. There have been a number of studies of moral development as seen by the Kohlberg cognitive development theory but not comparing it with another. The general outcome of those studies was that cognitive moral development could be increased by deliberate programs of improvement. For example, an oft-mentioned study by Blatt and Kohlberg (1975) found that groups of students who discussed moral dilemmas advanced on the average a third-of-a-stage on the six-stage scoring scale of that theory (and see below under school influence for other findings and references).

As part of their larger two-phase design, Haan et al. attempted to improve the moral development of the fifteen groups of university students and assess the nature of that development. Since the Kohlberg cognitive development theory assumes moral development to result from improvement in moral reasoning, and since Kohlberg and his associates have always used discussion of moral dilemmas as the means of improving moral reasoning, it was appropriate to employ the dilemmas here for the same purpose. Similarly, since the Haan interactional theory assumes moral problem-solving to occur in a social interaction setting, it was appropriate to have the groups of students engage in actual interaction by playing moral games as means of developing their moral problem-solving skills. It was also possible to determine whether the one activity, dilemma analysis or game playing, aided development of the opposite skill.

See pages 85-89 above again for an example of a group's discussion of a moral dilemma. A recorded except of a stressful game session is also given by Haan et al. (p. 164-166) but the interaction is difficult to follow. In brief, the game being played by a friendship group, four persons to a side, is NeoPd, which involves each playing a white or blue card. The rules were more complicated than those for the four-year-olds but in essence the same. Specifically, the pennies awarded depended on the coordination between the number of blues both groups turned up. Cooperation would give both groups moderate benefits, while attempts by one group to score heavily would penalize the other. If both groups tried to score heavily the result was a stalemate with no pay-off for either. In the excerpt one team is far ahead and both have agreed to play for moderate and equal points by avoiding playing blue cards. But the winning team breaks the agreement, all play blue, and again win points, while the losers go deeper into debt. Moments later the winners again violate their promise, think themselves clever, and act superior to the losers. When the losing team proposes that they be allowed to catch up, since the winners had broken their promises, the winners refused and seemed to have no sense of guilt at their dishonesty. At end, one of the losers reminds them of what they have been doing to win 50¢ -- their moral cost, but again the winners show no remorse.

Since the time period of the study was only 15 hours stretched over a few weeks, it was possible to expose the students to only a limited number of development-enhancing experiences and dramatic improvements were not expected. The focus was on why development occurs; specifically, what kinds of experiences lead to development, and what kinds of persons are likely to develop as a result of these experiences? Considerable hangs on ultimate answers to these questions for if it is found that cognitive (rational) disequilibrium is the essence of moral growth, that would suggest the usefulness of practice in thinking about moral dilemmas (as is often done in schools today), but if an interactional (social) disequilibrium is its essence, then experience in solving actual moral problems as groups would be indicated.

A complex analysis of results was made in order to learn the effects not only of the two methods of training but also of group structure (led or dominated), personal strategies of coping and defending, specific nature of the problem, and any sex differences in strategy. Here we must content ourselves with noting broad general results.

The amount of absolute change in either type of moral skill, as proposed by either theory, was not great. Employing a predetermined criterion of change, 26 percent gained in interactional skills, 16 percent gained in cognitive (reasoning) morality; 57 and 70 percent, respectively, stayed the same; and 17 and 14 percent decreased in competence (p. 249, 352). As these percentages indicate, more students increased their interactional skills as a result of the experience and more remained the same in moral reasoning ability.

Also, game playing resulted in greater gain in moral reasoning (cognitive morality) than did dilemma discussion, a finding contrary to an assumption of the cognitivists that discussion of hypothetical dilemmas is the most effective means of developing moral reasoning or judgement. Discussion of dilemmas produced no comparable gain in interactional morality (p. 270, 361).

When the students were divided into three groups -- gainers, stables (no change), and losers in competence, the following was found: (1) The stable students in both systems were rather similar. Although intellectually efficient and well-regulated, they were self-righteous, and in the eyes of their friends dominating, inflexible, and not very likeable. They seemed to need to protect themselves against the self-exposure of moral conflict and did not seek mutual resolution of the moral problems they and their friends faced (p. 272). (2) Students who gained in both systems also acted rather similarly. They were much involved in the moral experiences. At the end of the sessions, friends strengthened their judgements that those who made moral gains were straightforward and able to make clear arguments. Their comment suggested that the gainers in interactional skills typically tolerated ambiguity. Altogether, gainers seemed prepared to risk moral involvement and self-exposure and, when faced with conflict, did become involved (p. 272). (3) The two groups of students whose moral levels became depressed were not alike. Interactional losers were characteristically defensive and vacillating, showing self-effacing defenses, doubt, repression, and rationalization. Cognitive losers also were repressive, but they seemed intent on avoiding experiences of disequilibrium and their loss may have been only temporary, resulting from a desire to keep peace with their friends (p. 272).

Both theories assume that some manner of disequilibrium is necessary for moral development and from their findings Haan et al. conclude:

> *The kind of disequilibrium that made both interactional and cognitive development possible was passionate, stressful debate, not abstracted cognitive disagreement. This disequilibrium was not simply generalized stress but was, more specifically, the stress -- even the shock -- of discovering that one's friends and even one's self could morally violate, easily and unthinkingly.* As a result, morality comes to be seen as a delicate interchange that requires careful nourishment. And it involves the risk of self-exposing commitment; it means frequently attempting to right wrongs that people inevitably commit and frequently forgiving wrongs done to the self. Members of groups that functioned so smoothly that moral violations seldom occurred did not have these instructive experiences despite the fact that they usually acted effectively. This description of how and why

development occurred applied to cognitive morality equally as well as to interactional morality. (p. 273)

All this may be taken to mean that different types of morality-developing activity have their unique strengths but all must succeed in producing real, passionate involvement or they will fail. This is a large order when applied to, say, a roomful of adolescents who are concerned only with such immediacies as dating, popularity, fads and fashions, and spending-money.

Peer Influence

Age mates will be influencing values from childhood onward throughout lives -- first by playmates, then schoolmates, later marital-mates and occupational associates and others. Too, peer influence will be present in the midst of other of the influences that we survey here such as family and college.

It will be recalled that Piaget found that young children believe that rules are outside themselves and have a sort of physical reality, originating with adult authorities whose right to make rules is taken for granted. Later, sometime during the preadolescent years, there is a marked change in most children in their conception of rules. Now they have come to believe that rules are something that exist among equals, are agreed-upon by the parties concerned, and can be changed by mutual agreement (Maccoby, 1980, p. 308). Piaget reasoned that the young child perceives rules as real and absolute because they were imposed by parents who presented them as absolute. And it was not until the child began to interact with age-mates, as in games, did he have a chance to begin to perceive rules in the more mature, relative way. Thus, Piaget saw the peer group, not the family, as the source of more mature concepts about rules and authority.

Kohlberg reasoned in exactly the same way, feeling that the situation of equality between age-mates and especially their being at about the same stage of intellectual and moral maturity gave them an ideal opportunity to be testing moral ideals on each other. The Haan interactional theory assumes that all moral interactions are helping to produce moral maturity and those between equals will be especially facilitative.

This is an interaction rich with implications, for we can picture children and teenagers in constant daily interaction with peers, on playground, in classroom, at summer camp, at parties, etc., and in all of these interactions, in a setting of equality and freedom to speak, they may be giving and receiving value notions that gradually become settled convictions.

Without citing additional studies here, it may be mentioned that the Newcomb study of college girls (p. 143-153 below) was in considerable measure a study of peer influence. Similarly, the Haan et al. study of the moral development of university friendship groups, reviewed above, also was a study of peer group influence.

Family Influence, Late Adolescence and Adulthood

As mentioned, late adolescence, especially the college-age years, is a time of great flowering of interest in ideas, issues, causes, a time especially for trying out attitudes and values for the first time.

Since in our American society the nuclear family, consisting of parents and their children, is the basic unit of society, we would expect the parental influence to continue strong up until young adulthood.

Many studies of attitudes, dating from the beginning of social psychology in the 1930s, have shown similarity in attitudes between parents and maturing children, and we may be confident the same was true of values. For example, Jennings and Niemi (1968) found that 76 percent of a national sample of high school seniors favored the same political party as was favored by both of their parents. Earlier studies of similarity in political attitudes between adult children and parents, dating from the 1940's and 1950's, found that from two-thirds to three-fourths of voters voted for the party of their fathers, a remarkably high similarity (Lazarsfeld et al., 1944; Berelson et al., 1954). However, such similarity is not to be interpreted as showing that father was responsible for offspring's voting behavior -- both could have been exposed to the same information, belonged to same religion and social class, or faced the same economic problems, all distinct causes of attitudes. Too, similarity in political attitudes and voting behavior may represent a special case because ordinarily the choice is between only two political parties or two candidates. Attitudes on matters of dress, faith and morals, environment and pollution, and other issues of the day might show much less similarity.

Be that as it may, the student dissent of the 1960's and early 1970's, centering primarily in opposition to the Vietnam War and in civil rights, suggested the possibility that parental influence had weakened, that the students were rebelling against parental attitudes and values. A number of studies were done to investigate, guided generally by a pair of opposing hypotheses. The one, called the *socialization* hypothesis, assumed an essential similarity between parents and college-age children in attitudes and values, with the students reflecting the influence of parents. The other, called the *generational conflict* hypothesis, assumed that rebellion by the young against parental standards was a major cause for the dissent.

A first study, by Flacks (1967), found that while student political activists were more radical than their parents, their parents were clearly more liberal than other adults of their status. When the student activists were compared to a matched group of non-activists it was found that only 6 percent of non-activists' fathers described themselves as highly liberal or socialist, whereas 60 percent of the activists' fathers did so. Forty percent of the non-activists' fathers described themselves as conservative; none of the activists' fathers did so. Nor were the areas of agreement between the generations confined to political matters. Both non-activists and their parents tended to express conventional values toward achievement, material success, sexual morality, and religion. On the other hand, both activists and their parents tended to value intellectual and aesthetic activities, humanitarian concerns, and self-expression, and to devalue personal achievement, conventional morality, and conventional religion (See also Flacks, 1970).

A second study, by Keniston (1968), involved an intensive analysis of just a dozen activists who were participating in Vietnam Summer 1967, a project intended to arouse the public to oppose the Vietnam War. He found these activists to be complex persons. They were in good shape in the mental health sense -- open to their own feelings and motives, not notably hostile, rebellious, or suspicious. They were not strongly devoted to a political ideology, but rather to a set of basic values: justice, decency, equality, responsibility, nonviolence, and fairness. They were all going beyond anything their parents had ever done in the way of political action, but most felt a strong sense of continuity with their parent's values. When one was asked to come home and talk about what he was doing he told Keniston, "I'm looking forward to really trying to explain to them the kinds of things I feel, that I am a very personal embodiment of what they are, what they created in a son and what they brought me up to be." Keniston found that their previous family life usually had been warm, with mothers "achievement-demanding" but not threatening. Fathers were seen as not domineering and most as highly ethical, intellectually strong, principled, honest, politically involved, or idealistic, though some were seen as unsuccessful, acquiescent, weak, or inadequate. If any of the father's characteristics was rejected, it was not his principles but his failure to act upon them.

This last is a finding that emerges from most of these studies. When student activists criticized their parents, they usually were not rejecting parental values, but were complaining that their parents had not lived up to those values. When these students vigorously opposed the draft, war-related businesses and industries, discrimination, and other societal weaknesses, they usually were not acting out of rebellion against their parents but rather were protesting the fact that the society's institutions were not fulfilling the humanitarian values or practicing the equalitarian forms of decision-making they had come to know in their homes (Bem, 1970).

In a third study, Silvern and Nakamura (1973) took a close critical look at the two hypotheses and used as their subjects university students whose attitudes and behavior spanned the political spectrum from left to right. Where in previous studies the student supplied information on his parents' attitudes and values, here, with students' approval, parents were asked to complete a brief questionnaire. One question asked both student and parents to place themselves on a scale of general political position: radical left, strongly liberal, moderately liberal, moderately conservative, strongly conservative, or radical right. They confirmed the previously-found similarity in attitudes between students and parents, with liberal students coming generally from liberal homes and conservative students coming generally non-conservative homes. They also confirmed another finding, that students were more liberal than their parents all across the political spectrum. Relative to the left-to-right distribution of parents, the student distribution was shifted to the left, with liberal students farther to the left than liberal parents and relatively-conservative students more liberal than conservative parents, with some far enough to the left as to be liberal. While broadly confirming the socialization hypothesis, Silvern and Nakamura stress that their results point up additional liberalizing influences, such as books, teachers, and other things of the campus environment:

> Clearly in recent years there has been a campus zeitgeist which has encouraged students to move toward the left. In support of the argument that the contemporary intellectual and political milieu confronting college students encourages left-wing views is the evidence that left-wing, in comparison to other students, are more influenced by books, teachers, and other non-familial sources (Berns et al., 1972; Jansen et al., 1968). However, the effects of the college zeitgeist clearly operate in interaction with the influence of family background. The positive correlation between parents and offspring is after all evidence of that influence. Right-wing parents apparently exert a restraining effect on the influence of resocialization in college. Some of their offspring do remain toward the right. (p. 130)

Influence of College

The influence of the college environment has just been mentioned and we will see it again below in the study of the Bennington college girls. Other studies have attempted to assess the influence directly.

The *National Review* (1963) conducted a large-scale survey of twelve diverse American colleges and universities in 1961-62 and 1962-63. The schools were selected to represent a cross-section of kinds of colleges that have a liberal arts curriculum. Of all the sophomores, juniors, and seniors responding, nearly 70 percent reported that significant change had taken place in their political beliefs since entering college, and two-thirds of these had changed in a direction away from their precollege beliefs. In all but two of the twelve schools the change was in the liberal direction. At the other two schools (Marquette and Brandeis) the students were so liberal to begin with that there were few to switch. So, in effect, in all schools the change was toward liberalism.

Of the students who reported that their beliefs had changed since entering college, 40 percent listed lectures or assigned reading as the primary agent of change; increased thinking about political questions was given by 70 percent; and 10 percent gave personal contact with faculty members as an influence. The *National Review's* own conclusion was that the influence of the liberal arts faculty appeared to be paramount in determining the political complexion of students whose views had been flexible when they entered college.

Earlier studies had also reported general changes in outlook. Freedman (1960) reported significant increase in "psychological maturity," tolerance, liberality of religious beliefs, and acceptance of intellectual values over the four years of college among women students of about a half-dozen colleges. Sanford (1962) suggests from his research that students in college show significant changes in the direction of greater liberalism and sophistication in their political, social, and religious outlook. Webster et al. (1962) found evidence of broadening interests as well as changes in particular attitudes and values during the four years of college.

Coming nearer to the present, let us note again the findings, reported above, on student dissenters of the 1960's and 1970's. Though the emphasis in the reports of Flacks, Keniston, and others was on the family influence on these dissenters, all recognized an additional and immediate influence of the campus milieu. As mentioned, Silvern and Nakamura found evidence pointing up the campus influence and concluded in part, "Clearly in recent years there has been a campus zeitgeist which has encouraged students to move toward the left." (1973, p. 130)

Technically speaking, such studies as these do not prove that the college experience produced the changes of attitude and value reported. As Telford and Plant (1963) and others have pointed out, a control group of non-college young people would have been needed with which to compare the college students. Plant (1962) found, for example, that comparison groups of college-age persons who were not in college showed changes in attitude and ideology in the same direction but not as large as those made by students in college. He suggests the college may simply accelerate a change going on in the general population.

Surely no one would challenge the summary observation that the age period corresponding to the college years is a time of significant maturing in beliefs, attitudes, and values, and that the college experience often facilitates that maturing process.

Reference Group Influence

As the young person matures, typically she or he is out of the parental home more and more and exposed to additional attitude-value shaping influences. We have just seen how the college environment is adding its influence to that of parents in shaping students' attitudes and values. A potentially very important influence is the *reference group*, and as we shall see it can include parents as well as other groups.

Whenever people interact there is the possibility of one influencing another, especially when they interact in a continuing relationship, as would be the case between spouses, friends, work associates, fellow students, church or club members, next-door neighbors, or other continuing relationship. There is ample evidence of this influence on attitudes and beliefs. Campbell et al. (1954), for example, found a very considerable similarly in voting behavior between spouses (in about 90 percent of cases both voted for same candidate), friends (about 83 percent), and work associates (about 77 percent). Also, studies of group dynamics reveal that group norms (including shared beliefs, values, and codes of behavior) emerge when a group of strangers come together and form an enduring group, with the norms functioning as the cement that unifies the group and regulates member's interaction.

Granted that membership groups influence the values of their members, what happens when a person belongs to competing membership groups, and is it necessary that one belong to a group for it to be influential? The answer to both questions is to be found in the reference group. Newcomb (1943) was one of the first to recognize the phenomenon of the reference group and used the concept to explain his findings in the famous Bennington study, which is reviewed below. In brief, his college student subjects belonged to two membership groups, family and college community, which in most cases were opposite in attitudes and values. He found that one or the other functioned as the group of *identification* or *reference* for each student. He found also that one or the other could function as a *negative* reference group, having a repelling influence. Later it was realized that one need not belong to a group for it to function as reference group, which greatly expanded the possibility of group influence on the individual. For example, the League of Women Voters might function as a reference group for me, a male, influencing formation of my attitudes from a distance. Also, a reference group need not have a formal existence -- the vague groupings "young people" or "respectable people" may be the image in the person's mind. Too, the "reference group" may not be a group at all, but just a single key person, such as a respected peer or a well-known person.

Surely the most thorough study of peer, family, and reference group influence together was Newcomb's Bennington College study (1943). It is excellent for our purposes of understanding the origins of values, because both specific attitudes and general ideologies were involved (notably in the liberal and conservative orientations that underlay specific attitudes), and because of its depth of analysis which yielded considerable insight into the psychodynamics of attitude and value adoption. We will use it here as a vehicle to present and exemplify not only group influence but also the variety of personal factors that operate to influence selection or rejection of given attitudes and values.

These women students came predominantly from urban, economically-privileged families whose social attitudes were conservative. Over two-thirds of the parents belonged to the Republican party. Bennington was a newly-begun, small, very liberal, residential women's college located in rural Vermont. The members of the teaching staff were predominantly liberal, deeply concerned about social issues in a depression-torn nation and a war-threatened world, and felt a responsibility for encouraging the students to take an active interest in social and political problems. Thus the girls came from one world of attitudes and values and entered an opposite one. How they dealt with the conflict between conservative family influence and the liberal college atmosphere was the subject of Newcomb's study.

In general, the longer the girls were at Bennington the more politically liberal most of them became. During the presidential election campaign of 1936, for example, 66 percent of the parents favored the Republican candidate, Landon. Sixty-two percent of freshmen favored Landon, 42 percent of sophomores, and only 14 percent of juniors and seniors. Conversely, the percentage of students favoring more liberal candidates increased. Only 29 percent of freshmen favored Roosevelt, the Democratic candidate, as compared with 54 percent of juniors and seniors. Only 9 percent of freshmen endorsed either the Socialist or Communist presidential candidates, whereas 30 percent of juniors and seniors did so. But though the trend was from freshman conservatism to senior liberalism, it was not found in all students. Some changed markedly, others not at all, still others became more confirmed in their conservatism.

Newcomb's search for insight into these individual differences led him to study intensively 24 liberal and 19 conservative seniors. In interviews they were asked questions about the resemblance between their own attitudes and the attitudes of class majorities and leaders, about their parents' attitudes and the resemblance of their own attitudes to them, and related questions. Personality data also were obtained.

The general drift toward liberality is not difficult to understand. The faculty was liberal and intentionally or not was rewarding evidences of liberality in the students. By the time they had become juniors or seniors most students had become liberal, so were providing respected liberal models for the younger students. Families were far away, to be heard from only during vacations, so were at a disadvantage in presenting the conservative viewpoint. The information to which the students were exposed, from faculty, books, news reports, and, not least, events themselves tended heavily to favor the liberal point of view. Nor was their exposure to the liberal position brief; for most students it lasted for the full four academic years. In view of these facts it is remarkable that any girl failed to shift in the liberal direction.

Whether or not a girl adopted the liberal position or held to a conservative one depended on personal factors, especially her relationship to community and to her family.

Personal factors which may influence adoption of attitude-values. The following are factors that appeared to influence the liberal girls and are factors which operate generally in adoption of attitudes and values:

(a) *Need for beliefs and for a group with which to identify.* This point presents the subjective rationale for the reference group phenomenon. All of us are constantly "scanning" our environment in order to deal effectively with it. As part of this we seek information on the issues and problems of the day (today such problems are drug overuse, over-population, pollution, energy shortage, unemployment, etc.), seeking for facts, truth, and best courses of action, especially if others are expecting us to know something of these matters and to have a point of view. We also seek for groups and persons with whom to identify ourselves, for it adds to our sense of identity and security to picture ourselves as supported in our beliefs by others -- one feels uncomfortable standing alone. The two needs often go together, with the group supplying us both with our beliefs and with our support and identity.

A few of us may be so self-sufficient as to need little of the identity and security support, but all search for reliable, trustworthy sources of information (for all are dependent upon secondary sources of information), so are always looking for persons and groups who can satisfy this need. But apparently most of us are anything but certain as to the reality of things, so need both dependable sources of information and a sense of belonging and support for our beliefs.

Because a certain "rightness," reward value, and prestige was attached to the liberal position, and also because it was the prevailing campus outlook, for many or most of the girls the college community (or selected sub-groups and leaders) was their positive reference group. They looked to this group both for ideas and for support and identity. For some of these same girls their families functioned as a negative reference group, with family's ideas having negative emotional connotations. But for a minority of girls the situation was reversed, with family as positive reference, their ideas being respected and an identity with them and support from them being experienced. For these girls the college community was either a negative reference group or just not perceived as having any reference effect.

Here is a good example of the reference group phenomenon in action, taken from the comments of one of the seniors studied intensively by Newcomb:

Q6: "I was ripe for developing liberal or even radical opinions because so many of my friends at home were doing the same thing. So it was really wonderful that I could agree with all the people I respected here and the same time move in the direction that my home friends were going." (A girl characterized by considerable personal instability at first, but showing marked improvement.)

Though the concept of reference group takes us a long way in understanding the girls' shifts in belief, and in people's value adoptions generally, it does not account for all the reasons why the girls adopted their beliefs, so we need to look further.

(b) *Need for approval, to be accepted by the group, to belong.* This is a very basic form of human motivation and can explain some of the value adoptions of many of us. In simplest terms the formula is, "I will believe as they (or he) do if they will accept me." The comments of two of the seniors exemplify this motivation:

E22: "*Social security is the focus of it all with me.* I became steadily less conservative as long as I was *needing to gain in personal security, both with students and with faculty.* I developed some resentment against a few extreme radicals who don't really represent the college viewpoint, and that's why I changed my attitudes so far and no further." (A girl with a small personal following, otherwise not especially popular.)

Q57: "It's very simple. *I was so anxious to be accepted that I accepted the political complexion of the community here.* I just couldn't stand out against the crowd unless I had many friends and strong support." (Not a leader, but many close friends among leaders and nonconservatives.)

(c) *Need for respect, prestige, or admiration, to be seen as outstanding or a leader.* Another common human motive and cause of value adoption. Since liberalism is the norm at the college, proving oneself outstanding as a liberal could be expected to yield prestige. It didn't take some of the girls long to discover this, as indicated by the comments of these two seniors:

H32: "I accepted liberal attitudes here because *I had always secretly felt that my family was narrow and intolerant, and because such attitudes had prestige value.* It was all part of my generally expanding personality -- *I had never really been part of anything before.* I don't accept things without examining things, however, and I was sure I meant it before I changed." (One of those who has "agreed to differ" with parents.)

Q61:   "I met a whole body of new information here; I took a deep breath and plunged. When I talked about it at home my family began to treat me as if I had an adult mind. *Then too, my new opinions gave me the reputation here of being open-minded and capable of change.* I think I could have got really radical but I found it wasn't the way to get prestige here."

(d) *Rebellion from family domination, desire to be independent.* Because these are young persons who are in process of transition from the dependence of childhood to the independence of adulthood, it is to be expected that this motivation to break away and establish themselves as independent persons would be strong in a number of girls, and liberalism was perceived as the mark of independence. However, this motivation is not limited solely to young persons, for some of us are involved in lifelong struggles to free ourselves from dependence upon or dominance by family, spouse, church, or other and may adopt beliefs as part of an assertion of independence or of a new maturity. The following comments will exemplify:

Q7:   "*All my life I've resented the protection of governesses and parents.* What I most wanted here was the intellectual approval of teachers and the more advanced students. Then I found you can't be reactionary and be intellectually respectable." (Her traits of independence became more marked as she achieved academic distinction.)

Qx: "Every influence I felt tended to push me in the liberal direction: *my underdog complex, my need to be independent of my parents, and my anxiousness to be a leader here.*"

Q63:   "*I came to college to get away from my family,* who never had any respect for my mind. Becoming a radical meant thinking for myself and, figuratively, thumbing my nose at my family. *It also meant intellectual identification with the faculty and students that I most wanted to be like.*" (She has always felt oppressed by parental respectability and sibling achievements.)

(e) *You like the group (or person), therefore you like their ideas.* This heading seems to capture the essence of this reason for adopting a given value. That is, if you belong to a group and thoroughly enjoy the relationships, then without being aware of it you may find yourself reacting favorably to the beliefs being expressed and over time just "soak them up" and they become yours. No clear example of this cause is found in the comments of the girls, though its opposite is (see under "k" below), which is not surprising, as it is so subtle a process that the person himself might be quite unaware of its occurrence.

(f) *Need to know and understand, to actualize a hungry intellect, to find personal meaning in life.* This cluster of needs are seen most clearly in bright young people who, because they have alert minds, find themselves reaching out more and more, forever hungry for intellectual food, seeking comprehension of their worlds, grasping for pattern or unity. White (1976) called it a need for competence. Values are one very important outcome of this search. But this need, too, is by no means limited to the young; because we have curious minds throughout a lifetime and our grasp is always incomplete, we are pushed endlessly for new insights. Note in the comment of the first of these two girls how at first she was motivated by a need for prestige but upon getting it found that it was not enough:

Q43: "It didn't take me long to see that liberal attitudes had prestige value. But all the time I felt inwardly superior to persons who want public acclaim. Once I had arrived at a feeling of personal security, I could see that it wasn't important--it wasn't enough. *So many people have no security at all. I became liberal at first because of its prestige value.* I remain so because the problems around which my liberalism centers are important. What I want now is to be effective in solving the problems." (Another conspicuous leader, active in and out of college in liberal movements.)

Q21: "I simply got filled with new ideas here, and the only possible formulation of all of them was to adopt a radical approach. *I can't see my own position in the world in any other terms. The easy superficiality with which so many prestige-hounds here get 'liberal' only forced me to think it out more intensely.*" (A highly gifted girl, considered rather aloof.)

Now leaving the liberal girls and turning to the conservative ones, the fascinating question is, why didn't they also become liberal? Considering everything in favor of liberalism, something special must have been at work within each. In answering the question for these girls we may gain general insight into why certain values are adopted and why others, which perhaps should have been dropped, are held-to tenaciously. The following are factors that appeared to influence the conservative girls. Points *g* through *k* should be taken together since often all are at work within the same person as part of a single psychodynamic process:

(g) *Pronounced need for parental emotional support and security.* This state of affairs of a pronounced need for emotional support can exist if for some reason the person nears adulthood feeling inferior and insecure and unable to form satisfying relationships with age mates. The insecurity can cause the person to be inhibited and appear "mousy" and colorless and uninteresting to be around (or be the opposite, noisy and a show-off). It can make the person too eager to please and possessive, both of which drive others away. It may also force the person to make unusual demands upon others for emotional support and appreciation (admiration), while being unable to offer anything to the relationship in return, so others are repelled and no enduring relationship results. Whatever the specific traits, they tend to add up to interference with human relationships, leading often to such reactions by others as rejection, criticism, unfriendliness, or ignoring. Hence the person is thrown back on parents for support, and the vicious circle of dependence, insecurity, colorlessness, and hungering for acceptance and admiration continues.

(h) *Fear of rejection or disapproval by parents if their attitudes are opposed.* Whether the fear has any real foundation or not, if the person is somewhat insecure, parental approval may be precious and nothing may be done to risk its loss.

(i) *Resentment and hostility toward classmates.* If one wants to be liked, admired, listened to, sought out, and respected, as most of us do and as the insecure do especially, but instead are ignored, avoided, disliked, or criticized, then you easily find yourself feeling bitter and resentful toward classmates. This hostility colors one's behavior, perhaps causing one to be critical, fault-finding, defensive, and unfriendly (even though hungry for friendship), and worsens relationships still further, producing more resentment.

(j) *An insecurity-caused rigidity.* If one feels threatened, anxious, and insecure (even though none of these be consciously recognized), any new idea may also be threatening, so one resists and closes one's mind to it. Others may think you narrow-minded or stubborn. Only in situations where you feel free of threat, as when alone reading a book, can you let in an idea or two.

(k) *I dislike the group, therefore I dislike their ideas.* For various reasons, but especially because of feeling disliked, unappreciated, and rejected, one feels hostile toward the group, and the hostility extends over to their beliefs.

Though not all of the above five causal factors need have been operating in a given girl, all could have been in some of these college girls. Of course I could be wrong in my effort to spell out the subtle psychodynamics processes involved, but it seems safe to emphasize, as a minimum, the given girl's difficulty in forming satisfying human relationships, hence the feeling of rejection and isolation, and the resentment and consequent antipathy felt toward the liberals and their ideas. Here we have the essence of an explanation as to why many of the conservative girls could not establish themselves in the college community, hence could not regard it as a positive reference group, and, rather, either were antagonistic toward it (and had to look elsewhere for reference groups) or were just unaware of it because they were so socially isolated.

Generalizing beyond this special situation, we should recognize that feelings of inferiority or insecurity, fear of disapproval or rejection, feelings of hostility and resentment, and mental rigidity, either together or separately, can be influencing anyone of any age in his adoption or rejection of given values.

Newcomb describes one set of five conservative girls as apparently being overdependent upon one or both parents, stubborn or resistant with instructors, negativistic generally, and as having but average (two girls) or lower (three) prestige with classmates. The comments of two of the girls are indicative:

> E2: "Probably the feeling that (my instructors) didn't accept me led me to reject their opinions." (She estimates classmates as being only moderately less conservative than herself, but faculty as much less so.)
>
> F22: "I wanted to disagree with all the noisy liberals, but I was afraid and I couldn't. *So I built up a wall inside me against what they said. I found I couldn't compete, so I decided to stick to my father's ideas. For at least two years I've been insulated against all college influences.*" (She is chosen but once as a friend, and does not reciprocate that choice.)

Another set of five are much like the preceding five -- insecure in social relationships, extremely dependent upon parents, negativistic, stubborn or resistant, and of low prestige standings. But where the previous five are aware of their conservatism, these are not. They are either absorbed in small friendship groups of like-minded girls or are so thoroughly out of the larger college community as to be oblivious of majority attitudes. The following comments will exemplify:

> L12: "What I most wanted was to get over being a scared bunny. . . . I always resent doing the respectable thing just because it's the thing to do, but I didn't realize I was so different, politically, from my classmates. At least I agree with the few people I ever talk to about such matters." (Sociometric responses place her in a small, conservative group.)
>
> Q81: "I hated practically all my school life before coming here. I had the perfect inferiority complex, and I pulled out of school social life -- out of fear. I didn't intend to repeat that mistake here. . . . I've just begun to be successful in winning friendships, and I've been blissfully happy here." (She is described by teachers as

"pathologically belligerent"; she receives more than the average number of friendship choices, but reciprocates only one of them.)

(l) *Unusually close positive relationship with parents and respect for their views*. Newcomb reports that four of the five girls of another set were *not* negativistic or stubborn and resistant (rather, were cooperative), above average in prestige, and had close parental ties. All four were aware of the conflict between parents and college community and all quite consciously decided to "string along" with parents, feeling self-confident of holding their own in college in spite of being atypical in this respect. Note the strikingly different psychodynamics here from the previous girls. This point may be generalized to recognize that a close, positive relationship with anyone -- parent, friend, spouse -- can be influential in adoption of values, even where the majority of associates hold different values. The following comment will exemplify:

F32:   "*Family against faculty has been my struggle here*. As soon as I felt really secure here I decided not to let the college atmosphere affect me too much. Every time I've tried to rebel against my family I've found out how terribly wrong I am, and so I've naturally kept to my parents' attitudes." (While not particularly popular, she shows no bitterness and considerable satisfaction over her college experience.)

(m) *Concern for parental needs and feelings*. One of the girls in the preceding set is an only child in a one-parent family and is aware of how important she is to her mother, how much she could hurt the mother by adopting alien attitudes (another cause of values that can be generalized beyond the specific case):

Q73:   "*I'm all my mother has in the world. It's considered intellectually superior here to be liberal or radical. This puts me on the defensive,* as I refuse to consider my mother beneath me intellectually, as so many other students do. Apart from this, I have loved every aspect of college life." (A popular girl, many of whose friends are among the nonconservative college leaders.)

(n) *Unaware of community attitudes and hence uninfluenced*. In a final set of four girls, all of whom were unaware of their conservatism, one was uninfluenced by community attitudes mainly because she was engaged to be married and thoroughly involved in that relationship; another was a local "town girl" of working-class parentage who had to devote much time to self-support and studies, and continued to regard parents as reference group; another was a science major who belonged to a small group of like-minded science majors whose only interests were in science and who served as reference group for each other; the fourth was given to severe emotional upsets and felt alone and helpless except when with her parents.

In general, if for some reason one does not know of prevailing values of course one cannot adopt them.

Glancing back over the list of points, it will be evident that this study has provided us with a rather thorough array of social-personal causes for adoption (or rejection) of values.

Newcomb also provides us with a sequel to this fine study (Newcomb, Koenig, Flacks, & Warwick, 1969). A follow-up study of the Bennington graduates was made between 1961-1964, to find out what had happened to their attitudes over that 25 year period. In general, the liberal girls continued to be liberal. For example, in 1960 sixty-two percent of Bennington graduates favored admitting Red China to the United Nations, 85 percent approved of Negro student sit-ins and picketing, and 79 percent favored medicare (all very liberal stands at that time). Of the about 60 percent of women who were politically active, 66 percent had worked for the Democratic party and other parties and candidates of the left, whereas only 27 percent had worked for the Republican party or other parties and candidates of the right.

These findings have special interest to us relative values because they show that more than specific attitudes were involved, that broad attitudes or values were being acquired in college and continued beyond. This is shown by the fact that the specific issues had changed dramatically over the 25 years, from, say, the issue of whether workers had the right to join unions and strike to the issue of admitting China to the United Nations, but the liberal or conservative orientations had continued. Of course "liberal" or "conservative" are not satisfactory names for their values, and rather we have to infer such specific values as those of equality or traditionalism as being involved in the liberalism or conservatism.

Newcomb's own explanation of the stability of attitude was that the women chose new reference groups, notably friends and husbands, after college which were compatible with and supportive of their attitudes. For example, 67 percent of the women who were above the median in conservativism in college married men who preferred Nixon (Republican) over Kennedy (Democrat), whereas only 33 percent of the relatively-liberal preferred Nixon. So we have support for the idea that to some considerable extent we pick for associates people who share our attitudes and values, which in turn strengthens those beliefs and insulates us from alternatives.

School Influence

In societies that have the institution of the school one of its basic functions has always been that of teaching the young the common values of the society.

These are communicated via teacher's emphases, lesson books, discipline, modeling and imitation, peer influence, and other.

To exemplify the past influence of school and books, a study by De Charms and Moeller (1962) may be reviewed, entitled, "Values expressed in children's readers: 1800-1950." Guided by several lines of social theory (those of Weber, Riesman, Whyte, and McClelland) they postulated that reading-books used in American elementary schools over the period 1800-1950 would show decrease in certain value-teachings and increase in others. Specifically, they postulated that the readers would show a decrease in *achievement* themes (termed "achievement imagery") over that period (i.e., presentation of achievement as desirable); would show a decrease in *moral* teaching; and would show an increase in *affiliation* themes or imagery (i.e., presentation of such things as friendship as desirable). Here is a good obvious example, taken from the *McGuffey's Second Eclectic Reader,* published in 1879, presenting the theme of industriousness or, broadly, achievement:

THE FIRESIDE

1. One winter night, Mrs. Lord and her two little girls sat by a bright fire in their pleasant home. The girls were sewing, and their mother was busy at her knitting.

2. At last, Katie finished her work, and, looking up, said, "Mother, I think the fire is brighter than usual. How I love to hear it crackle!"

3. "And I was about to say," cried Mary, "that this is a better light than we had last night."

4. "My dears," said their mother, "it must be that you feel happier than usual to-night. Perhaps that is the reason why you think the fire better, and the light brighter."

5. "But, mother," said Mary, "I do not see why we are happier now than we were then; for last night cousin Jane was here, and we played 'Puss in the corner' and 'Blind man' until we all were tired."

6. "I know! I know why!" said Katie. "It is because we have all been doing something useful to-night. We feel happy because we have been busy."

7. "You are right, my dear," said their mother. "I am glad you have both learned that there may be something more pleasant than play, and, at the same time, more instructive."

De Charms and Moeller found that achievement imagery increased throughout the nineteenth century up until about 1890, and then began to decline until 1950. Moral teaching declined steadily and strikingly with hardly any present in the readers by 1950. Affiliation imagery showed a modest uneven increase over the century and a half.

Though these results show more decrease than increase in value teaching in American school books, they do serve to exemplify the use of school and education to implant values. Of course we should not assume that the same changes have taken place in the school books of other countries. To the contrary, we should expect textbooks to be used today in many countries, especially the newly independent ones that are trying to establish a common ideology and values, deliberately to teach values, for the school is such a logical avenue of value communication. Nor should we overlook the possibility that at some future date community leaders in our own country will decide that shared values are necessary and are becoming too few and will again decide to use school and textbooks for the purpose of developing them.

In light of the above-reported findings of Piaget and Kohlberg on the need for a degree of intellectual maturity before moral values can be grasped, we might guess that some part of the value teaching that appeared in elementary school books in centuries past fell on uncomprehending ears (more exactly, unconceptualizing minds). Rereading "The Fireside" example above, it is likely that some of the value messages were too subtle to be grasped, unless reinforced by the teacher. Too, we can picture many a child stumbling through the reading lesson, doing well to pronounce the words correctly and totally missing the value message.

In a paper entitled *Ethics and Moral Precepts Taught in Schools of Japan and the United States*, Lanham (1979) has compared the attitudes toward the teaching of ethics and the specific moral-ethical concepts appearing in school books of the two countries.

In Japan, unlike the United States, there has been no dearth of academic interest in the teaching of ethics, with many articles written by educators on their ethics courses.

A course on morality was taught in Japan before Word War II and emphasized nationalism, militarism, and Emperor worship. This was banned by the U.S. Occupation Forces; after the peace treaty it was not reinstated by Japanese educators out of fear of a return to militarism. However, some mothers feared their children might mature without proper training, so an entirely new course, titled *Dotoku*, was introduced in 1958 and made compulsory in 1962. A special period of one hour once a week was set aside for teaching the subject. The course has been controversial, in part out of fear that it might be used for conservative political purposes, but Lanham reports that the text editors have been sensitive to public opinion, and local school boards, in consultation with faculty, decide which specific publications will be used, and deletions are possible.

Some of the same virtues appear in both the old pre-war and new post-war readers, such as: don't give others trouble, take care of your health, return lost possessions to its owner, and report an injury to another's property, even though an inadvertent act. These teachings are reinforced in the home. Stressed also are patience, perseverance, diligence, hard work, orderliness and planning ahead. Attention in both old and new readers is given to those forms of ethics that involve interpersonal relationships of forgiveness, gratitude, kindliness, and benevolence. But lessons encouraging ancestor worship, esteem for teacher, and filial piety have been deleted. The new books also place high emphasis upon the kind of courage that involves opposition to the group in deference to a morally just position.

Turning to the American side, and the old McGuffey Readers, the idea of helping the poor and unfortunate is more prevalent than in its Japanese counterpart, though benevolence is strong in both. Another common theme is friendship and the misery of the child who is shunned by others. The more recent Golden Rule (GR) books also have stories describing the misery of an isolated child and have happy endings when later accepted by peers. The GR books are concerned with kindliness but not politeness. Selflessness and fairness are given more attention than in their Japanese counterpart.

The idealized figures of the Japanese pre-war books tended to be soldiers or the Emperor with stories of soldiers or generals who commit suicide for a noble cause or die in battle; now they are persons who have contributed to science, technology, and humanities and one story features an airline hostess who remained calm in the face of danger. In the McGuffey readers, too, patriotism, war heroes, and nationalism were important and continued to be so in the GR books.

In various ways the GR books present things American as superior to all others, a common national tendency and perhaps so ingrained that the text writers were unaware of it. (In recent decades two contradictory tendencies have been observable -- a damning of certain American ways as though they were unique American failings, whereas actually they are to be seen in other countries, sometimes in worse form, side by side with this conviction that all things American are superior to all else.) The Japanese books are much more international. As an example, Lanham asked ten- and eleven-year-old children in both countries, "If given a choice, who of the past would you most like to be?" The percentage of persons mentioned who were foreign was sixty for the Japanese and nine for the U.S. (Lincoln fared three times as well in Japan.)

A major difference between the books of the two countries lies in their treatment of perseverance. In the Japanese books perseverance in the face of adversity appears more often than any other virtue. The first grade reader contains the story of a small boy who remained out in the bitter cold, though exhausted, to help his father complete his farm chores. Later readers have stories of scientists and other great men who succeed in spite of adversity or infirmity. Teacher's manuals instruct in the encouragement of perseverance and also in the related virtues of ambition and resourcefulness. (No wonder Japan is a leader in science and industry.)   The American texts do not stress perseverance though resourcefulness has always been an esteemed national trait. Lanham says that development of self-confidence has a higher priority among American educators so teacher will avoid placing the child in potentially frustrating situations, hence giving little opportunity for perseverance. Each society pays its price -- fewer American children are outstanding scholars or artists, but more Japanese experience the frustration of failure, are crushed by it, and commit suicide.

Recent books of both countries are sophisticated in their presentation of moral material with no "preaching" and no obvious villains or heroes. Rather, the stories include boys and girls who solve the kinds of personal and social problems that confront them in daily life. The moral in a story often is implied rather than stated.

Stories in the Japanese books tend to be more realistic, many telling of the unkindness, lack of consideration and meanness of children to another, and the writers feel no need to supply an ending, happy or otherwise. American stories are given endings, usually with virtue being rewarded and fault recognized or punished.

Democracy is idealized in both countries, but Lanham feels that there is more practice of democracy in the Japanese schools in that the children are expected to settle their own disputes, with instructors there in the background helping them to develop skills in group process. She feels, too, that children there get better preparation in the home for group functioning, for the relationship in the home is more equalitarian.

> My investigations show a strong Japanese emphasis on getting the child to understand; i.e., having him want of his own volition to do that which is acceptable and proper. Force is rarely used. When the child resists, parental response is more like the way an American relates to another adult rather than to his or her child. In Japan, for instance, a child's request is generally granted when a parent is unable to change his mind. The parent's ultimate concern is the importance to the child of his desire, not who should have authority in the situation. By contrast, in the United States, some degree of denial and restraint is felt necessary in order to teach the child self-control. The American parent engages in an unrecognized assumption that restraints imposed forcibly from without automatically lead to the child's imposition of discipline upon himself at some later date -- a hypothesis that as yet has not been adequately tested. (p. 14)

The reader may note that their talking with the child and trying to get him to understand seems much the same technique, called "induction," as used by American parents who are effective in the moral development of their children (see

p. 111, above). And Lanham's comment that here some amount of restraint and denial are considered necessary to develop self-control likely is a common folk assumption, but the hypothesis has been tested and found wanting. Warmth and structuring have been found to be the essential ingredients for development of self-control, with some amount of restraint and denial acceptable in a context of warmth. In the Japanese home the warmth or acceptance ordinarily is present and there is a notable amount of structuring, but it is very subtle -- it is rare to see a child throw a tantrum or otherwise be irritated and I never saw a parent publicly become angry and start shouting. Lanham likely is right that there is much more of the kind of relationship she describes to be seen in Japan than here.

The time period of Lanham's research was the 1960s. It would be desirable to see what has happened in both countries since, but no comparative report could be located.

It might be noted that teachers are influencing children's values in more ways than through these textbooks and courses. This happens because teachers inescapably must function as parent surrogates through about the first six or eight grades, so must be teaching the children morals and broad values in their daily interactions, perhaps doing so with little awareness of what they are doing. For example, if a child takes the possession of another, teacher must not only see that the object is returned but try to teach a concept of personal ownership and attach a "shouldn't take" moral prohibition to it. It is a reasonable guess that these will be about the same basic morals as must be taught children everywhere because of the necessities of social living -- truth telling, honesty, fairness, sharing, not attacking and hurting, and obedience to authority.

Another informal influence on school children's ethics will be peer interaction of the children themselves, for the school day will be full of such interactions, many never observed by teacher or other adult. We might guess that concensual, rather than unique, values will be emerging as each youngster interacts with a number of other children, each time learning that child's conception of what "ought" to be.

Still another influence will be the values actually practiced by teachers and administrators. Extolling the virtues of democracy may have little effect if there is no practice of it within the school. Lanham (p. 16) reports that she saw considerable evidence of the practice of the virtues taught in the Dotoku books. Purpel and Ryan (1976, Ch. 5) discuss the moral education that is received from the "hidden curriculum," and mention specifically the classroom culture, the moral messages conveyed in such extra curricular activities as competitive athletics, student culture (i.e., peer culture, such as children's developing and enforcing rules in playground games), and school culture (e.g., punctuality and neatness are good, cheating is bad, school loyalty is good, respect for adults is good). In light of all the informal sources of value learning in the school setting, these writers and others say that value education will occur in the schools no matter what the official policy and even if the policy is to avoid value teaching altogether.

Lanham mentions that there has been no dearth of academic interest in Japan in the teaching of ethics, unlike in the United States. Some part of this difference will be due to the different histories of the two countries and composition of populations. The Japanese are a remarkably homogeneous people. The country is an island nation with an oceanic barrier to outside influence. Over the centuries they borrowed from Chinese culture but never were invaded nor experienced mass immigration of alien peoples. Unlike most other areas of Asia, they escaped occupation and exploitation and "cultural invasion" by Europeans. Up until W. W. II they were able to pick and choose what from the outside they would let in. Post-W. W. II brought a radical re-examination of old ways, but the American military occupation was remarkably benign, with very little dictation in the realm of values, and it was the Japanese themselves who chose to change the content of ethics courses after the war. Consequence of all this is that the Japanese educators come to the task of planning texts and programs with a considerable base of agreement among themselves as to which values to include and with comparable support and agreement from the community.

Contrast this with the history and present composition of the population of the United States. From the outset immigrants have poured in from unique groupings and societies, early from distinct European societies and in the present century literally from societies all over the world, and it continues strongly today. Many of the immigrant groups came because they wanted to follow unique ways of life and values. Where is our common value ground? Add to this the American valuing of individualism, which itself invites every person to have his own unique world of values. Add also our different views as to which institutions of the society have the value-shaping responsibility -- some feeling the home should do it solely, Christians perhaps feeling it a function of church and Sunday-school, most feeling it a function of the schools, but a few feeling suspicious of any effort from any direction and want their children to have no moral instruction.

So the mandate of the schools is unclear both as to the specific values to teach and as to extent of their involvement, with teachers criticized both for their efforts and lack of effort along these lines. The decentralized system of American education, while having its strengths, contributes to the confusion, as one school district will have one program, a neighboring one another, and any may be vulnerable to the special biases of individual parents or school board members. Consequence of all this for teachers is that they must be cautious rather than enthusiastic. Sometimes it is simpler to delete instruction rather than face possible dissent and contention.

Yet in spite of conflicting views as to the schools' role, educators do assume an obligation and programs flourish.

How to develop values? Granted that the schools have a mandate, however mixed, to teach values, how are values to be taught? They cannot be taught straightforwardly as can, say, arithmetic or vocabulary, and long ago teachers gave up such obvious techniques as moral exhortation or requiring memorization of lists of virtues. (But this is what I had to do when I joined the Boy Scouts, at about age 10 or 12. We were required to learn both the "Scout's law" and "Scout's oath," and one consisted of a list of about a dozen ideal traits, the only ones of which I now remember are: A scout is trustworthy, cheerful, thrifty, brave, clean, and reverent. Though I memorized the list so thoroughly that for years I could rattle off the entire dozen instantly, it was just a mere list of words; none was really conceptualized and made a functional part of myself and it never occurred to me to practice them. This is the usual fate of mere memorizations.)

Several methods are described in the education textbooks, but apparently there have been no systematic experiments in the schools where two or more methods of developing values were tested under controlled conditions and outcomes carefully assessed. The Haan et al. (1985) study, mentioned at several points above, is the only one of the type known to me; it was not intended as a test of methods to be used in schools, but did test two methods and its results are generally applicable. It will be recalled that its purpose was to study both moral action in a here-and-now situation and moral development. To produce development, the university students, under the one condition, were had to analyze moral dilemmas in individual interviews and also discuss dilemmas in group sessions. This procedure was intended to represent the technique of Kohlberg (cognitive-developmental theory) and be a test of any gain in moral reasoning. The other had the students engage in games involving moral interaction, and was intended to be situations of actual daily moral interaction, and its outcome be a test of any increase in moral interaction skill (Haan's social interaction theory). These results are summarized above (p. 137-138); as indicated, there is a slight favoring of the social interaction method, with numerous qualifications. Though this may be the only comparative study thus far, numerous studies on single questions have been done, especially on the Kohlberg theory, as it has been around for several decades and its unique nature has invited both controversy and experiment. The Haan theory is too recent to have had much use in the schools as yet.

A survey was made of recent books on the teaching of values in the schools. Nearly all were concerned with the more narrow topic of moral values, though the term is used loosely and likely few educators differentiate the traditional morals (honesty, faithfulness, etc.) and valued traits. Too, an important change has come in the meaning of "moral." When De Charms and Moeller, above, report a drop to zero in the teaching of morals in the McGuffey readers, they are referring to the teaching of the Ten Commandment-type of morals; today moral education usually means the development of skill in making moral judgements on ethical problems and there is no direct reference to such virtues as honesty, courage, and unselfishness.

As to methods, there has been a striking shift away from teaching any specific value, moral or otherwise, in favor of teaching skills in dealing with moral issues and problems. Purpel and Ryan (1976) state this point of view well when they write, "What the public schools must do is not 'teach morals' but teach appropriate ways of responding to moral issues and concerns. Our basic attitude toward moral education is that it should involve careful and sensitive inquiry into moral questions." (p. 57) This happens to be a convenient, uncontroversial way of dealing with an otherwise controversial domain in a pluralistic, multi-valued society, though this not given as reason for present approaches.

Though no advocacy for the teaching of single values was found in the literature, there is no doubt that it occurs informally, for reasons of the above-mentioned "hidden curriculum" and other, especially with the elementary-level children who need quite specific guidance in learning and practicing given behaviors and are not yet capable of benefiting much from classroom discussion of moral value problems.

An indication of values actually being developed in American (and British) schools is found in a report by Connell (1976) who compares moral education in China, USSR, England, and United States. He says the person who is objective and uncommitted, who is able to get along pleasantly and helpfully with other people, and who is interested in his own individual development and success is the kind of student our American educators appear to be trying to produce. The approach to social studies best illustrates the first of these qualities; the emphasis is on finding the facts, appreciating different points of view, and understanding the problem or process being studied. An understanding of controversy is developed, and opinions may be formed, but there is no commitment to act in any way and teacher is required to be impartial to avoid influencing. But on some political matters there is effort to inculcate firm beliefs: patriotism is insisted upon, parliamentary democracy is always seen as ideal in principle, and the traits of character and moral virtue which help to make and preserve a strong and democratic nation are seen to be good, proper, and worthy of inculcation (p. 41).

As to the second, the foreign observer is always impressed by the facility with which American students talk with him and with fellow students, by their skill in handling group discussions, and by the poise and responsibility they show in a variety of social situations. This ability is a result of long practice and a continual emphasis from earliest school days on social skills (p. 41). (Most of Connell's comment on these two points has to do with skills or traits not values; but to the extent it is thought to be good and desirable by parents, teachers, and students themselves, it is a value.)

As to the last, almost every statement of educational purpose will somewhere indicate that one of the main goals is to enable each individual to develop to the full extent of his capacity. Individual effort is encouraged throughout and individual excellence is rewarded both by formal grading, placement, and promotion and informally by teacher and parental praise and support. Students are expected to join teams and other group activities, but even here individual success tends to be sought (p. 42).

The method of *values clarification* has had wide use and, as of 1976, is reported to be the most widely used. Its creators are Roths, Harmin, and Simon, as presented in *Values and Teaching: Working with Values in the Classroom* (1966). As its name indicates, its purpose is to clarify one's values. No particular set of values are advocated. No person's or institution's values are held up for emulation. The intention is for the individual to get in touch with his own values, bring them to the surface, and reflect upon them. Some of its strengths are that it is easily learned by the teacher and there are ample instructional materials, it can be used to deal with contemporary problems in the student's lives so produces involvement, teacher does not have to impose her own views, and teachers say it works (Purpel & Ryan, 1976, p. 73).

Lockwood (1976) points out that the value issues addressed in value clarification are primarily related to making decisions about personal preferences. That is, the questions raised direct the student to consider how he chooses to lead his life, what career he seeks, how he uses his leisure time, what kind of a person he wants to be, what kind of people he admires, and what actions he would take in different situations. It appears not to be as useful in examining larger, impersonal moral issues and in revealing "the basic principles, criteria, or standards by which we are to determine what we morally ought to do, what is morally right or wrong, and what our moral rights are." (Frankena, in Lockwood, p. 165)

Values clarification appears, at least by default, to hold the view that all values are equally valid. The accepting role of the teacher, the admonition to avoid moralizing, the avoidance of conflict, and the nurturent and trusting environment yield the distinct impression that all decisions arrived at through the prescribed process are equally defensible and acceptable (Lockwood, p. 165). Such value relativism is commendable when helping young person's clarify goals, interests, and desired traits, but not with such larger public issues as whether to permit euthanasia, pornography, and abortion.

Though the method of *cognitive development* of Kohlberg may not be the most used method today, it is the one that dominates the literature (it is reported that, as of 1985, 3000 school districts were using it). As with the value clarification method, it stresses open peer discussion, but there the similarity ends as its purpose is quite different. Its goal is to stimulate movement in the person to the next stage of moral reasoning.

As explained before, Kohlberg started his research by asking people how they would respond to specific moral dilemmas (recall the case of Heinz who had to decide whether to steal a medicine for his gravely-ill wife). As a result of interviewing persons of different ages Kohlberg formulated his theory of stages of moral reasoning. In one specific study he followed the development of fifty boys from age ten to age twenty-five, by asking them at three-year intervals how and why they would resolve a set of eleven dilemmas. It was found that changes in moral thinking go step by step through the six stages, with one person's development stopping or becoming fixed at any one of the six stages. As a result of such studies the reasoning which describes and defines each stage has been thoroughly worked-out and a scoring system devised for determining the stage of each person. (Chapters descriptive of the theory and method appear in many books, some by Kohlberg himself, as in Purpel and Ryan, 1976, Ch. 12,13. This book also has evaluative chapters relative to its educational application. The whole of Arbuthnot and Faust, 1981, is devoted to the use of the technique in the schools and deals with theory, methods, and problems, and is well-written. The book edited by Berkowitz and Oser, 1985, takes the theory and method as its point of departure; has a chapter by Kohlberg on the just community, which represents some of his most recent thinking; has a useful chapter by Berkowitz, Ch. 8, containing an analysis of research findings and problems; and has chapters on use of the method in clinical, industrial, and other settings.)

The methodology was developed for use in studying the cognitive-moral development of individuals but early was adapted for use in high schools, with whole groups of students, to try to increase their quality of moral reasoning. Peer moral discussion is the heart of the method, typically using hypothetical moral dilemmas as subject of discussion. Blatt (1969) working under Kohlberg's direction, found that, on the average, the students advanced one-third of a stage in moral reasoning. This has been a typical outcome in numerous later studies. As a result of experimentation it was decided that exposure to reasoning one stage above one's own was desirable for growth, that interaction among students who were at various stages of growth was desirable, that teacher involvement in helping the group was useful, and that real cognitive interaction between the students is necessary for growth. Berkowitz (1985, Ch. 8) discusses all of these in light of the research and finds the one-stage-ahead strategy to be of doubtful value, that the mixture of stages is valuable and a good substitute for the one-stage-ahead (and for use of adult leaders who otherwise must be supplying the expert one-stage-ahead guidance), teacher facilitation is not necessary for growth, though may be helpful in keeping the peer interaction on-track, and what is absolutely necessary is real cognitive disputation among peers which is producing states of disequilibrium -- is making them think.

A minor problem with the method is that some high school students are disinterested or become bored; hypothetical dilemmas are too far removed from their adolescent worlds to have any meaning.

A major concern or uncertainty has been the significance of any gain in moral reasoning or maturity. A person might emerge from a semester of discussions able to give more mature reasons for making choices on the dilemmas but have no more motivation to do anything about moral issues than when he began. Moral reasoning and discussion is not intended outrightly to develop the "ought to act" feeling, the motivation. It is intended to transfer from the hypothetical dilemmas to *reasoning* on real-life dilemmas. Kohlberg (1984, p. 34) reports that studies empirically demonstrate a relationship between the hypothetical reasoning and the real-life judgements, but that we don't know from those studies whether change in moral judgement from educational programs would actually lead to change in moral action. Several useful outcomes might be suggested. First, improvement in moral reasoning is its own justification in producing a liberally-educated person, much in the same sense that study of history or evolution has no practical purpose but is self-expanding. Second, from the reasoning activity there is a good chance of producing better decisions and consequent actions, when life thrusts conflicts upon us. Third, once a person has been led to think about a particular issue for the first time and to hear different points of view about it, and thus to look at it from different perspectives himself, and to have to "chew on it" for a time, there *may* result a readiness to act when need arises. At least, this last is a way people acquire beliefs and attitudes, and attitudes involve action tendencies. Fourth, this method holds up not only just and fair ends as solutions to dilemmas, but also forces member of the group to recognize the need for fair and just means of dealing with each other. Hence it calls for an equalitarian outlook and the practice of real democracy and has far-reaching implications for the functioning of all manner of group and of whole nations (this point distilled from Kohlberg's chapter on the just community, 1985, Ch. 2).

Kohlberg has always been critical of the teaching of specific moral behaviors, calling it the "bag of virtues" approach, but in some of his latest writing (1985) has found merit in the old teaching of virtues approach, apparently in good part because teachers felt it desirable. But he qualifies as to *how* it is to be done, rejecting deliberate indoctrination in favor of an *advocacy* approach. That is, teacher should be an advocate for certain moral content, such as honesty, but instead of indoctrinating, by authority, should appeal to sense of justice, respect the student as an autonomous moral agent, and see self as but one among equals in the dialogue (1985, p. 34-35). This is an important qualification but seems quite similar to the orientation of teachers, especially the Japanese, in Lanham's report above.

One interesting line of research has been investigation of the relationship between parent's stage of moral reasoning and childrearing practices and child's stage of moral reasoning. Parikh (1980) found that both were influential and tended to go together. That is, parents who were at a relatively high stage of moral reasoning tended to use effective conscience-forming childrearing techniques. Specifically, instead of punishing and scolding, parents would use inductions, talking and reasoning with him, emphasizing especially the harm to the other of his actions and "how would you feel if he did that to you." As we reported in an earlier section above, use of inductions in a context of warmth helps produce a child with a strong conscience.

Religion-Church Influence

Religion should be one of the most obvious shapers of morals and values since a significant portion of any of the world's main religions is moral-ethical teaching. But we live in a time of weakening influence and uncertainty as to effect on lives.

It is a remarkable thing that morals have such a prominent place in religions in that a religion could exist solely to meet man's need to comprehend the mysterious and unknown, give meaning to existence, and help him cope with his helplessness in the face of disease, pain, death, wars, and natural forces and calamities. This alone would be a large undertaking. Of course every society must have its moral-ethical rules in order for its members to interact with each other and live in peace, but was it necessary that they become a part of the religion? Apparently there have been different reasons for it; sometimes the people have reasoned that only the moral person could receive divine guidance and protection or deserve it, or that he alone could attain salvation -- a common assumption -- or could attain enlightenment or find peace of mind. A different view is that progress toward enlightenment transforms a person so much that inescapably he is a moral-ethical person and need make no special effort in that direction.

Perhaps the world's most straightforward account of the relationship between enlightenment, with its inherent peace of mind, and ethics and morals is found in the first sermon of the Buddha. His insight, after long searching, was that all existence is marked by suffering (sickness, old age, death, unpleasant experiences, disappointments, frustrations, etc.), that suffering has a cause and can be brought to an end, and that there is a specific life-pathway to end it. This way is the Noble Eightfold Path involving:

1. Right understanding: Having a real understanding of the nature of suffering, its origin, and extinction.
2. Right thought: Living a life of malice toward none, of resolve to harm no living creature, and free of sensual lust.

3. Right speech: Abstaining from lying, tale-bearing, harsh words, and idle gossip.
4. Right action: Abstention from injuring living beings, from stealing, and unlawful sexual intercourse.
5. Right livelihood: Avoiding occupations involving fortunetelling, usury, war, killing of animals, and trading in intoxicants, slaves, and weapons.
6. Right effort: Putting forth the effort to begin and continue the practice of the above activities.
7. Right mindfulness: Practicing meditation to attain such insights as that all physical and mental states, pleasant or unpleasant, are transitory.
8. Right concentration: Becoming capable of going beyond ordinary reasoning and reflection into higher states of intuition (Ross, 1953, p. 108-115)

Note the various moral-ethical requirements -- truthfulness, charity, kindness, self-control, etc., and the implicit reasoning that one cannot make progress toward escape from suffering without behaving this way.

A somewhat opposite causal sequence is found in the *Bhagvad Gita*, though here, too, it is assumed that living a moral life is necessary for progress toward self-realization. As Gandhi (1959) has put it, man is not at peace with himself until he has attained self-realization, which is a sense of unity with the Divine essence. The way to attain self-realization is through renunciation of the fruits of action. That is, as long as we live we must act, must carry on the daily activities of life and experience the possibility of attachment to possessions, life, egoisms, appetites, and much more. So worldly pursuits are inevitable. It is the fruits of action that must be given up in favor of desireless action. More specifically, it is not a total abandonment of goals and purposes; rather one may be wholly engrossed in a chosen activity, fully involved in the adventure of living and anticipating its rewards. As Gandhi (p. 8) put it, let no one consider renunciation to mean a lack of fruits of action for the renouncer. Renunciation means absence of attachment to or striving for the fruits of action themselves, hence not becoming irritated, worried, or desperate at failure to attain desired ends.

So the person who has become non-attached in the midst of the involvements of life may possess such virtues as these: jealous of none, a fount of mercy, without egoism and selfishness, ever-forgiving, always contented, not afraid of others, treats friend and foe alike, untouched by respect or disrespect, loves silence and solitude, and has a disciplined reason (p. 8).

Note that these virtues are the consequence of self-realization or enlightenment, not the cause of it.

Christianity derives mainly from a combination of Jewish and Greek thought, as adapted by early Christians and elaborated by later Christian thinkers.

Ideals of conduct and moral prescriptions have always been a prominent part of the religion, though it is difficult to get an impression of all the different sorts of ideals and morals that have been emphasized, because they are found scattered about in writings spanning the centuries, and apparently no attempt was ever made to collect them in one place. Because of this diversity as to source, a certain amount of contradiction is to be expected, some of the ethics advocated are too ideal to permit their practice or else are preached but rarely practiced, and certain of the morals of past centuries would be regarded today as immoral, such as waging holy wars and crusades against people of other religions, or even against other sects of Christians, because it was the will of God and therefore just. At least it would be good to know which of the old values are still influential, for that is our present concern, but there is no way of telling even that since Christians are such a diverse lot, so we must content ourselves with a few examples of the probably important.

The Greek contribution was mainly general, though certain of the ideas of Plato, Aristotle, the Stoics, and others may have influenced Christian values during the centuries following the Christians' discovery of Greek thought. Christianity derives mainly from Judaism, as the early Christians were themselves Jews, saw themselves as continuing the ancient heritage and automatically accepted the holy writings of the Jews -- the books of the Old Testament -- as their own. In due course these became the major portion of the Bible. The Bible is at once an ancient document and a powerful contemporary influence on the lives and values of peoples belonging to the Christian tradition. It would be difficult to exaggerate its role as a value influencer, for it is read by the millions, studied and discussed, the source weekly church sermons, and the inspiration of innumerable religious tracts. Many Christians regard it as divinely inspired, the very word of God, so give it highest possible veracity and authority.

Of the books of the Old Testament, two may be singled out as exemplifying moral instruction and values generally -- *Deuteronomy* for the former and *Proverbs* for the latter.

In *Deuteronomy* we are introduced to Yahweh, the deity of the Hebrews, who they understood to be something of a super-person, with certain all-too-human attributes. Moses explains that Yahweh had made a compact (covenant) with the Hebrews when he brought them out of Egypt, that they were his chosen people and he would help them in numerous ways, including defeating and slaying the peoples of cities in their path, but they must obey him. Among his orders were that they must obey the Ten Commandments. The first four can only be appreciated when it is understood that Yahweh is telling them emphatically "I am the Lord thy God, which brought thee out of the land of Egypt, from the house of bondage." So, he continues: Thou shalt have no other gods before me, and Thou shalt not make any graven images of them; Thou shalt not bow down unto them or serve them; Thou shalt not take the name of the Lord thy God in vain; and Thou shalt keep the

Sabbath day, for the seventh day is the Sabbath of the Lord thy God. The remaining six, the ones usually mentioned, are: Thou shalt honor thy father and thy mother; Thou shalt not kill; Neither shalt thou commit adultery; Neither shalt thou steal; Neither shalt thou bear false witness against they neighbor; Neither shalt thou covet . . . any thing that is thy neighbor's. All these latter are practical and necessary moral values for community living. A number of comparable moral instructions are given elsewhere in Deuteronomy, especially pertaining to sharing. Throughout we are given to understand that Yahweh is a stern but helpful god who will serve his people well if obeyed but will punish severely if disobeyed. So at a point the people are told that if they will harken diligently to the voice the Lord thy God and do all his commandments "the Lord thy God will set thee on high above all the nations of the earth" (and there follows a long list of blessings that he will bestow). But, if they will not harken to the voice of the Lord thy God nor do all his commandments "all these curses shall come upon thee" (and follows a long list of curses, vexations, pestilences, and disease that he will bring, some quite terrible). At another point the people are told to *fear* the Lord thy God and keep his commandments; but a few sentences later they are admonished to *love* the Lord thy God with all thy heart, with all thy soul, and with all thy might, a strange combination of sentiments, though in both cases it is an "order," a moral command.

In time the Hebrews concluded that Yahweh had other attributes, such as that he cared nothing for ceremonial worship but only for justice and righteousness, that he was loving as well as harsh. Micah summed up his finer qualities with these moving memorable words: "He hath showed thee, Oh man, what is good; and what does the Lord require of thee, but to do justly, and to love mercy, and to walk humbly with thy God?" This is of course also a statement of ideal human values, and not unattainable either.

Yahweh later became the Christian God and Muslim Allah and of course those two faiths also assume that God exists and is master of all our destinies. Also, there is but one god -- "our" god, and apparently all three faiths came to regard all of this as a moral matter. One had to believe in God or face punishment in this life and damnation in the next, and other people's belief in their gods was equally sinful. There has been change in these beliefs in our time but it was only yesterday that one felt the pressure to believe, and missionaries are still sent off to far parts of the world to convert people to the one true faith and save their souls.

The book of *Proverbs* does not contain any "thou shalts" and "thou shalt nots" as does *Deuteronomy*, but does give an impression of some of the values of the ancient Hebrews. They turn out not to be different from those of today. Proverbs is primarily a compendium of bits of advice to the young men just entering adulthood. It is a hodge-podge of types of statements, coming from many sources, most but a sentence long. Some do not really say anything as no specific behavior is mentioned, as in this one, "The righteous hate what is false, but the wicked bring shame and disgrace." Quite many state the wisdom of the common man, some of it thought-provoking, as in this oft-quoted one, "A gentle answer turneth away wrath, but harsh words stir up anger." An excellent bit of advice! Some state moral judgements outrightly, as in this one "He who despises his neighbor sins, but blessed is he who is kind to the needy." Some allow us to infer a trait to be valued (by anyone), though the proverb does not word it that way, as in this one, "A patient man has great understanding, but a quick-tempered man displays folly." The inference is of course that patience in anyone is to be valued and quickness of temper disvalued.

Here, then, are some of the values that are mentioned: trust in the Lord and not in oneself; violence and sexual immorality (specifically, associating with an adulteress) are to be avoided; a quarrelsome wife is to be condemned; quarrelsome, quick-tempered men are also denounced; home should be a place of love (a different sort of value from the preceding); gossiping is a source of trouble; and control of the tongue to be admired; the parent should instruct the child; and discipline is necessary for his well-being ("He who spares the rod hates his son, but he who loves him is careful to discipline him." Compare with the familiar "spare the rod and spoil the child."); diligence and hard work are praiseworthy; and laziness, especially sleeping during the harvest, is condemned; generally, wealth is connected with righteousness and poverty with wickedness, but some verses link riches with wickedness; honesty and justice are praised repeatedly; a ruler should defend the rights of the poor and needy; those who are kind to the needy are blessed; the proud and arrogant are damned; drunkards are the epitome of the fool; wise is the son who listens to his father. There is also an epilogue on the wife of noble character and each trait mentioned can be regarded as a valued trait, such as her keeping her family well fed and clothed, is kind to the poor, speaks with wisdom, and does not "eat the bread of idleness."

Turning to the New Testament and the ministry of Jesus, his teachings contain both the general moral exhortation that people discover and do the will of God and a number of specific moral-ethical judgements. The general moral teaching is the essence of his entire ministry so finds restatement in various wordings over and over again. Where one of the Greek philosophers might have said in a neutral manner, "This is the Divine scheme of things, do as you wish about it," Jesus felt his whole purpose in being was to promote the truth, to help people discover and do the will of God, and it had a moral urgency -- it is necessary that you know and do God's will! Sometimes he speaks in chiding, condemnatory tones -- "you hypocrites," at others he explains in positive terms. Once he said, "When you see a cloud rising in the west you say at once, 'A shower is coming'; and so it happens. And when you see the south wind blowing, you say, 'There will be scorching heat'; and it happens. You hypocrites! You know how to interpret appearance of earth and sky; but why do you not know how to interpret

the present time?" (Why do you not know how out of touch you are with the
kingdom of heaven.) At another time he was asked what he regarded as the greatest
commandment in the (Hebrew) Law, and he replied, "You shall love the Lord your
God with all your heart, and with all your soul, and with all your mind. This is the
great and first commandment. And a second is like it, you shall love your neighbor
as yourself. On these two commandments depend all the laws and the prophets."

Most of Jesus' specific moral teachings are gathered together in the Gospel
of Matthew as the Sermon on the Mount (Matthew 5:1 - 7:27). They are:

> Let your light shine before men that they may see your good deeds and
> praise your Father in heaven (which probably means that you should
> behave morally so that you may be a model and inspiration for others).
>
> Do not violate the commandments of the Law and Prophets (that is, the Old
> Testament).
>
> Not only should you not commit murder, but you should avoid anger
> toward others, should avoid insult, and should make peace with an
> adversary before worshiping.
>
> Not only should you avoid adultery but should avoid adulterous thoughts
> toward a women.
>
> Divorce causes a woman to become an adulteress, so avoid divorce except
> for unfaithfulness.
>
> Avoid swearing oaths of any sort.
>
> Instead of "an eye for an eye, a tooth for a tooth," resist not evil persons if
> attacked, and turn the other cheek; likewise if forced to go a mile, go
> two with him, and give or lend to anyone who asks.
>
> Love not only your neighbor, but also your enemy and pray for those who
> persecute you. (Angell and Helms, p. 408, have useful comment on the
> interpretation of "love" here.)
>
> When giving to the needy do not announce it to the world with trumpets; do
> it in secret (your Father will know and reward you).
>
> Pray in private and do it sincerely.
>
> When fasting do not make a show of it.
>
> Do not store up treasures on earth, rather store up merit in heaven.
>
> Do not worry about your life, where the next meal will come from, or about
> your body or what you will wear.
>
> Judge not others or you too will be judged.
>
> Ask for guidance from your Father and it will be given.
>
> Do unto others what you would have them do unto you, for this sums up
> the whole teaching of the Laws and Prophets.
>
> Do the will of the Father and avoid false prophets.

This is a remarkable list of ethical teachings and, as Muller (1957, p. 151) has aptly commented, "Almost all Westerners, including agnostics, revere the teaching; almost none, including the most orthodox Christians, really believe its plain injunctions of non-attachment and non-violence." It has been suggested that Jesus expected the world soon to come to an end -- he spoke often of the coming day of judgement -- so was urging people to prepare for that, hence moralizing that they not lay up treasures on earth or resist evil or take thought of the morrow. But another interpretation is that he was not anticipating the world's end and was simply describing ideal moral conduct, knowing that mere mortals could not fully attain it, but offering acceptance by God of imperfect persons who are trying. Whatever the case, some of the teachings are unrealistic so cannot be proposed as standards for daily practice, but the list does define an ideal way of life and ideals have an important role in human life, however unattainable.

Jesus has had another value role for Christians, that of a model who inspires emulation. Because of his teaching it is inferred that as a person he was kind, forgiving, modest, peaceful, tolerant, helpful, and unselfish, and his responding to pleas to heal the dying and crippled suggests a compassionate nature. But he knew what he believed and had the courage of the missionary, sometimes criticizing and scolding. Apparently, too, he was quite a leader, judging from his drawing disciples to him.

The apostle Paul, who singlehandedly did so much to shape Christianity (his long letters were the first written statements of the new faith) made one contribution that was to have far-reaching consequences. Apparently he experienced impulses and actions that produced guilt and self-condemnation, and failed often to walk the high spiritual road. This he called "sin" and says of himself, "I do not understand what I do. For what I want to do I do not do, but what I hate I do. . . . As it is, it is no longer I myself who do it, but it is sin living in me. I know that nothing good lives in me, that is, in my sinful nature. For I have the desire to do what is good, but I cannot carry it out." He generalizes this into a law of nature: "When I want to do good, evil is right there with me. For in my inner being I delight in God's law; but I see another law at work in the members of my body waging war against the law of my mind and making me a prisoner of the law of sin at work within my members. What a wretched man I am!" He concluded that everyone experiences sin and formulated the principle of Original Sin, that all humans are born in sin. Then in answer to his question, "Who will rescue me from this body of death?" his reply was, "Thanks be to God -- through Jesus Christ our Lord." Here his answer for everyone is the doctrine of Christ the Redeemer who atones for the sins of all men since the fall of Adam. So he had reason to preach eloquently of the life "in Christ," and of how it could make others, as it had him, a "new creature," reborn to love, joy, peace, and goodness. He taught this gospel of hope and charity throughout a life filled with peril, privation and pain (Muller, 1957, p. 155-161).

Unfortunately, the doctrine of original sin was subject to more literal interpretations and over the centuries untold millions of Christians have been led to conceive of themselves as morally depraved and to search within for evidences of immorality, feel guilty, and damn themselves. George Bernard Shaw commented that it was Paul who converted Christianity into a religion that caused millions of people to regard their own common nature with horror and the religious life to become a denial of life.

The *Seven Deadly* (or *Cardinal*) *Sins* date back to the early history of Christian monasticism and were formally grouped together as early as the 6th century by Pope Gregory the Great, though probably all are to be found somewhere in the Old Testament and all turn up in other religious traditions of the world -- they are the natural failings of mankind. They are: pride or vainglory; covetousness; lust (meaning an inordinate or illicit sexual desire); envy; gluttony, which usually includes drunkenness; anger; and sloth (laziness). The 13th century theologian, St. Thomas Aquinas discusses them in his *Summa Theologica* and, of special interest to the student of values, they were popular themes of morality plays in the Middle Ages.

If we chose to search for them, numerous examples of failure to practice professed values or even of ignoble values could be found in the history of Christianity, but let us conclude this brief historical survey with one of Christianity's most noble statements of personal values -- the prayer of St. Francis of Assisi:

> Lord, make me an instrument of Thy Peace . . .Where there is hatred, let me sow love; where there is injury, pardon; where there is doubt, faith; where there is despair, hope; where there is darkness, light; where there is sadness, joy.
>
> O Divine Master, grant that I may not so much seek to be consoled as to console; to be understood, as to understand; to be loved, as to love; For it is in giving that we receive; it is in pardoning that we are pardoned; and it is in dying that we are born to Eternal Life.

Though the historic Christian moral-ethical tradition is clear enough, the picture is unclear as to how well the church teaches its values today. Potentially it should be effective, for unlike religions elsewhere in the world, Christians practice congregational worship with instructive moral sermons, operate Sunday schools to teach the children Christian morality, and often have adult study groups as well. But how to teach Christian virtues if few attend church?

Apparently Protestantism has always depended upon family, school, and community to do much of its teaching. Westerhoff (1970, p. 15) mentions that for many years the law of Massachusetts required that all families catechize their children and servants at least once a week. While the law was not always obeyed there was little question about the importance of the family for religious nurture and instruction. Similarly, the common schools, which became the public schools, were expected to teach faith and morals to children of the Protestant denominations (the Catholics had no liking for this and have always operated their own schools). Children in many of the town schools of New England learned their alphabet thus: "A = In Adam's fall, we sinned all," to "Z = Zacchaeus, he did climb a tree his Lord to see." Though the Constitution decreed a separation of church and state, which was spelled out in subsequent Supreme Court decisions, the separation actually came slowly because Christian or Protestant ethics were so much a part of the fabric of the culture. We have seen above how the early McGuffey readers contained moral lessons and only slowly reduced the moral content into the present century.

What about the Sunday schools, did they take up the slack caused by the secularization of the public school? It was informative to learn that Sunday schools were begun in England in 1780, to teach, not religion, but ordinary literacy skills to poor factory-employed children who could not afford to take time off to attend school on week-days. Such schools soon spread to this country, the intent being the same: "to aid ignorant and lawless children" (p. 17). Churchmen were opposed to these schools, sometimes calling them an instrument of the devil; but since the Bible usually was used as the lesson book, it was an easy evolution over to holding Sunday schools on church property and giving them a more religious coloring. During the westward settlement of the country often the Sunday school provided both the general and religious education of the children of the frontier, such as it was. As public school systems developed the public and Sunday schools became mutually supportive institutions, with the public school the primary agency for religious education and the latter teaching the special tenets of the given Protestant sect. "The importance of the one-hour-a-week Sunday schools run by volunteers can be understood only on the basis of the widespread Protestant dependence upon the public school for the fundamental aspects of religious education." (p. 18)

Up until the recent past the assumption among Protestants was that all begin life as sinners and until the person accepted Christianity he was lost. Acceptance involved basically learning Christian beliefs -- learning questions and answers of the catechism, learning portions of the Bible itself, and learning church dogma. A Christian was one who professed such dogma as the divinity of Jesus, and Christianity the one true faith, and knew something of Bible and church history. It is hard to tell whether there was any emphasis on practicing Christian ethics as part of the conversion; evidently it was just taken for granted.

By mid-twentieth century much had happened within Protestantism and different points of view existed as to what Christian educators should be attempting to do and how it is to be accomplished, paralleling the same concerns in public education.

Westerhoff poses the question, What is it that Christian educators hope people will learn? -- and presents two contrasting answers. The first is the historic answer, with conversations with church school teachers revealing that they understand education as primarily imparting information. They believe that children, youth, and sometimes adults need to be told what the Bible says, what occurred in the history of the church, what Christians believe, and what right and wrong behavior is. Parents, too, are saying we need to reemphasize such information in church education.

Westerhoff himself does not believe that this is the best way to teach Christian faith, and describes an alternative in these passages:

> When we say we want to communicate the Christian faith, what do we mean? Do we want to teach information about the Christian faith, or do we want to introduce persons to the Christian faith? If the second is our goal, how do we accomplish it? What is faith?
>
> Most often faith is misunderstood as a set of specific beliefs expressed through special words. People explain, "To be a Christian is to believe that . . ." But Christian faith does not involve believing that particular statements are true. It certainly does not mean intellectual assent to a creed or certain words found in a translation of the Bible. . . .
>
> To understand a man's faith we must get inside the way he sees the world. Faith is best comprehended as a person's frame of reference, as the eyes through which he looks at life and views his own life. All our beliefs, feelings, and actions issue from our faith. Our faith in turn issues from our life experience. Therefore, in order for a person to be introduced to the Christian faith, education is going to have to be understood as more than classroom instruction, more than imparting information about what the Bible says, what occurred in the history of the church, what Christians believe, or what right and wrong behavior is. . . .
>
> Our faith issues from our experiences; its meaning, however, is acquired by a process of action and reflection. We discover what the Christian frame of reference implies by acting and reflecting with those who share that faith. For that reason, church education also needs to change its focus from learning about Christian doctrine and tradition to learning how a Christian acts and thinks. . . .

To learn the process of thinking in the light of a Christian frame of reference implies opportunities for practice. Involvement and participation are essential. (p. 26-30)

It is evident from these comments and from ideas expressed elsewhere in his book that Westerhoff's conception of Christian faith involves a functional set of insights and values for dealing with personal and community problems, including a motivation, a sense of duty, to involve oneself in the community. These can be developed only by actually getting involved.

Because many fewer people today attend church and Sunday school, the burden of moral training falls the more on the home and public schools. But the institution of the family is also eroding. To be sure, many families are doing the character-shaping job well, but many families are temporary, or harried one-parent, or parents-too-busy, or morally indifferent and doing their job in a hit-or-miss manner or poorly.

This places the greater burden on the public schools. As mentioned under the preceding topic, their mandate has been somewhat uncertain and to some extent has been a controversial thankless task, but in the main the responsibility has been accepted. However, the American public school is expected to be all things, do all things, in shaping the youth of the country, at once producing an adult who is scientifically informed, mathematically capable, civically concerned and participative, mentally and physically healthy, occupationally prepared, and now morally sensitive as well! How much can they do in a day or a year?

Are our children receiving an adequate character training today, and, if not, who will be responsible for it in modern societies?

Influence of Myth, Drama, Folk Story, Epic, Movie, Etc.

These influences tend to be informal in nature yet, one may guess, sometimes powerful. Their role will differ greatly from society to society, in some less-literate cultures being a major influence. Since there is no body of research evidence upon which to draw, let me exemplify broadly by describing an observation made in India.

I was visiting a city in central India and on this day was out wandering the narrow streets, taking in sights and smells and observing the people at their daily lives. Coming upon an open space between the buildings, I observed a group of passersby assembled, sitting on their heels (as is the usual mode of sitting in that part of the world), listening to an older man who appeared to be telling a story. His delivery was animated, half-narration and half-acting, and he clearly had his audience's attention, with the group increasing steadily as more and more stopped to listen. Since he was speaking in one of the local languages, I could not understand him, but often heard the words "Rama," "Sita," "Hanuman," and

"Ravana," so knew that he was telling a story from their great epic, the *Ramayana*. Later I was able to question an Indian colleague about my experience and he explained that what I had observed was by no means unusual.

Storytellers will go to places where people may gather, sit, and begin a story (I am hazy as to the identity of the storytellers but have an impression that they are Brahmins, members of the old priest-teacher-scholar caste, but common folk like their audience). The *Ramayana* is age-old, rich in story themes of kings, great warriors, semi-human gods with miraculous powers, evil demons, virtuous women, great battles, acts of virtue and heroism. And it is the perfect vehicle for teaching values. As a few examples, Rama, the young hero prince, without any objection, obeys the order of his father, the king, to go live the life of a penniless hermit in the forest (value: obedience to elders). Sita, Rama's beautiful young wife, chooses to give up the life of luxury of the palace, to which she has always been accustomed, to go to the forest and share the hard life of her husband because she feels it is the duty of a wife always to be at husband's side and to suffer adversity with him (devotion to husband). Later Sita is abducted by the demon king, Ravana, whose passion for her is aroused at first sight, and throughout her imprisonment remains faithful to her husband and is prepared to die rather than sacrifice her virtue (marital fidelity). Lakshmana, Rama's younger brother, also chooses to go live in the forest with his brother, rather than remain in the palace in anticipation of succeeding to the crown, and distinguishes himself for bravery in battles in the effort to rescue Sita (devotion, unselfishness, loyalty, courage). Dasaratha, the old king who was led by one of his queens, a scheming greedy woman, to order Rama's banishment, is used in the epic as a model of still other virtues, for when he wishes to rescind the hateful order of banishment of his beloved son she reminds him that a promise is a promise and not even a king should break it, and furthermore if he is truly committed to the path of Dharma (here, literally, obedience to the Divine law) then he must fulfill his promise (trustworthiness, obedience to a higher law). Hanuman, the human-like monkey god, who is an extremely popular folk hero, joins the effort to rescue Sita and displays great cleverness, daring, and courage (intelligence, bravery). Even the demon-king, Ravana, who is caused by his passion to abduct Sita and carry her off, is good for value "mileage" -- as villains always are, for he exemplifies the misery caused by uncontrolled lust (self-control, moderation).

The *Ramayana* is also presented in drama form and it might be mentioned too that centuries ago it spread beyond India, throughout Southeast Asia and out into the islands of present-day Indonesia, where today it is enacted through the night, using puppet cut-out figures (wayang) held up against a backlighted screen.

Legend and folk story. Such an observation as the one in India invites thinking of comparable epics, folk stories, and dramas here and in other countries.

Western culture has its literary epics, such as the Iliad and Odyssey and Beowulf, but these are not well-known nor apparently used for moral teaching purposes. Better known are the legends of King Arthur and The Round Table, and Robin Hood. The Bible contains many incidents that traditionally have been used to teach morals and values. Every culture has its folk stories and often these contain "moral messages" embedded in the plot. Similarly, many children's stories contain moral themes. A delightful example comes to mind -- Pinocchio. Recall that his wooden nose grew longer each time he told a lie -- a very explicit moral message!

The Russians have wonderful folk stories often full of imagination which sometimes have moral themes as well.

One such Russian legend, elaborated by Tolstoy, tells of an ambitious peasant, Pakhon, who hungered for lands of his own. Learning from a transient merchant that ample land was to be had far to the east, from the nomadic Bashkirs, he resolved to go there.

After traveling for days and days he reached the high prairie country of the Bashkirs. These people lived on the open prairie in felt tents, moving from place to place with their herds. They neither ploughed the ground nor fenced it and their lands stretched to the horizon.

Pakhon inquired about buying land and was told by the chief that they had plenty to sell. When asked the price he replied, "One thousand rubles a day." This was a strange reply, so Pakhon asked, "What kind of measure is a day?" "How many acres are there in it?" The chief replied that they had no way to measure acres, so they sold by the day -- as much as Pakhon could walk around in a day would be his, and a day's price would be a thousand rubles. Pakhon thought it a tremendous bargain and replied that a man could walk around a great amount in a day. The chief laughed and said, "It is all yours, but there is one condition, if you do not come back in one day to the place from where you started, your money is lost."

Pakhon could not sleep that night, thinking all the time of how much land he could walk in a day and of all the uses he could make of it and the profit to be had. He would become a rich landowner and have land to spare to rent as well. He was up at daybreak, eager to get started. Out on a rise on the open prairie the chief marked a spot on the ground with his cap, saying, "From here you will start and here you will come back. Whatever portion you encircle from sunrise to sunset will be yours." Pakhon took out the money and put it on the cap.

Just as the sun was peeping over the eastern horizon Pakhon took off his coat, attached bread and water to his belt, pulled up his boot-legs, took spade in hand, and started out. Walking steadily in an easterly direction he stopped now and then to dig a small boundary marker and from time to time would look back to where the chief and the others waited on the rise, deciding each time whether to go on or turn a corner. And each time decided to go a bit further, as the land looked so rich and it would be a shame to pass it up. Finally, when the waiting group had become so tiny as to look like black ants he decided he had gone far enough, so dug a prominent corner marker, and turned sharply to the left and began walking in that direction.

By now the sun was high, Pakhon was feeling hot and hungry, and getting tired. He stopped for a brief rest and food, took off his now heavy boots, and resumed walking. After continuing several hours in this direction he was about to make another turn to the left but upon seeing a fine little valley just ahead decided to include it before making the corner marker and turning.

Now looking toward the distant cluster, they could barely be seen through the shimmering heat haze of mid-afternoon. Pakhon realized he would have to hurry if he was to complete pacing the remaining two sides so he increased his stride. But soon it became evident that he could not cover the same distances as the first two sides so he quickly dug a third corner marker, and headed straight for the distant cluster.

Walking had become hard, he was thirsty, and he had cut and hurt his feet. He wanted to rest, but he could not for he would not get back by sundown. In spite of the pain he kept increasing his stride, and as it was still far, he began to trot. As he ran, his shirt and trousers stuck to his body from the sweating, his mouth was cottony dry, his heart pounded in his chest, and he gasped for air.

He ran and ran, and as he approached the rise the Bashkirs shouted encouragement, for only a tiny rim of the sun now shone above the horizon. He ran with all his might up the rise toward the cap, collapsing forward on it just as the sun disappeared.

"You are a fine fellow" cried the chief, amused at Pakhon's desperate exertions, "You have come into a lot of land." Pakhon did not hear him; he was dead. (Adapted from Tolstoy, 1904).

Vitz (1990) has written forcefully for a theory that narratives (stories) are a central factor in a person's moral development, and supported the theory with a variety of theory concepts and findings on *narrative thought*. Bruner (1986) especially has proposed that mental life is made up of two different modes of thought, one *propositional* and the other *narrative*. Propositional thinking is the one we use when faced with an objective problem and is best known as the reasoning used by the scientist in his work. By contrast, narrative thought presents concrete human and interpersonal situations in order to demonstrate their particular validity. It is descriptive of reality and is a way of seeing that aims at the true and real. Specifically, the story mode requires imagination, an understanding of human intention, and an appreciation of the particulars of time and place (Vitz, p. 710). It is this manner of thinking that Vitz feels is critical in moral development, and he proposes that educators return to the various sorts of narratives (stories, plays, films, etc.) as a means of teaching morals.

Drama. Because of its life-like portrayal, drama has always had the potential for strong moral and value influence. We quickly become personally involved in the plot and identify with the actors, for the duration totally forgetting that it is all make-believe. Part of the involvement may be moral.

In the Middle Ages morality plays were popular and a common theme was the struggle of vices and virtues for the soul of man. The vices commonly would be drawn from the seven deadly sins, so one might have a character representing Greed, another Lust, another Rage, and so on. Of course the virtuous, the "good guys," always prevailed, and the sinners always punished, perhaps falling through a trap-door down into a fiery hell.

In time morality plays largely disappeared but not the use of drama to present moral themes. Throughout the nineteenth century and into the twentieth the melodrama was popular. Originally a play interspersed with singing and instrumental music, eventually the singing was eliminated and the instrumental music used to emphasize the action. Melodrama evokes images of rapid action and sudden crises, such as the midnight abduction of the heroine, but the morality theme is there throughout, with right and virtue always triumphing in the end, and the despicable villain getting his just desserts.

It is probable that the rise of motion pictures hastened the demise of the melodrama; at least the pictures continued the same tradition. Perhaps its most obvious form was the "western." Early in the movie the characters of the plot would come on the screen and even the children noisily seated down-front could guess at once who the "good guys" and "bad guys" were, because the good guys would be clean-shaven and handsome (according to a north-European standard) and the big cowboy hats they wore would be of a light color. The bad guys had a shifty look and dark complexions with often a dark moustache -- and of course wore big dark hats. The heroine always had a wholesome country-girl look. The great appeal of the western, especially to the small fry, was all of the fast action -- galloping horses, fist fights, gun battles, train robberies -- but a bad guy never won out over a good guy and never rode off into the sunset with the heroine. (I wonder now, looking back to childhood, whether any of the dozens of westerns seen had any influence on my moral development. I suspect we developed a rather good understanding of such things as fairness and honesty, but I don't recall ever saying to myself "I'm going to be that way." If there was an influence it was subtle.)

Of course television in turn largely displaced the films so we would need to analyze the content of T.V. programs, especially those for children, to discover the present moral influence.

Models. With the example of the Ramayana in mind the special role of models in value adoptions may be noted. Just as the various figures of that epic provided flesh-and-blood models that one could idealize, identify with, and emulate, so too elsewhere, models have a powerful role in value shaping. Surely it is safe to say that every nation has its folk heroes who are used for the purpose of modeling specific virtues, persons comparable to our Washington, Jefferson, Franklin, and Lincoln. Each religious tradition has its "saints."

The model can be an historic person or a half-imaginary legendary one, or even be wholly fictional; but if fictional he or she must have a reality in the minds of the people, comparable, say, to Shakespeare's Hamlet. Of course, the model may be living or was recently so. Surely Martin Luther King provides a good example here, not only because he was an admirable man, but also because black Americans need their own value models with whom they can identify.

Nearly all such figures will model positive values, but there will be a few, like Ravana above, who are widely known as villains (bad guys, traitors, devils, etc.) and who model negative values.

In part these models gain their influence because people hold them up as models of virtue and constantly draw attention to them. But beyond this, we seem to be looking for persons to idealize -- apparently some special need on our part. Whether this need is universal I cannot say, but I have noted evidence of it in such diverse cultures as Japan, China, India, Middle-East, as well as in European-derived societies.

Probably the name "Frank Merriwell" means nothing to present-day Americans, but from 1896 to 1916 Gilbert Patten, under the pen name of Burt L. Standish, wrote 986 Merriwell installments in *Tip Top Weekly*, and these stories were later reissued in 208 volumes by Street and Smith. It is estimated by Patten's publishers that 500 million Merriwell books were published in the United States, leaving Tom Swift, the Rover Boys and the Bible far behind.

Frank Merriwell was intended to be the ideal, the value model of the American boy and young man. He was a student at Yale, an outstanding athlete at every sport and a brilliant well-traveled person. But his greatest strength was honor. In the confrontations of yesteryear he stood tall, ready to stun the sour of heart, to thump the toadies and the bullies.

Listen to him, from his sick bed, exhorting team-mates before the Harvard-Yale football game: "Each of you must play his hardest every moment. . . . Fight as Yale fights in the last ditches. . . . Never say die! never let up!"

Watch him hours later, still addled with fever, stagger onto the gridiron. The Yale men saw him and were astounded. For a moment they could hardly believe their senses. Taking a punt on the Yale ten-yard line, he zigged, zagged, and tore on, 20, 30, 40 yards. High and fair like a flying bird he sprang over the last Harvard defender, then struck the ground, stumbled, fell to his knees, staggered up, fell again; and with a last effort, literally shot across the line for a touchdown just as the whistle blew ending the game.

Frank forgives; Frank holds no grudges; Frank would sooner keep his word of honor than personal laurels. He was a veritable United Fund of charity, giving tips right and left.

Fisticuffs were common to Merriwell's environment; let personal honor or the name of good old Yale be besmirched and -- pow! -- the fists are flying. For example, when a gambler disguised as a Princeton man caused trouble, "Frank leaped from the doorway and caught the fellow a terrible blow upon the face." But Frank's aggression in defense of principle was diluted by saintly sympathy. After battering a thug into unconsciousness, Frank stands by to help him up, and the now-repentant thug goes off a reformed man, saying "youse makes me want ter do der square t'ing."

While Merriwell had a way of winning enemies to his side, he lived in a remarkably hostile world. Lesser athletes, jealous of his prowess, schemed against him; scholars tried to frame him as a cheat on examinations; fickle classmates snubbed him at Mory's, the student hangout. But through it all Frank remained the hero that he was: honest, loyal, decent, faithful, and true-blue!

(The above was freely adapted from an article by Sheward Hagerty, titled "The hero: he was honest, decent, and true-blue; In 1970 is he a square?" which appeared in the Yale Alumni Magazine, November, 1970. Hagerty's purpose is to describe this fictitious hero of yesteryear and to wonder whether today he would be considered a "square" -- someone lacking sophistication. If so, have heroic figures of his sort gone out of fashion? And who are today's real-life heroes for the young people? Are heroes still needed for the moral and value development of young people?)

Influence of Information (Beliefs)

A well-recognized source of attitudes is the information or facts to which one is exposed. For example, when the facts became known about the alarming increase in world population many people adopted attitudes favorable to family planning. There is no reason to assume that information is not also influential in the formation of values, but it will not be as simple a process as the example would suggest. Indeed, the example is more complex than might appear, for one interprets the population increase *relative to* one or more value premises, such as that of the worth of human life, and the new attitude is a result of a combining of the information with the values. Values can be so fundamental as to constitute "first premises" of existence and themselves be so taken for granted that their existence be overlooked. Hence they may be more the shaper of the information coming in than being shaped.

This is an old point of concern and controversy among students of the subject. It came up especially when scientists and other scholars wanted to be able to assert that they were making statements of fact (stating existential propositions) free of any value coloring or distortion. But others maintained that value elements are never absent, and at least one scholar, Ray Lepley (1943), in a paper entitled "The Identity of Fact and Value," argued that the separation of the two categories results solely from our conventional habits of thought. For example, when the scientist says, "these are the facts of nature as we have discovered them by scientific experiment," he thinks he is escaping the tainting of values, but actually he is not, for the statement is made in the context of his highest values: truth, validity, correctness.

Granted the inseparability of fact and value, still it may be said that information, now in the form of subjective beliefs, plays its part in the shaping of values. Here is exemplification from Kluckhohn (1954). If the nature of human nature is conceived as intrinsically evil, men are not enjoined to behave like gods; though if human nature is believed to be perfectible, they may be. The Navaho think of the natural order as potentially harmonious. It is therefore a prime value of Navaho ceremonialism to maintain, promote, or restore this potential harmony.

Among facts that influence values are certain existential ones, two main ones being that ill-health is painful and life-threatening and that death is frightening. These give rise to the nearly universal valuing of physical well-being and life.

As we have suggested before, anthropologists have a useful concept in the *value-orientation* which is an interblending of both value and existential elements. Florence Kluckhohn and her associates (1961) have been especially vigorous in its employment in cross-cultural research.

Impact of events. Closely related to and often indistinguishable from the above "information" is the impact of events. A cluster of related examples would be the events pertaining to the environment: destruction of the high-altitude ozone shield, producing danger of increased skin cancer; pollution of the air by autos and power plants, creating dangerous, ugly smog, poisoning lakes and killing forests; pollution of streams and oceans, endangering both human health and marine life; increasing mountains of garbage, creating both health hazards and problems of disposal; an apparent gradual warming of the planet creating likelihood of permanent alterations of the earth's climate; and encroachments upon nature everywhere, threatening extermination of additional whole species, upsetting of natural balances, depletion of natural resources, and an increasing drabness and ugliness as natural beauty is lost.

Any and all of these events naturally cause thinking persons a sense of concern or alarm and provoke new attitudes and mobilize existing values. Notable throughout these events has been the role of the communicators -- newspapers, science magazines, special T.V. programs, reports by the environmental groups (Sierra Club, National Wildlife Federation, Greenpeace, etc.), Earth Day celebrations, demonstrators and protestors, etc.. Since few of us can observe the above conditions at first-hand, we are dependent upon the communicators; and the communicators often wish to do more than just inform -- they want to mobilize attitudes, evoke values, and produce action. Increasingly of late, as the movement has gained momentum, there has been more advice on "What you can do personally" to help solve the problem, as by reducing temperature of home or office or recycle newspaper and bottles. To people who already have a conscience, these messages readily evoke a sense of "I *ought* to be recycling (etc.);" they are rousing the powerful voice of conscience.

Values Derived From More-Basic Values

A possible origin of a value is a still-more-basic value. Actually, many of our values already are as basic as they can get and effort at explanation of "why" introduces an artificiality; it forces an intellectual cast on something that at this rock-bottom point is essentially nonrational. The something is *felt* as right or good, not reasoned to be. Still, some of our values are based on more basic values. Suppose I value self-development and am asked why I value it. After thought, I am able to mention such things as valuing the actualization of potential, the having of a richness of experience, increased effectiveness or skill at doing what one undertakes to do, and escape from the tyranny and enslavement of the immediate environment. Dembo (1960) pursued this very line of inquiry, asking her respondents to say why each given wish (value) was wanted. Her subjects found it difficult to go deeper but many were able to mention more basic values when encouraged and helped.

Deliberate Efforts to Change Values

It seemed likely that a number of studies would be found on the deliberate changing of people's values by one means or another, but only the two studies below by Rokeach and his associates were found. Applied efforts to change values, and related beliefs and attitudes, occur in prisons and reformatories, in the military as part of indoctrination, perhaps in some occupational training programs (as when the new employee is taught to lie to the customer), and likely in other places.

There is no doubt, too, that efforts to shape people's beliefs and values have occurred often in history. Likely every king or dictator in modern times who has planned to embark on a war has had to try in advance to generate popular support, and every military adventure gets presented as a "just" war, undertaken to protect cherished values of freedom, homeland, faith, or whatever. Two good modern examples of such deliberate programs were the Nazi efforts to reshape the thinking of an entire nation and the Chinese Communist's "thought reform" program.

The Nazi's gained complete control of all avenues of communication in Germany and then systematically went about reshaping everyone's understanding of history and his attitudes and values -- die for the Fatherland and realize Germany's manifest destiny, live as the noble Teutonic knights lived, restore Aryan racial purity, etc.. This is not the place to go into all the specific and cruel methods used -- they were diabolically effective, and it must suffice to say that if any "fact" is repeated often enough, and there is no competing message, eventually it will be believed. This was the Nazi strategy.

The thought reform program of the Chinese Communists was begun soon after the revolution and used on professors, students, former officials of the previous government, and other intellectuals. It also was used in modified form on American prisoners of war during the Korean War, where it was called "brainwashing." (Something of the sort was also used in Vietnam at end of that war.)

This reform activity was carried out in special "revolutionary colleges" and Lifton (1957, 1966, Ch. 19) reports that the program had four phases. The first phase was a time of getting settled and becoming acquainted with each other; the atmosphere was relaxed and an effort made to make everyone feel at ease and among friends. Lectures were given on the evils of the old society and on the ideals of the new China. Thought reform was presented as morally uplifting, harmonizing, and therapeutic of the old "disease."

In the next phase formal courses begin, with long, "heavy" lectures on history from the Marxist point of view and on various phases of Communist ideology, these accompanied by interminable small-group sessions where the lectures are discussed and a first "thought summary" written.

Now in third phase comes a marked change, a shift from the intellectual and ideological to the personal and emotional. The thought summary is subjected to extensive criticism from all sides and the student now is expected to subject himself to extensive and continuous self-examination, self-criticism, and confession. If he pretends to be a "new man" to escape the harassment his ruse is quickly recognized and completely rejected. He must thoroughly self-examine and self-criticize. Most get caught up in the confession compulsion and vie to outdo each other in the frankness, completeness, and luridness of their confessions. At end of this period a great mass, revival-like meeting is held and students with particularly "evil" pasts present lurid accounts of their past political and personal sins.

The last phase involves the writing of a final comprehensive thought summary or final confession. It requires about ten days to prepare and is subjected to prolonged and penetrating criticism. The confession ends with an emphasis on remaining liabilities and a solemn resolve to continue to self-improve.

All of the pressure of these last two phases generates fear and anxiety and conflict in everyone, since one never knew what the final outcome would be. Also, there were feelings of guilt and shame, as arousing these was a purpose of the program.

Surely so intensive an experience resulted in a new person in everyone? Lifton says the outcomes were mixed: some, especially the young, were thoroughly converted; others resisted the heavy-handedness from the outset and never changed inwardly; the great majority fell in-between, partially convinced, but primarily concerned with adapting themselves to this great stress and assuring their futures under the new regime.

The first Rokeach study (1973a, Ch. 8-13) involved attempting to change values and attitudes of university students by making them aware of possible contradictions between their values of *equality* and *freedom* and their self-conceptions. The assumption was that an experienced contradiction would lead to internal changes toward making values and self-conceptions consistent. The sense of this reasoning is that if you see yourself as a humane, kindly person with a feeling for the welfare of your fellowman, and information comes your way that your not-so-high stand on equality-among-men contradicts your self-image, then either your self-image will change to be consistent with your stand (your value) or the value will change to conform with the self-image. Rokeach (p. 120) postulated that contradictions are resolved so that self-conceptions will, at the least, be maintained and, if at all possibly, enhanced.

In the experiment the students were had at one time to rank the value terms of the Rokeach *Value Survey*, which included *freedom* and *equality*, and later given information which could be interpreted as contradicting these rankings (p. 235-237). Specifically, to arouse a state of self-dissatisfaction the experimenter offered this brief interpretation of the average finding on the ranking of the value terms:

> Apparently, Michigan State students value *freedom* far more highly than they value *equality*. This suggests that MSU students in general are much more interested in their own freedom than they are in freedom for other people.

The students were had to rank the value terms again several times between 3 weeks and 17 months later and differences between first and later rankings analyzed. Several of the results were: (1) subjects expressing satisfaction with their *equality* and *freedom* rankings changed the least as compared with the other subgroups, (2) subjects who were dissatisfied with both their rankings of these two values markedly raised their rankings of both, (3) those dissatisfied with one but not the other usually changed the dissatisfied ranking upward. Other measures were taken and results found but need no be reported here. In follow-up studies other of the value terms of the questionnaire were employed, namely a *world of beauty* in one (Hollen, 1972), and self-control (*self-disciplined*) in another with smokers (Conroy, Katkin, and Barnette, 1973). These, too, supported the original experimental hypothesis.

The other study (Ball-Rokeach, Rokeach, and Grube, 1984) was intended to be a more real-life or "average-citizen" extension of the previous study on university students, this time using television as the medium of communication and ordinary daytime viewers in an area of the state of Washington as subjects. Specifically, attitude or value influencing material was introduced into regularly scheduled programming, with the material presented by the regularly-appearing professional actors. Viewers were told the results of a previous national opinion-poll, followed by an attempt to arouse an emotional experience of self-dissatisfaction or self-satisfaction among them, the researchers assuming that they normally would think of themselves as lovers of democracy or as lovers of natural beauty. For instance, one of the hosts of the television program told his viewers,

> Americans feel that *freedom* is important. They rank it third. But they also feel that *equality* is considerably less important . . . they rank it twelfth . . . what does that mean? Does it suggest that Americans as a whole are much more interested in their own freedom than they are in freedom for other people? (1984, p. 74)

Later in the program the other host made similar remarks about Americans' low ranking of *a world of beauty*.

Measures of the values of a sample of viewers were obtained before and after this television program was aired. It was found that the average ranking of the three values -- *equality, freedom, a world of beauty* -- had increased four weeks after viewers watched the 30-minute program, but only for viewers who watched the program without interruption. There were also consistent attitude and behavioral changes. The researchers' explanation was the same as in the earlier studies -- arousal of feelings of self-dissatisfaction leading to value change toward consistency.

Though the findings of this study may not seem very impressive when seen against the daily barrage of attitude-and-action-shaping messages coming over T.V. from advertisers, political candidates, or special interest groups, this study apparently is the only one of its kind thus far and required considerable initiative and planning.

The scarcity of studies thus far surely is due largely to difficulty in conducting them, but ethical consideration often enter the picture as well and may deter the would-be researcher from proceeding. Rokeach (1973a, p. 335-37) has a special section on the ethical implications of such value-changing research, and there is good reason for concern in the light of history, for tomorrow's dictator may choose to use today's social scientist's research findings for harmful ends. Rokeach himself submitted his proposal for the first study above to a university-wide review committee for approval and in addition formulated three ethical criteria to guide experimental work designed to attempt to produce lasting conceptual and behavioral change. Two were that the review committee must find the proposed (value) change compatible with the assumptions of a democratic society, and, second, be in the interest of all humanity. On the basis of these criteria research intended to *decrease* such values as freedom and equality would not be ethically permissible. The third criterion had to do with use of deception and stated that false feedback about one's own or other's values and behavior is ethically indefensible. Rokeach adds that perhaps the most frightening possible practical application of his work is to the political area.

Haan et al. (1985), whose research on moral values is mentioned at several points in these pages, writes in a similar vein about doing research on moral development and action. "Thus the question for researchers is, Which value *should* they approve by choosing it as the target of their investigations? Plainly, scientists *ought* to choose a value that could conceivably be endorsed by humankind. . . ." (p. 47)

Personal Experiencing as Origin of Values

It will be recalled that a distinction was made between evaluative and worth values in Chapter 2. The evaluative involve a sense of right-wrong, good-bad, should-should not, etc. of the object or activity; the worth involve a non-evaluative sense of important, worthy, valuable, meaningful, etc.. Though a strict separation of the two types is not warranted, they do tend to have different origins, with the evaluative deriving largely from influences from others, of the sorts we have been surveying thus far, whereas worth values derive largely from direct personal experiencing. Some of the sorts of direct experiencing that create worth values may now be surveyed, our question being, what can be giving a person a sense of the importance or worth of something?

The felt worth of anything derives from the quality of experiencing with it, as when one enjoys exercise and games and therefore conceives of them as having personal worth. Since quality of experiencing is the determiner of valuing, then anything giving joy, fulfillment, satisfaction, contentment, relief, pleasure, etc. can become valued, and anything giving their opposites of distress, displeasure, anguish, pain, discontent, etc. can become negatively valued. Though we are in no position to enumerate all of the qualities of experiencing that can give rise to values, we owe it to ourselves to form some conception of their extent. At first glance it might seem appropriate to try to list all such terms as joy, contentment, relief, anguish, pain, etc. that describe qualities of experiencing; but only a few of these name specific qualities of experiencing (e.g., physical pain) and the rest are just general labels (joy comes in many flavors). The forms of experiencing below are intended to get us beyond generalities and suggest as specific a conception as possible of the extent of this domain of values, yet it should be taken for what it is, the gropings of one mind for insight into such values.

(a) *Values from motives.* A large category of experiencing is that connected with motives. In Chapter 2 it was proposed that motives create values, as when desire for pleasant sensory experiences leads one to have sensory experiences, and may lead to one's forming a conception of the desirability (value) of such experiences. Thus almost any recurring motive that is of any significance may create a value. Though the number of possible human motives cannot be unlimited, it can be very large. One fairly complete listing was presented in Table 1 (pg. 41) and the reader is asked to turn to it again.

As was suggested in Chapter 2, pg. 40, each motive may be assumed to create at least implicit value and often gives rise to a conceptualized (explicit) value as well. Examples were given from the table. Another might be "attaining love and positive identifications with people and groups" (third group of abundancy motives). Here the implicit value would be the having of love and positive identifications and the value concept would be the feeling that love and identification are worthy and desirable. "Establishing moral and other values" (from the fourth group of abundancy motives) is interesting relative to our concern with values. The authors are saying that people are motivated to establish values, and we add that one may feel that having values is desirable. (As the perceptive reader may soon discover, some of these motives may themselves be derived from values, with the value supplying the motivation. In such cases, our formulation of motive-creating-value should not be used because of its circularity).

Thus using the table and reading through it in detail we may get an idea of the range of values that can flow from motives. And with such concrete experiencing possibilities before us as hunger, pain, sensory pleasure and aversion, curiosity, sense of accomplishment, feeling liked, feeling inferior, and joy of play let us note again that the source of worth values are these specific qualities of personal experiencing, and not the evaluative assertion of another that it is good or desirable. To be sure, groups do put evaluations on forms of experiencing, as when the experiencing of physical pain or joy of play are labeled "bad," but that is another matter and moves us back into the domain of evaluative values. As another qualification, it may be noted that some amount of "borrowing" of these worth values occurs, as when I accept another's assertion that sensory pleasure is desirable (worthy).

(b) *Values from interests.* Interests are but a special form of motivation, so the same psychodynamics apply. My interest in painting or my neighbor's interest in cycling are not values automatically; but if the activities give us feelings of meaningfulness or worthwhileness, then they are values.

(c) *Values from emotions.* The emotional states of fear, anger, love, depression, irritation, grief, hate, anxiety, irritation, jealousy, joy, wonder, etc. are themselves qualities of experiencing. Each may come to be conceptualized by the experiencer as desirable or undesirable in the worth sense. The emotions of fear, anger, and depression are widely given negative value because of an inherent unpleasantness, and love, joy, and delight or elation given positive value for the opposite reason.

A number of the emotions also carry evaluative labels in the various societies of the world, surely because such emotions as anger in its various forms, fear in its various forms, and jealousy and envy are disruptive of interpersonal relationships and orderly group process.

(d) *Values from personal relationships.* Because of affection, companionship, and perhaps admiration the husband or wife values the mate. For much the same feelings the parents value the child or a person values his friend. The citizen may value a public figure because of his/her admirable qualities. In general, persons may become objects of value because of the feelings held toward them.

(e) *Unique qualities of temperament.* Unique qualities of temperament can lead to unique values. One is reminded here of the essential idea of Spranger's (1928) theory, which was that each person is so uniquely composed as to find certain experiences especially meaningful. Specifically, the assumption was that one person is so composed as to have frequent aesthetic experiences and to find them especially meaningful (valued). Another is so composed as to be oriented toward human interactions and concerns (love of people) and to value them. Another as to have religious experiences and to find value in them. Another as to have analytic intellectual experiences and to find them worthwhile. And another to have commercial, business-world type experiences and to find them personally rewarding. Though common sense suggests that such temperament orientations, with associated values, as these exist, Spranger did no research on the matter and the subject remains largely explored. If these six exist it may be guessed that a number of other such unique temperament disposition also exist, each predisposing its possessor to special sorts of experiences that are especially meaningful, hence valued.

(f) *Unusual mental states.* Apparently humans have always valued having certain unusual mental states. The experience itself is so special that the person attaches value to it and seeks its repetition. There is evidence going far back in history of efforts to induce trances, visions, out-of-body states, unusual sensory experiences, mystical states, illuminations or profound insights, and the like. Such efforts are found in the history of advanced cultures and the anthropological literature is full of such efforts and experiences in folk cultures. Sometimes peoples have resorted to use of fermented beer-type substances to induce unusual states en masse and have used certain plant substances such as peyote, mescaline, opium, and hashish, to induce altered states of consciousness. Among some peoples these drug-induced altered states have been given a profound religious-type significance or value. Today, the wide availability of intoxicants and drugs permits people to take them just to "get drunk" or have a "high" and their over-use constitutes a huge world-wide problem, impressive if tragic evidence of the valuing of unusual mental states.

(g) *Practical-functional needs*. Practical or functional needs create a great array of worth values. We value our houses for the shelter and perhaps the prestige they afford, we value hundreds of tools and gadgets for the practical needs they serve, we value our automobiles for the pleasure and usefulness they provide, etc.. This is the domain of the economist, for often these values can be expressed in monetary terms, and the interplay of such values and their far-flung ramifications create complex economic systems. It will serve our purpose here simply to recognize the existence of such values and the practical needs that create them.

Self-Selection and Commitment As Origin of Values

We would be remiss if we did not recognize that one source of values is self-selection. That is, one may look over an array of value alternatives and make a deliberate choice from among them (or, even if no actual choosing occurs, still make a deliberate commitment to given values). Of course the choice will not be totally "out of the blue," with no antecedent influences. Rather, all of the above determinants potentially could be influencing one person or another, especially such things as parents or historic models, admired groups or esteemed friends, or personal temperament (the sort of pre-disposition that leads one person spontaneously to value wildlife and nature when these are brought to his attention and leads another to value exploitation of nature for want of any feeling for other forms of life). But though there will be ample predisposition, this does not contradict the fact that at some point in adulthood we can and many of us do make choices from among value alternatives and do make commitments to live by those values. The life of Vera Brittain, summarized below, nicely exemplifies this choice-making process.

Functional Needs as Origins of Values

In the preceding chapter a number of functions or roles of values were mentioned, such as to give meaning to existence, create favorable self-concepts, facilitate interpersonal relationships, etc.. Here we should recognize that functional needs are a reason for the acquisition of values. This is but a borrowing of insight from social psychologists as to the origins of attitudes. Initially they assumed that attitudes were straightforwardly learned from significant others (parents, mates, friends, etc.); then, one by one, other causes were recognized and in due course about a half-dozen *functions* of attitudes were identified. As proposed by one or another writer, they are adopted out of a need to: (a) create an orderly (inner) world having clarity and stability; (b) maximize rewards and minimize losses in the game of life; (c) mediate interpersonal relationships and produce compatibility; (d) satisfy needs for affiliation and approval; (e) create a favorable self-image and express ideal self-concepts; and (f) express deeply held beliefs and values. This array is so broad that almost any attitude or value can be fitted in somewhere as being adaptive or functional. Though criticized later on certain technical grounds, none of these causes has ever been rejected as incorrect.

The above-reviewed Newcomb study of Bennington College girls nicely exemplifies this point, as nearly all of the attitudes of these girls had been adopted for functional-adaptive reasons. Note again their adoption by one girl or another for such reasons as peer-group approval, to be regarded as a leader, to express resentment and hostility toward the college community, to express independence from parents, to satisfy need for a reliable source of information, to gratify a need to know and understand one's world, and others. Another more-detailed exemplification of functional factors will be seen in the report on the feminist-pacifist Vera Brittain, just below.

The functional determinants have great importance in our understanding the origins of individual values. They might be thought of as operating in addition to such more obvious influences as teaching and modeling of values by parents and others, and in often subtle ways determining which values the person will attend to and adopt.

Vera Brittain: A Case Report of the Emergence of Beliefs, Attitudes and Values

It is desirable, if possible, to supplement presentation of general causes of values and attitudes with individual case reports. These bring the shaping process to life and often remind us of comparable value emergences in our own lives.

One such individual report is that of Stewart and Healy (1986) on the British feminist and pacifist writer and activist Vera Brittain.

Brittain (1893-1970) lived in an era of social and political turmoil in Great Britain. She was raised in a provincial upper middle class family and her life spanned a time of struggle by women for equal rights and two world wars, all coming at crucial periods in her personal development.

Stewart and Healy propose that any formulation of the relationship between personal experience and political action should take account of (1) the centrality of political values in an individual's identity; (2) the individual's life stage and life history; and (3) the individual's current situation, including the reference group that frames the individual's perception of the situation. In their analysis of Vera Brittain they conclude that political events taking place in adolescence shaped her broad ideological commitments, and that political events in later life were experienced as demanding expression of beliefs formed earlier. Finally, with the appearance of a need to be "generative," or to contribute to the future, Brittain experienced a strong need to translate her beliefs and values into responsible political action (p. 11-12).

More specifically, they reason that the development of Brittain's feminist and pacifist ideologies differed somewhat: her feminist beliefs were formed early and grew directly out of her personal experience; her pacifist beliefs grew more gradually from the convergence of personal and international events (namely, the impact of the first world war) (p. 12).

Stewart and Healy set the stage for their description of the development of Brittain's feminist convictions by noting, following Mannheim (1952) and Erikson (1965, 1968), that in late adolescence, probably around 17, the person begins to be open to attitude-shaping influences and starts to experiment with ideas. Erikson proposed that a major task of late adolescence is development of an *identity*, and the experimentation with beliefs and attitudes is part of the identity-discovery process. He assumed, too, that identity must ultimately include commitment to a set of values.

Brittain's feminism developed early and might be pictured as resulting from the interplay of (a) a bright mind and independent spirit; (b) anti-feminist sentiments from her father; and (c) ample exposure to feminist ideas, especially at her school. Her talent and independence of spirit are evident throughout, the latter especially in her winning admission to Oxford University, against her family's wishes, to study to be a writer. As to the anti-feminism, she describes herself as the daughter of a provincial Edwardian family which regarded the subservience of women as part of the natural order of creation. In a diary[1] entry for November 15, 1913, when she was 20, she describes a conversation with her father about religion:

> Finally he ended up by saying that I didn't know what I was talking about, and it was ridiculous a little slip of a girl arguing with him about what I didn't understand etc.
>
> Of course I have always known . . . that he has nothing but contempt for me and my knowledge, just as he has at heart for all women, because he believes them for some unknown reason to be inferior to him. . . . (1982, p. 41)

Her wording here might give the impression that her father did indeed feel contempt for her, but that is most unlikely in view of her being the very antithesis of a cowed, inferior-feeling girl. Even while describing his behavior toward her she is manifesting her self-sufficiency and objective-mindedness about the father's attitudes. Likely she had had a good relationship with her father through the

---

[1] All quotations from unpublished letters and diaries that follow are from the Estate of Vera Brittain, reproduced by permission of the William Ready Division of Archives and Research collections, McMaster University Library, Hamilton, Ontario, Canada.

growing up years but now, as she approaches maturity and begins to interact with him as an intellectual equal, she runs afoul of his attitudes about the place of women. But apart from the father's attitudes, another diary entry shows that she is aware of the broad reality of limited opportunities for women as compared with men (Brittain, 1982, pp. 39-31).

As to the exposure to feminist ideas, Brittain reports in her autobiography that she had "first acquired the feminist tendencies" at her school, and that they were "developed by the clamorous drama of the suffragette movement far away in London" (1933/1980 p. 58).[2] As Brittain's retrospective appreciation of the "older" feminists, written in 1928 (June 20) for the *Manchester Guardian*, recalled:

> The name of Mrs. Pankhurst was a familiar echo in my schooldays -- an echo that became louder as her exploits gathered publicity and I grew to the self-important maturity of a prefect. Our headmistress was an ardent if discreet feminist, and some of the older girls were occasionally taken to village suffrage meetings of a suitably moderate type.

This same teacher introduced Brittain to the ideas of leading feminists of the time (see 1933/1980, pp. 38-39), and -- most crucially -- lent her Olive Schreiner's (1911) *Woman and Labour* as soon as it came out. Stewart and Healy add that the eventual importance of Schreiner's thinking for Brittain's own feminism cannot be over-estimated (and cite Bishop, 1983, in further support). Both shared a passionate conviction that the cause of women's devaluation lay in their exclusion from most forms of productive work and a faith that increased status for women would help prevent war. Brittain eventually wrote it was Schreiner's book that "supplied the theory that linked my personal resentments with the public activity of the suffragettes" (*Manchester Guardian*, June 20, 1928).

Speaking most broadly and in retrospect, Brittain generally traced her feminism back to her adolescent school experiences:

> Thus it was in St. Monica's garden . . . that I first visualized in rapt childish ecstasy a world in which women would no longer be the second-rate, unimportant creatures that they were now considered, but the equal and respected companions of men. (1933/1980, p. 41)

---

[2] The 1980 edition of the autobiography, *Testament of Youth*, published by Seaview Books, is now out of print and copyright has reverted to Paul Berry, her literary executor, and Virago Press, London. The book is currently published by Viking Penguin, 1989.

Stewart and Healy conclude that the combination of early exposure to sexist attitudes at home, a temperamental inclination to autonomy and resentment of injustice, and the capacity and tendency to see connections between her fate and that of all women prepared the way for Brittain's adolescent responses to feminist ideology when she read and heard about it from a trusted and admired mentor.

Once her feminism had developed, probably by about 1911, it broadened to the point where she reacted to events in terms of their sexist and feminist implications. Thus, in August 1914 she responded to the outbreak of war by reflecting on the role of women (and herself) in it: "Today I started the only work it seems possible as yet for women to do -- the making of garments for soldiers" (1982, p. 89). She could write later

> feminism . . . is not . . . merely a particular form of propaganda; it is an attitude towards life, resentful against conventional restrictions, but essentially constructive in its reaching out to a wider freedom and a more independent self-sufficiency. (*Manchester Guardian*, January 16, 1929)

Perhaps because of the centrality of feminism in her identity, as well as her ideology, it changed very little in its broad outlines over six decades. Nevertheless, as her life situation changed, the specific preoccupations illuminated by her feminism also changed (Stewart and Healy, p. 16). She married in 1925 and bore two children. This change in status, to wife and mother, led her to focus on different problems faced by women. There was plenty to keep her busy throughout these decades as the status of women changed only slowly and some of the topics she wrote on in the 1930s are still timely today. As World War II approached she increasingly set aside her work in behalf of women in favor of work for peace, but after the war resumed this work.

In contrast to her feminism, her pacifism developed later and gradually, taking shape in the course of the first war.

In the summer and fall of 1914 World War I was just beginning. Previous to its onset war had seemed to be something remote and unimaginable to her -- something to be followed in the newspapers but would never have to be lived personally.

At outbreak of the war Brittain expressed both excitement and trepidation. On August 3 she wrote in her diary:

> To-day has been far too exciting to enable me at all to feel like sleep -- in fact it is one of the most thrilling I have ever lived through. . . . That which has been so long anticipated by some and scoffed at by others has come to pass at last -- Armageddon in Europe! (1982, p. 84)

These brief lines deserve special note for they may well capture the spirit of the whole of Europe at the outbreak of the war. There had not been a major war in Europe for more than forty years (and none involving the whole of Europe for even longer) and no one had experienced the carnage and horror of modern warfare. Garraty and Gay (1972) aptly express the mood of the time:

> With what innocence, with what enthusiasm, did the Europeans of 1914 respond to the tocsin! No one foresaw even the contours of the disaster ahead, and most people welcomed the war as a great patriotic adventure. After a decade of worsening crises and a spiraling arms race, they had come to expect a final showdown, but after decades of peace, they had forgotten what war was like and few had an inkling that a modern war would multiply the terrors of earlier conflicts. Europeans marched off to battle with something close to exultation, proud in their patriotism and certain of their cause, confident of a victorious end in a short time. It was the last time in our civilization that war could be greeted in this fashion. (p. 981)

But Brittain's excitement must be taken with caution, and Stewart and Healy say that even at this early point she was not completely pro-war. Rather, she was quite conflicted (p. 19). On September 3, she described her reaction to the news that her brother Edward was going to war: "I will not say anything but that I am glad, but I can not pretend not to be sorry" (1982, p. 102). Her ambivalence was also evident in terms of the less personal and more national perspective. Upon hearing (in August 1914) of a major British victory over Germany resulting in 25,000 German deaths, she wrote:

> I am incapable of feeling glad at such a wholesale slaughter of the Germans, whatever use it may be to us. I can only think of the 25,000 mothers who bore & reared those men with toil, & of the wives & families, never ardent for war or for a quarrel with us, which they leave behind them. (1982, p. 90)

So even at this early point in Brittain's experience with war, an awareness of its implications for personal loss on both sides of the battle lines is to be seen.

Brittain's greatest personal interest, and therefore the potential for the greatest personal loss, centered on Roland Leighton, her future fiancé and the person with whom she most looked forward to attending Oxford. On August 21 she wrote in her diary of her joy that Leighton, owing to his defective eyesight, had not passed the necessary exam for serving in the army, so could not go. Also, that she was glad because she did not want that brilliant intellect to be wasted and that most promising career to be spoilt at its outset (1982, p. 94). There is also evidence that she thought war was especially wasteful of talented individuals in general, regardless of national origin. Thus she expressed in her diary that hope that the rumor of the death of the violinist Kreisler, an officer in the Austrian Army, was false, and that geniuses such as he because of their value to humanity, should not be allowed in the army. Stewart and Healy continue:

> Ultimately Leighton succeeded in his effort to join the war effort. The discussions between Brittain and Leighton about the war mirrored the ambivalence toward war that we see in Brittain herself. We can see in her early reactions to the war a mixture of beliefs: that individuals have a moral obligation to serve their country, that war provides an opportunity for heroism (Gorham, 1985), and that war results in both personal loss and a waste of human talent that transcends national boundaries (Mellown, 1983a).

At the same time that it was becoming clear that the men closest to her (Edward and Roland) would soon be in the midst of fighting, Brittain was becoming aware of the large-scale human tragedy inherent in war. In her diary in January 1915, Brittain responded to a letter from her father who wrote of young men she knew who had already died fighting for Great Britain. She wrote, "This war takes them all, 'the eloquent the young the beautiful & brave' and I don't feel as if there can be *any* justification for that" (1982, p. 150).

The last time she saw Leighton before his departure for the front, Brittain forced him to analyze his reason for wanting to go. She acknowledged his desire for personal heroism: "I know well enough really why he wants to go, why, if I were a man I should want to go." Nevertheless, she told him, "I could not pretend to be glad, that I was no heroine" (1982, p. 157).

Even so, the first letters that Brittain received from Leighton detailing the conditions of life in the trenches at the front stimulated both an intellectual interest and personal anxiety:

> His letter filled me with a queer exultation & yet anxiety & dread. If only I could share those experiences with him I should glory in them; as it is, the thought of all those guns he heard fills me with apprehension. (1982, p. 175)

On April 25, 1915, Brittain wrote to Leighton:

> The terrible things you mention & describe fill me, when the first horror is over, with a sort of infinite pity I have a never felt before. . . . Is it [the war] really all for nothing -- for an empty name -- an ideal? Last time I saw you it was I who said that and you who denied it. Was I really right, & will

the issue really not be worth one of the lives that have been sacrificed for it?" (letter to Leighton, April 25, 1915)

From this passage we can derive indications of the future direction of Brittain's development. Here she responded to her first real knowledge of the realities of battle with an "infinite pity." She strongly questioned the value of the war, focusing on the human lives wasted for an empty ideal. Yet Brittain still felt the obligation to serve -- though she channeled this energy not toward her country's prosecution of the war but to minimizing personal tragedy and human suffering, the by-products of war.

Brittain's ambivalent pacifist orientation continued to develop throughout 1915. She thus left Oxford in the spring to become a nurse -- to alleviates suffering resulting from the war, while describing this as "serving my king & country" (Brittain, 1982, p. 262). She continued to exchange letters with Leighton who remained at the front (and to whom she had become engaged late in 1915). In October, as she prepared for her new nursing job in London and Edward's departure to the front, she wrote a powerful statement about her view of war to Leighton:

The more I think of this War, the more terribly incongruous seems to me the contrast between the immense importance of the individual, and calm ruthlessness with which hundreds of individuals are mown down at once by an impersonal gun. Postal Service, ASC, RAMC, Taxes, Hospitals, etc. -- all perfectly organized simply to afford the greatest facility to the Science of Death -- in its noble work of interrupting and nullifying all the other sciences that make for life. . . . Public opinion has made it a high and lofty virtue for us women to countenance the departure of such as these and you to regions where they will probably be slaughtered in a brutally degrading fashion in which we would never allow animals to be slaughtered. This, I suppose is "the something elemental, something beautiful" that you find in War! To the saner mind it seems more like a reason for shutting up half the nation in a criminal lunatic asylum. (letter to Leighton, October 10, 1915)

Though she later apologized for the letter, it clearly expressed some deeply felt views about war.

On December 23, 1915, Roland Leighton died of war wounds and Brittain's first experience of personal tragedy caused her to question the value of heroism. "I ask myself in anguish of mind, 'Was it heroism entirely or was it folly?'" (Brittain, 1982, p. 309).

Brittain pursued her duty to her country in spite of her increasing questioning of the value of war, and she was ordered to Malta in September

1916 (Brittain, 1982, p. 328). While in Malta, nursing the war wounded, she learned that two close friends had died. Shortly before learning of these deaths Brittain wrote to her brother about the way in which the war was losing its political meaning as its personal significance increased:

> The longer the War goes on, the more one's concern in the whole immense business seems to centre itself upon the few beings still left that one cares about, and the less upon the general issue of the struggle. One's personal interest wears one's patriotism threadbare by this time. (1933/1980, p. 338)

After returning to England for a while, Brittain managed to arrange a coveted assignment nursing in a hospital close to the fighting in France. Brittain arrived in France in august 1917, and attempted to rededicate herself to the patriotic ideal that England's cause in the war was just (Brittain, 1933/1980, p. 370). Brittain soon experienced what was perhaps the ultimate paradox in her personal experience of the war; the hospital where she nursed assigned Brittain to a ward for German prisoners. Comforting a German soldier she was

> . . . thinking how ridiculous it was that I should be holding this man's hand in friendship when perhaps, only a week or two earlier, Edward up at Ypres has been doing his best to kill him. The world was mad and we were all victims; that was the only way to look at it. These shattered, dying boys and I were paying alike for a situation that none of us had desired or done anything to bring about. (Brittain, 1933/1980, p. 376)

Thus, Britain arrived at the conclusion, through personal loss and direct personal experience of the destruction of war, that there were only victims of war. Still, she held to her belief in the importance of working to minimize the effects of war on others wherever possible.

By the fall of 1918, after her brother's death, Brittain had lost the ideals that, until this time, had continued to motivate her to fight the suffering caused by war:

> At that stage of the War, I decided indignantly, I did not propose to submit to pious dissertations on my duty to God, King, and Country. That voracious trio had already deprived me of all that I valued most in life, and if the interminable process of attrition lasted much longer, the poor surviving remnants of the writer's career that I once prepared for so fiercely would vanish into limbo with the men whom I had loved. My only hope now was to become the complete automaton, working mechanically and no

longer even pretending to be animated by ideals. Thought was too dangerous; if once I began to think out exactly why my friends had died and I was working, quite dreadful things might suddenly happen. (Brittain, 1933/1980, p. 450) (Stewart and Healy, pp. 20-22)

In this statement it is clear that all ideological support for the war has been lost. Specifically, war was no longer an opportunity for heroism and patriotism, but had become *only* a destructive force, with victims on all sides.

Stewart and Healy summarize that by the end of World War I, three factors had converged to create what they term Brittain's "psychological pacifism" -- that is, a pacifism in reality, even if not yet formally declared as such: (1) her changed understanding of war, which had shifted from a vague, idealized image of an opportunity for individuals to perform "heroic" deeds, to a concrete, detailed sense of the horrors and demands of war; (2) her increased awareness of the destruction of war, both for enemies and allies; and (3) her personal losses sustained over time as a result of the deaths of her fiance, brother, and two close friends (p. 23).

The remarkable thing about this phase of her life was the slow transition taking place within her, apparently produced almost entirely from within. Unlike the feminist conversion, no one was there at her side urging a pacifist ideology upon her nor were pacifist publications at hand. To the contrary, in wartime governments engage in systematic efforts to keep up "war morale" by a play on such deeply held values and beliefs as duty to king and country, patriotism, doing your fair share, sacrifice for the common good, making the world safe for democracy, overcoming of evil (the enemy), doing the will of God ("God is with us!"). The whole British populace was strongly motivated by various of these values and daily reinforcing each other's commitment to the war effort. So her conviction against war was emerging in spite of all outward influence to the contrary. An independent soul indeed!

But it was not until after the war that her pacifist ideology finally crystalized. At Oxford she decided to study history instead of English in order to understand better how the war calamity had happened and how to prevent another -- "It's my job, now, to find out all about it, and to try to prevent it, in so far as one person can, from happening to other people in days to come" (1933/1980, p. 471).

During the 1920s and 30s she spent much time working for peace -- writing, lecturing, assisting international peace organizations and the like. In 1937 she joined the Peace Pledge Union, thereby publicly promising never to support any war in any way. The civil war in Spain was by then underway and she was one of the few British authors to express unwillingness to support the struggle against Facism taking place there. A statement published at that time shows how thoroughly formulated her pacifist beliefs and values had become:

As an uncompromising pacifist, I hold war to be a crime against humanity, whoever fights it and against whomever it is fought. I believe in liberty, democracy, free thought and free speech. I detest Fascism and all that it stands for, but I do not believe that we shall destroy it by fighting it. And I do not feel that we serve either the Spanish people or the cause of civilisation by continuing to make Spain the battle-ground for a new series of Wars of Religion. (pamphlet "Authors Take Sides on the Spanish War," published in December 1937). (Stewart and Healy, p. 24)

She continued to hold to her position during World War II, now against much the same war spirit as prevailed during the first war (a pacifist in wartime often is a reviled and hated person, accused of aiding the enemy, sometimes physically attacked in public and sometimes imprisoned). Though Brittain was not physically abused, she had to endure a special sort of suffering for three years. Out of concern for their safety, and as part of a government evacuation scheme, their two children were sent to the U.S. in 1940, to stay with friends. Parting from them was painful, but she hoped to be able to visit them from time to time or call them back if conditions improved. But the British authorities denied her an exit permit (probably out of fear that she would lecture on pacifism in the U.S.), so she was separated from them for three years. Indicative of her suffering was this entry in her diary on January 1, 1943: "If only, only, I could get the children back! Life without them gets more, not less, like a double amputation, and every achievement is dust and ashes."

We tend to emphasize such external causes of values as parental, church, and community influences and unwittingly neglect movements from within the person himself. Brittain admirably exemplifies this latter influence, for when we ask what it was about the unequal status of women and what about the calamity of war that moved her as they did, we find ourselves recognizing something about her very makeup that led her to react as she did against both.

CHAPTER 5

ASSESSMENT OF VALUES

This chapter will present all the types of value assessment methods that could be identified together with examples and pertinent comment. Its purpose is to give the reader who may know little or nothing of value assessment an overall picture of the possibilities but will not go into detail on any.

Since some readers will have an impression that technical knowledge is required to do values research and that all methods require statistical refinement, they may be assured that anyone can study values and the most sensitive techniques are the simplest and require no statistical refinement.

The chapter is divided into two parts. The first surveys specific value-assessment methods; the second discusses general problems or considerations in value assessment.

Specific Value Assessment Methods

Interview

The interview is the oldest and simplest method of learning a person's values. Together with observation it has always been used by anthropologists to learn the ways and values of peoples around the world. It can be used by anyone with a minimum of training and is potentially the most sensitive of methods, as the interviewer can follow-up initial questions with further queries, seek clarification, pursue interesting comments, and learn something of the strength or importance of each value. Not only is it flexible but also it can be used with persons whose level of literacy precludes use of printed instruments. Its major limitation is its time-consumingness which bars its use with large numbers of respondents. One solution is to combine intensive interviewing of a limited number of persons, perhaps a random sample of the total, with giving of questionnaires to the total large group. Of course its effectiveness depends upon the skill of the interviewer, but it is much the same skill that one employs in everyday conversation when questioning someone, not something requiring special training. Main thing is to create an informal, friendly, conversational atmosphere so that the respondent feels free of threat, is relaxed, and senses that the interviewer is genuinely interested. (Anyone who feels inexperienced should of course seek the opportunity to practice under supervision).

When beginning an inquiry into a person's values, it may not be fruitful to begin by asking "What are your values?" because unless the person has had occasion to be thinking about values, as in a college course, likely he will be able to think of very few -- perhaps just several moral values. Each of us possesses many values, but as we have seen they are of different sorts, and most are just lived and evoked in particular situations, rather than thought about. So some sort of structuring of the interview is advisable.

Structured interview. Quite a variety of structurings are possible, but the simplest is just a list of questions or topics to work through. One research example will be given here and others given below under more specific headings.

One of the most intriguing examples of structure was Tamara Dembo's (1960, pgs. 86-87) first question: "At the birth of your next child there will be a fairy present, and this fairy says that you can have seven wishes for your child, wishes which will come true. What are your seven wishes for the child, for the whole life of the child?"

Before asking the question she would first thank the person for coming, seat him/her, request permission to record the interview and turn on the recorder, seat herself, and ask two questions in rapid succession: "Are you married?" and "Do you have children?" The questions were presumed to facilitate the emotional involvement of participants and their answers dictated the wording of the instructions. If the person was married and had children then the "at the birth of your next child" opening was used. In general, the wording would be altered depending upon marital status, age, ability to have children, or other characteristics of the person. But even when the child had to be that of a friend, the subjects still readily and seriously involved themselves in the task!

Following this first phase, she repeats one by one the seven wishes that have been given, asking the person to analyze why it is valued.

> I now turn to the method used to induce subjects to analyze their zero-level values, i.e., to determine their components:
>
> The experimenter took the first wish mentioned by a subject in the first experiment -- let us use "health" as an example -- and said to the subject, "What do you mean by health?" To transpositions of the zero-level value into value-guarding terms, e.g., "absence of disease and crippling," or into definitions, e.g., "proper functioning of the body," the experimenter

indicated that such responses were not acceptable. To transpositions, the experimenter replied, "What I am asking for is what is positive about health." To definitions, the experimenter replied by stating, "I am not asking you to define health. I want you to describe to me what health actually means to you. How does it feel to be healthy?" A subject might protest that feelings cannot be described. In such cases, the experimenter assured the subject that many people tend to doubt their ability to analyze feelings, but eventually find that they can do so. Finally, under this sort of questioning and redirecting, subjects were able to describe feelings, thus bringing out the components of zero-level values. The process was repeated for each of the zero-level values wished for a child by subjects.

It is evident that she felt values to be analyzable into something more basic. I don't know of another theorist who has made this assumption and it is something that deserves further exploration. There is a danger of forcing the person to go beyond actual experiencing and invent answers to satisfy the interviewer, but there is also a possibility of real growth of insight on the part of the interviewee.

In another phase of her research she tells subjects who have gone through the above phases that another fairy will come and grant seven wishes to the person himself. This also is followed-up as above. The main purpose of this phase is to see how similar or different the values (wishes) are for child and for self.

Interviews structured by imaginary situations, conversations, anecdotes, etc.. A variety of specifics are possible here, limited only by the imagination of the investigator. Imaginary situations and anecdotes have a special appeal that abstract questions lack and persons of all levels of education quickly involve themselves. A good example is the interview material developed by F. Kluckhohn and Strodtbeck (1961) in which they describe in real-life terms several different life situations and ask for a personal choice by the respondent and a judgement by him as to how others of his group also would react (see pgs. 27-29, ch. 1, above, for the rationale of this research project). Their purpose was to develop an interview instrument to measure the dominant and variant value orientations found in five different cultures -- Spanish-American, Anglo-American (Mormon and Texas Homesteaders), Hopi and Navaho Indian. The interview schedule consists of a posing of 22 situations calling for a judgement between two or three possible reactions, the first of which is the following:

1. Job Choice
   A man needed a job and had a chance to work for two men. The two bosses were different. Listen to what they were like and say which you think would be the best one to work for.

A   One boss was a fair enough man, and he gave somewhat
(Doing) higher pay than most men, but he was the kind of boss who insisted
         that men work hard, stick on the job. He did not like it at all when a
         worker sometimes just knocked off work for a while to go on a trip
         or to have a day or so of fun, and he thought it was right not to take
         such a worker back on the job.

B   The other paid just average wages but he was not so firm. He
(Being) understood that a worker would sometimes just not turn up -- would
         be off on a trip or having a little fun for a day or two. When his
         men did this he would take them back without saying too much.

(Part one)
Which of these men do you believe that it would be better to work for in
    most casts?
Which of these men would most other_____think it better to work for?

(Part two)
Which kind of boss do you believe that it is better to be in most cases?
Which kind of boss would most other_____think it better to be?

Interviews structured with longer stories (or narrative questionnaires). In addition to structuring interviews with descriptions of situations and anecdotes, it is possible to use longer stories either read aloud by experimenter or respondent reads to self as a narrative questionnaire. As the story unfolds one character will express his belief that such and such should be done, another will disagree and make an alternative proposal, and perhaps a third and fourth characters will offer still other proposals. Such a posing of alternative values or expressions of value continue throughout the story, with a number of sets having been presented in total (though not a great number, as there is not enough space in the story for them). Instructions invite the subject to state the alternative he favors (oral form) or to underline or make marginal note (questionnaire form). The natural plot for such a story is the founding of a new community or society, where decisions must be made on such things as child rearing, education, community organization (communal, individualistic, etc.), political arrangements, interpersonal relationships, etc.. Specifically, the plot can begin on an adventurous romantic note by having the group sail away to a remote island, or trek to a distant uninhabited mountain valley, or, perhaps most appropriate of all for our time, blast off in a spaceship bound for a distant galaxy. A good place to start in preparing oneself to write such a narrative is in the books on utopias, past and present. They make interesting reading in their own right (see Holloway, 1966). One that might be especially helpful is Aldous Huxley's *Island*. One "good" that he emphasized and built into his island utopia was the use of drugs to expand consciousness and enrich existence. He and *Island* bear their share of the blame for the drug addiction that swept the country; surely he hadn't the slightest notion as he wrote that his ideas -- so ideal -- would have such a tragic effect.

There is at least one such narrative in existence, prepared by Carter (1956) and titled "Koloman: A Modern Utopia." It poses alternatives pertaining to education, role of women, morality and its enforcement, race relations and equality, ownership of industry and wealth, religion, and form of government.

Interviews structured with hypothetical moral dilemmas. Brief descriptions of moral dilemmas have been used extensively in studies of moral development, especially by Piaget, Kohlberg and his associates, and Haan and her associates (see in Chapter 4 above for summaries of this research). The respondent, child or adult, either reads or hears the story and is then questioned about what should be done. Kohlberg's (1983) best known dilemma is the one involving Heinz, whose wife is fatally ill with cancer. A local druggist has a medicine that may save her but its price is too high for Heinz to afford. Heinz in desperation breaks into the drugstore. The question to the respondent is: should Heinz have done it?

Haan and her associates (1985) presented four moral dilemmas to each university-student respondent during each of three interviews (and also used dilemmas in group discussion sessions). Here are two:

PEACE CORPS CANDIDATE
Andrew is a recent college graduate who has been offered a job with the Peace Corps. He has always wanted to help less fortunate people in other countries, and he enjoys traveling. However, his mother has a severe chronic illness and must stay home most of the time. He is her only child.
(See above in Chapter 3, pages 85-89, for a group discussion of this dilemma.)
SCHOOL AND MIGRANT WORK
Juan is a 13-year-old in eighth grade in public school. He and his family are migrant laborers and each year his father takes him out of school for about four months to work in the fields. This is necessary for the family to have enough to live on. Juan is a very bright student and likes school. Until sixth grade he could keep up his work enough to pass each year. His schoolwork is getting more difficult and he failed last year. Juan's teacher is concerned about him and the cycle of poverty that passes from generation to generation. She has to decide whether or not to report his parents to the authorities and force them to leave him in school for the full year.

Interviews structured with questionnaires. Questionnaires are discussed below in their own right; here it may be mentioned that questionnaires may also be used as discussion material in interview. The typical question might be, "Why did you make that choice (mark that way on the questionnaire)?" Potentially, much can be learned about a person by discussing his various questionnaire responses.

Surely some questionnaires are better discussion vehicles than others though I know of no opinions on the matter. One questionnaire that is rich in discussion possibilities is the Morris (1956) *Ways to Live* questionnaire. The thirteen ways to live, by their very nature as sketches of ideal patterns of living, invite comment. Too, because each is of paragraph length, many persons will notice certain things in them and miss others and react positively (value) to some parts of the "way" but dislike others, and only by discussion can this selectivity of value be assessed. In addition, likely many a person conceives of the ideal way to live as combining elements from different "ways" and this can be brought out only by discussion. (See below for more on this questionnaire.)

Interview structured with pictures. Pictures may be used to elicit values. There is one well-known tell-a-story-about-the-picture technique in existence, the Thematic Apperception Test (TAT), which was devised to elicit stories involving certain sorts of needs or motives. With proper alternative instructions people can be induced to make-up at least simple stories involving values, or, as an even simpler method, value alternatives can be posed, using the picture figures as possessors of the given values, and the respondent asked to choose and comment. The task is much the same as in the above structured interview techniques, but the pictorial material may make it especially appealing with some respondents, children especially.

Structured group discussion or interview. In addition to individual interviews, it is sometimes desirable to interview two or more persons together and take advantage of the interaction. (There is no rule on size of the group but common sense suggests no more than about six persons.) Because discussion can get lively, usually it is desirable to record everything and analyze later.

Excerpts from von Mering's recordings of structured group discussions provide a good example (1961). Members of two Southwestern American communities, identified as Texas Homesteaders and Rimrock Mormon, were had to discuss the many alleged and observed difficulties Navaho Indians encounter in their struggles to adjust to the dominant white culture (p. 245). Discussions were led by an associate of the researcher and each group consisted of three persons, ten groups in all.

Discussion was prompted by a scripted ten-minute stimulus conversation and continued for about an hour (p. 244).

Below are selected excerpts from the group discussions, but not all from the same group of three discussants (the symbols in parentheses identify all of these discussants as Homesteaders (H); the following number identifies the discussion session number 1, 3, 4, or 5; and the final letter and number the individual subject 1, 9, etc.).

1) I don't care how we have the school for them, but I believe they must be given an opportunity to go to school -- if it can be -- no, it must be. It's a problem for every community out here. (H #1, S #1)

2) Anywhere they are, they should have the opportunity. On the reservation I don't think it should be different from any other place. Whether they are on the reservation or not. People oughtn't just think it can be done different, they must know what they have to do in this sort of thing. (H #1, S #9)

3) You know you're their neighbor and you know you wouldn't want to cheat them out of anything -- you just can't sit and let things happen to them when something's wrong -- you know is not right for anybody. (H #3, S #0)

4) . . . I believe it'd take time, but we ought to go and work on it, help 'em and I think it ought to be done . . . it must be done; we must want to care; I am sure of that. (H #4, S #11)

5) Well, now, you know there's no need to just keep them in misery -- you just don't do that to anyone. Nobody gets no good out of that, excepting if you don't give a damn. (H #4, S #10)

6) Well, I think I -- really they should -- they should -- we should -- you know -- respect them and work 'em when they can and help 'em when you can, just like any other person. This is something we must do; it's everybody's job in a way . . . . If a Navaho wants to do good, but it goes wrong you can't just turn your back on him. (H #4, S #11)

7) Maybe they might have -- fleas -- well, you know a lot of people are afraid of 'em because they're -- they may have lice or something like that. Well, that's an awful reason to just shove some fellow human being around instead of trying to help them. (H #5, S #14)

8) Doctrines I don't know anything about; if they go over there to worship God, I think that should be enough. I think the other man's church -- well, he can have his pick. He does what he thinks is right. He ought to be able to do it. Like anyone else. It don't do no good to be offended by what they think. (H #5, S #13) (p. 178)

These comments by the Texas Homesteaders are especially good examples of values, as the values themselves are so evident, and they are coming from ordinary folk, and uttered in the course of ordinary conversation (but, to be sure, contrived situations rather than completely ordinary). Note the frequency of the use of such value-key words as "must," "should," "right," and "ought." (Incidentally, this book contains many examples such as the above and in their concreteness should provide the student of values with interesting reading. But he might find himself mystified by many of the categories and examples. The key is to be found on pages 74-78, notably in his category "existential values." These are what psychologists generally call beliefs, cognitions, concepts or constructs, or, in von Mering's words "what has been called 'is' assumptions about the physical and social world." This is an entirely different conception of values from the one being employed here. In our understanding beliefs are involved in values (as the "is" component) and help determine values, but beliefs themselves are not conceptions of the desirable (values), and represent a different domain of human experiencing. Thorough inter-blendings of "is" and "ought," belief and value, give us "value orientations." Because the book contains so much exemplification of beliefs in action, it should be of special interest to the student of cognitive processes.)

A recent use of structured group discussion was that of Haan et al. (1985), the stimulus material in this case being hypothetical moral dilemmas.

The technique has much in its favor as it can come close to eliciting values as they are experienced and expressed in life, without too much experimental artificiality. But because the values are being expressed in a group discussion setting, there is the possibility of group-induced distortions. A timid person, for example, might express values in agreement with those being expressed by more forceful group members, but not really believe what he was saying. One would need to be sensitive to the dynamics of the given group and perhaps make allowances. There is also the possibility of a change in value position from one discussion session to the next, again influenced by the group dynamics of the moment. It is Haan's (1985) theoretical position that this, and more, is exactly what is happening in real-life value interactions between people, so is the very thing to be observing, rather than just set, pre-existing values.

Questionnaires

There are a number of value questionnaires in existence but as compared with the full domain of values they are very few and the researcher who wishes to use a questionnaire likely will need to prepare his own. (This has been the case, too, in doing attitude research, with most investigators having to prepare appropriate questionnaires. An apt example was the need of a biology student for a questionnaire to learn attitudes toward use of the wilderness -- keep it untouched, permit pack trips, open it with roads, etc.. Most existing attitude scales had to do with such things as prejudice and social distance and this person's need was utterly different.) Specific values assessment methods, primarily questionnaires, may be located in several places. Braithwaite and Scott (1990) have a chapter on value measures. Some will be found in *The Tenth Mental Measurement Yearbook* (1989) and its supplements and in *Tests in Print III* (1983), both published by the Buros Institute of Mental Measurements, the University of Nebraska Press, Lincoln, Nebraska. General reference sources for locating values techniques and research studies are the *Psychological Abstracts, Sociological Abstracts,* and *Social Sciences Index.*

Though not as flexible and sensitive as the interview, questionnaires have the virtue of permitting study of the values of a number of persons at one time. Fortunately, preparation of a value questionnaire can be quite simple, as each statement (question) can be treated as an entity unto itself with no need to add-up scores, and the meaning of each statement can be so obvious that common problems of questionnaire preparation, such as determining validity and interpreting scores, are avoided. As with attitude questionnaires, the simple Likert-type response scheme can be used (very important, important, neither (neutral), unimportant, very unimportant) and other value words substituted for "important."

Of published value questionnaires, the best-known by far is the Rokeach *Value Survey.* Let us look at it as an example of questionnaire construction, though keeping in mind that other constructors have used somewhat different methods.

Rokeach (1973) needed a broad range questionnaire, rather than one limited to a particular type of value. It has two distinct parts, each composed of eighteen terms. The eighteen adjectives of the part termed "instrumental values" came from a long list of 555 trait names prepared by Anderson (1968), who in turn got his list from a monumental lexicon of 18,000 trait names compiled by Allport and Odbert (1936). The 18 were chosen according to such criteria as: representing the most important values of American society, expressing positive rather than negative values, being self-descriptive, and permitting one readily to admit to having the trait without appearing to be immodest, vain, or boastful (and see pg. 29-30 for other criteria). Rokeach assumed that there might be five or six dozen additional valued traits, but felt that a list of more than 18 would become too difficult to rank in order of personal importance.

The following will exemplify the list of 18 traits (because it is copyrighted the entire questionnaire cannot be reproduced here; see Rokeach, 1973, for the whole of it):

> Ambitious (hard-working, aspiring)
> Broadminded (open-minded)
> Capable (competent, effective)

The other 18 concepts, termed "terminal values," were selected from a much longer list, assembled from various sources. Rejections were guided by such considerations as avoiding terms having much the same meaning or being too specific (general concepts were needed). Probably the main selection criterion was terms describing goals and social arrangements that Americans value, such as an exciting life or attaining salvation. Half of these 18 were selected to represent personal (intrapersonal) values -- examples: *peace of mind* and *salvation*, and the other half to represent social (interpersonal) values -- examples: *world peace* and *brotherhood* (p. 8).

The following will exemplify the list of 18 concepts:

A Comfortable Life (a prosperous life)
An Exciting Life (a stimulating, active life)
A World at Peace (free of war and conflict)

The format of this questionnaire is among the best in that each term is followed by a clarifying word or phrase, and in the commercially published form each term is printed on a gummed sticker and respondent can move them about like a deck of cards, ordering and reordering until satisfied (and even remove from the form and re-stick if he changes his mind). Many value concepts would require more than a single word for their description so would have to be longer than Rokeach's main terms, but brevity is desirable to the extent possible.

The *Value Survey* exemplifies what was said at the outset, that a questionnaire can be constructed by simply treating each concept as an entity unto itself with no need to add-up scores and deal with certain technical problems (discussed further below). However, because Rokeach preferred to have respondents *rank* the concepts from most valued to least, he made all 18 concepts relative to each other in the mind of the person, so they no longer could be treated as independent of each other. It is possible to *rate* each independently, which Rokeach also did experimentally, and of course to do both. Rokeach found the results from the two methods to correlate highly, so continued to prefer the ranking. Rokeach has compiled a remarkable amount of technical-statistical information on the *Value Survey* (much of it appearing in *The Nature of Human Values*, 1973), nearly all of it ranking results.

Leaving Rokeach and commenting on questionnaires generally, they vary in the length of their concepts, varying from single words to full paragraphs, though the latter are unusual and I know of only one, the Morris *Ways to Live* (1956) whose statements are so long. With such long statements there is always a question as to what is being perceived by the reader and producing the reaction, for inevitably they contain more than one concept. One reader might focus on one concept, one another, with perhaps few responding to the total way of life, as was Morris' intention. Several attempts have been made to find out either what in the wording was determining the judgement of the respondent (Kilby, 1963) or to identify discrepancy within the paragraph (Dempsey & Dukes, 1966). (The Kilby adaptation involved attempting to cut each of the Morris statements in half plus adding one additional way to live, resulting in a 28-item questionnaire.) These analytic efforts do not mean, though, that such long statements should be avoided. To the contrary, the main consideration should be doing full justice to the concept -- in this case description of whole complex personal and cultural ways to live -- and means must be found to assess the reactions. Building on Morris' excellent pioneering, surely other and perhaps better questionnaires of the type can be developed. This one has been especially useful in cross-national studies of values, where it was used with college students in eight major nations (Morris, 1956) and subsequently used in other nations.

The following are the instructions for rating the thirteen ways to live (they may also be ranked), followed by Way 1, again reproduced in full (and see pages 15-16, Ch. 1, for the key sentences of the other twelve Ways).

Instructions: Below are described thirteen ways to live which various persons at various times have advocated and followed.

Indicate by numbers which you are to write in the margin how much you yourself like or dislike each of them. Do them in order. Do not read ahead.

Remember that it is not a question of what kind of life you now lead, or the kind of life you think it prudent to live in our society, or the kind of life you think good for other persons, *but simply the kind of life you personally would like to live.*

Use the following scale of numbers, placing one of them in the margin alongside each of the ways to live:

7 I like it *very much*
6 I like it *quite a lot*
5 I like it *slightly*
4 I am *indifferent* to it
3 I dislike it *slightly*
2 I dislike it *quite a lot*
1 I dislike it *very much*

WAY 1: In this "design for living" the individual actively participates in the social life of his community, not to change it primarily, but to understand, appreciate, and preserve the best that man has attained. Excessive desires should be avoided and moderation sought. One wants the good things of life but in an orderly way. Life is to have clarity, balance, refinement, control. Vulgarity, great enthusiasm, irrational behavior, impatience, indulgence are to be avoided. Friendship is to be esteemed but not easy intimacy with many people. Life is to have discipline, intelligibility, good manners, predictability. Social changes are to be made slowly and carefully, so that what has been achieved in human culture is not lost. The individual should be active physically and socially, but not in a hectic or radical way. Restraint and intelligence should give order to an active life.

To the other extreme, a remarkably simple two-value questionnaire is the work-values questionnaire of Blood, which apparently has no formal name but which we might call here the *Work Ethic Questionnaire.* It was inspired by Weber's assumption that a special set of values, the Protestant ethic, came into being with the rise of Protestantism in Northern Europe, was brought to this country by the Puritans and others, and has continued strong into the present century. The questionnaire is composed of but eight statements, four of which are in agreement with the Protestant ethic ideals (pro-Protestant ethic) and the other four not in agreement (non-Protestant ethic). In one study in which it was used, a replication and extension of Blood's (1969) original study, Aldag and Brief (1975) found a number of correlations between work value scores and affective responses (general satisfaction, internal work motivation, supervisory satisfaction, etc.), perceived task dimensions (skill, variety, task significance, etc.), and perceived leader behavior for a group of 131 hourly employees of a manufacturing firm. It may be found in Blood (1969).

It is reproduced in entirety below:

1. When the workday is finished, a person should forget his job and enjoy himself.
2. Hard work makes a man a better person.
3. The principal purpose of a man's job is to provide him with the means of enjoying his free time.
4. Wasting time is as bad as wasting money.
5. Whenever possible a person should relax and accept life as it is, rather than always striving for unreachable goals.
6. A good indication of a man's worth is how well he does his job.
7. If all other things are equal, it is better to have a job with a lot of responsibility than one with little responsibility.
8. People who "do things the easy way" are the smart ones.

Open-ended questionnaire. Perhaps the simplest of questionnaires is the open-ended type, where a question is asked that requires a written response. The method is exemplified by questions from a questionnaire used by Gillespie and Allport (1955) in a cross-national study that focused on youth's outlook on the future. A variety of sorts of questions were asked, most not concerned with values (e.g., "Would you like to have more friends than you now have? Yes____ No ___"). The questions intended to elicit value reactions were the following:

a. What two things would you most like to have that you don't now have?
b. As a parent, what two specific lessons will you try hardest to teach your children?

c. What two things would you like your child most to have that you yourself did not have?

d. For what end would you be willing to make the greatest sacrifice of personal comfort, time, and money?

e. What are the two worst things that could conceivably happen to you during your lifetime?

f. If you should receive a large sum of money five years from now, what would you do with it?

g. What two things could you conceivably accomplish during your lifetime that you would be most proud of?

(Let me insert a personal observation here. I used most of the above questions in a questionnaire that was given to Indian university students. The question "What are the two worst things . . .?" often was left unanswered by women students, especially by the more mature ones. Inquiry as to why revealed that any answer given might be tempting fate to make it come true, and they did not want to take any chances. Obviously, evidence of a fatalistic outlook, but one by no means limited to the Indians. To most of us today "fate" has the simple meaning of "predetermined," but to Greeks and Romans the Fates were three goddesses who determined human destiny.)

In my own work in the international (cross-cultural) study of values I came to the conclusion that the ideal stimulus concept would consist of the main term, perhaps in bold print (e.g., WISDOM), followed by three or four clarifying descriptive phrases or synonyms (perhaps in parentheses). The synonyms help make clear the meaning of the main concept and they are a great help to translators when translating into another language (attaining equivalence in meaning is impossible but the phrases and synonyms go a long way in telling the translator which English meaning of the main term was intended, and they also help on the translated side, now in the other language, in clarifying that meaning). Contrarily, lists of single adjectives with no synonyms, as in adjective check lists, invite the respondent to supply his own meaning. Once in India I used "homely" in an adjective check-list and found to my surprise that many young Indians checked it as self-descriptive, whereas young Americans rarely did. The Indians were using the meaning derived from the British of "home-loving."

Exemplifying this format is the omnibus *Clarification of Values* questionnaire, which is presented in full in Appendix A, pgs 237-242.

Its composition was dictated by a desire to get into one questionnaire all the goals and values that I could think of, so has a variety of types in it. It was prepared out of a need for a questionnaire that could be used in college classes to exemplify types of values and help students clarify their own values, rather than any specific research need. Its "catch-all" nature will be evident and can be shortened (or lengthened) to suit any research or teaching need, and a variety of response schemes can be used. It may be reproduced without permission. Below are sample items taken from it:

1. RELIGIOUSNESS -- having a faith, worship and seeking Divine guidance, prayer or meditation, acts of faith.
2. SOLVING SOCIETY'S PROBLEMS -- attacking the problems that face us (disease, malnutrition, flood, etc.) and working toward their solution, making the world a fit place in which to live, mastering nature and putting it to work for us, willingness to work in science and industry.
3. LEADERSHIP -- influencing others, carrying out my ideas, winning positions of responsibility, perhaps being in charge of groups of people or organizations.
4. SENSORY PLEASURE -- seeking and enjoying sensory impressions, as from foods, sounds, sights, feelings, odors, colors, forms, movement, music, poetry, sunshine, swimming, dancing, perfumes, flower scents, etc..

Response methods vary. A simple one is to instruct the respondent to *check* those statements describing behavior that is right or important to him. A common response format is to provide a *rating scale* for each item, such as an adaptation of the familiar Likert five-position scale (strongly value, value,uncertain-neutral, disvalue, strongly disvalue). Another is to request a *ranking*, from highest value to lowest, as is done with the Rokeach questionnaire. Another is to *combine rating* and *ranking*, as by asking the subject first to rate all of the choices and then, using another set of instructions, ask him to rank all of the choices that had been given high rating. This is a way of forcing persons who have given high ratings to many of the choices to refine their judgements. If desired, subjects can be asked to limit this final list of highest values to five, ten, or however many choices are wished. This is one way of revealing importance or strength, but it is not an outright indication and other steps should be taken to ascertain importance. A well-known variation and refinement on the ranking procedure is to arrange for a *paired-comparison* of value choices, which is accomplished by presenting them two-by-two for choice between them, with every choice paired once with every other. This method can be used with only a limited number of items, as the pairing in effect multiplies the number of choices and the whole can become unduly long, hence it is a logical method to use after the list has been reduced by some other method. Though paired-comparison and ranking basically are the same thing, the activity of comparing each single value concept with every other in distinct pairs is a much more refined method and an excellent one to use with value choices.

The *semantic differential method*, devised by Osgood (1959) is a response method that should be mentioned, lest it be overlooked. It involves asking respondents to react to the value concepts by means of lists of bipolar adjectives, such as: important-unimportant, good-bad, fast-slow, interesting-uninteresting, useful-useless. The pairs are arranged across the page with spaces between to allow respondent to indicate degree of feeling, as is shown in the example at end of this section.

This technique, or a variant, is the logical extension of our ordinary response methods of eliciting a judgement of importance or value, for often there is more to the person's value than just the basic commitment. For sure there will be beliefs and images -- the value's cognitive elements -- and often there will attendant feelings that shade off into the inexpressible. It adds to our understanding if we can learn some of these addition qualities of people's values. To convey an idea of the potential, imagine using a list of the adjective pairs to elicit a reaction to an architectural work or a painting. We might get from a viewer a reaction toward the architectural work that it is light, traditional, soft, pleasant, feminine, beautiful, serene, spacious, impractical, strong, and simple. Some of these will be qualities that the person might not think of if asked to describe the structure and he might not even be aware that he had such subjective meanings. Of course value concepts are not concrete objects like buildings and paintings so might not be expected to evoke such an array of feelings, but something will be there and its exploration should be fascinating.

Osgood was not pointed in the direction of study of individuals and their values. Rather, he and his associates were interested in the general subject of denotative (actual, literal) and connotative (surplus, subjective) meanings of words and objects. From their research, using long lists of adjective pairs as the response medium, they concluded that the main connotative reaction to anything could be described as primarily evaluative (true, good, etc.), and secondarily as potent (strong, powerful, etc.) and active (active, quick, etc.).

In one thorough study Osgood, Ware, and Morris (1961) used Morris' thirteen *Ways to Live* as the stimulus concepts and used 26 adjective pairs for reacting to them, using college students as subjects, and a summary of the findings will give an impression of how the technique was used. The 26 adjectives were selected to represent the three clusterings of the adjectives (factors) -- "evaluation," "potency," "activity," plus four minor ones: "stability," "receptivity," "novelty," and "tautness." But here, when used to react solely to value propositions, these factors dissolved and three new ones emerged, named "successfulness," "predictability," and "kindness." Successfulness is the old evaluation factor (timely, successful, true, good, positive, wise, versus their opposites), plus elements of potency (strong, powerful vs. opposites), plus elements of activity (active, quick vs. opposites), and elements of receptivity (savory, interesting, colorful vs. opposites). The predictability factor is made up mainly of predictable, stable, calm, colorless, slow, old, straight, wise vs. opposites. The kindness factor is made up mainly of kind, soft, warm, rounded, beautiful, and feminine vs. opposites. This study definitely shows that when value concepts are used as the stimulus material respondents tend to use many more adjectives in an evaluative way; it also shows that the clustering or factors change depending upon the concept being judged.

Though lists of pairs of adjectives are to be found in the literature (see especially Osgood et al., 1957, p. 53-55, and Snider and Osgood, 1968), the values researcher will need to assemble his own and the above factors will be of little help (unless he wishes to pursue factor-analytic inquiry). Because of possible pitfalls, it is well to experiment with lists in advance of doing studies and ask trial subjects to give feedback.

A usual arrangement is to use sets of five to ten pairs of adjectives, with half or more evaluative and the rest clearly non-evaluative, with the latter interspersed on the page with the evaluatives (see example below). This is to prevent response sets, the tendency to fall into a pattern of ranking all the evaluatives the same. Subjects will tend to mark even the non-evaluatives as evaluatives; for example, strong-weak, active-passive, and quick-slow readily get turned into evaluatives with strong, active, and quick becoming synonymous with good. If one does succeed in finding pairs that defy conversion, e.g., warm-cool, soft-hard, new-old, then some respondents will be mystified and ask how the concept (e.g., *friendship and affection*) can be either warm or cool, soft or hard?

Should the reader wish to experiment with using adjective pairs to uncover the sorts of images and feelings mentioned above in connection with art and architecture try to think of *descriptive* pairs that reflect nuances of feeling and combine a number of these with just a few evaluative pairs, and in the instructions make clear the purpose of the questionnaire. Suggestive possibilities are: risky-safe, growth promoting-growth inhibiting, costly-inexpensive, simple-complex, serene-troubled, calm-ruffled, safe-dangerous, adventurous-cautious, freeing-restraining, active-passive, stable-unstable, colorful-neutral, traditional-modern, feminine-masculine, soft-hard, slow-fast, vigorous-restrained, changing-unchanging, varied-uniform.

As with other response methods, the problem of assessing strength and commitment arises here as well. As the example below indicates, there is space on the seven-position scale for a person to indicate *very* important, good, valuable, etc., but it would be desirable to see confirming evidence before assuming that strength and commitment was being measured in most subjects. I have tried using special instructions to try to induce a critical state of mind and recommend that others try doing the same. (Example: "Please give special significance to *important-unimportant*. Be guided by this question: How *personally* important or vital in my life today is this way to live? *Our interest here is in locating those ways that are really important to you, that involve the heart or deep convictions."*)

The following will exemplify a possible semantic differential answer form. This one has been marked to show how it might look when completed. Subject is provided with one set of adjectives for each value concept to be judged.

A subject responded to the concept "A life of adventure is the best way to live," by filling out the set of adjectives as follows:

Way 1	Very	Quite	Slightly	Neutral	Slightly	Quite	Very	
Interesting		X						Uninteresting
Slow							X	Fast
Unimportant					X			Important
New				X				Old
Good		X						Bad
Passive							X	Active
Worthless					X			Valuable
Unusual	X							Usual
Colorless						X		Colorful
Like		X						Dislike

Public Opinion Polling

Though questionnaires have an extensive use in school settings, they have a limited usefulness elsewhere because some people cannot read well enough to understand them or are simply unwilling to make the effort, or cannot take the time from work or whatever to complete them. This has led to the use of very brief printed or oral questionnaires and specifically to the development of the public opinion polling interview (still another type of interview).

A good example of a brief printed questionnaire is the ten-item goals questionnaire of Centers (1948) which he used in his research on factory workers and managers. Each brief statement was printed on a card, and the entire deck would be handed to the workman with instructions that he should sort through the deck, picking the statements that expressed his feelings (in this particular study they were to make first, second, and third choice, but all could be ranked in importance). It was appropriate to the literacy levels of the workers and could be completed in a few minutes with little interference with work activities. It is reproduced below, but note that the identifying terms "Leadership," "Esteem," etc. did not appear on the cards:

1. Leadership - A job where you could be a leader.
2. Interesting experience - A very interesting job.
3. Esteem - A job where you would be looked upon very highly by your fellowmen.
4. Power - A job where you could be boss.
5. Security - A job which you were absolutely sure of keeping.
6. Self-Expression - A job where you could express your feelings, ideas, talent, or skill.
7. Profit - A very highly paid job.
8. Fame - A job where you could make a name for yourself, or become famous.
9. Social Service - A job where you could help other people.
10. Independence - A job where you could work more or less on your own.

Though we are not concerned here with results of its use, it might be mentioned that the manual workers chose both *independence* and *security* with equal frequency while managerial, professional, and other white-collar workers chose *self-expression* above all others.

(Needing a brief questionnaire for demonstration purposes and for my own research, I prepared an extension of the Centers questionnaire, titled *Survey of Personal Goals*, using longer more descriptive statements and increased the number to 15. It was used in a cross-national study (Kilby, 1965) and used regularly in my classes to exemplify goals and values.)

Following an early embarrassing error of prediction of the outcome of a presidential election (1936), because the survey had been done by telephone, the public-opinion polling organizations employed door-to-door interviews and fairly satisfactory sampling techniques. Later, when nearly every household had a telephone, they went back to telephone interviews and, judging from my own experience in being called and interviewed, quite a number of questions are asked and typically on a variety of topics (one may wonder as to how many people have trouble with the questions or grow tired or irritated).

Since opinion polling has been going on for many years, there now exists an extensive database of answers on a variety of topics, collected by the various polling organizations. For many topics it is possible to compare recent replies with earlier ones and thus chart recent social history. Most of the database consists of replies to specific questions so falls in the domain of opinion or attitude, but some has enough generality to be regarded as value expression or permits an inference of values. A good example is the replies to a series of questions on pollution of lakes and rivers, contaminated drinking water, disposal of hazardous wastes, and air pollution. By strikingly high percentages of 75% or higher the American public was in favor of all measures to assure clean air and water, stop acid rain and clean up hazardous wastes, and these attitudes were held in spite of the qualification in the question that jobs might be lost if the clean-up measures were carried out. One poll in the late 1980s found that 85% wanted the Clean Air Act to be made even stricter. Unquestionably, one or more fundamental values are involved here, for certain the near-universal one of concern for health, life, and well-being and perhaps others pertaining to the well-being of the environment in its own right or even its aesthetic aspect.

For the value researcher, an opinion survey is a good way to assess values on a broad scale, such as to learn values held by large portions of the American populace, but as we mention below under "Sampling" such surveys are costly and few behavioral scientists are able to arrange it. One who did was Rokeach, who had his *Value Survey* given to a national sample in 1968 (Rokeach 1973, Ch. 3-5).

Incidentally, there is also need for a values database, comparable to that for attitudes. The polling organizations could supply part of it, and in addition a fairly simple way to accumulate it would be for researchers to deposit copies of information from their studies -- value concepts studied, findings, subjects, etc. -- in a central clearinghouse. A catalog of value concepts could be assembled and drawn upon by researchers for their studies. Foreign investigators should also be drawn in and invited to deposit their data and use the catalog and make additions to it reflective of their own cultures. It is late to be assembling world-wide information on values as "world culture" (to use an apt term) has spread so widely as to replace or dilute many indigenous values around the world -- a loss comparable to the loss of plant and animal varieties around the world. But "better late than never."

Observation

Together with the interview, this is one of anthropology's traditional methods. The anthropologist might go to some distant place, perhaps a village in New Guinea or a town in China, take up residence, and make observations of the people as they carried on their daily lives (taking detailed notes), interviewing as language skills permitted, and from all this make inferences as to the people's beliefs and values. This manner of free observation is subject to certain errors, the main one being that different observers attend to different things and may interpret in quite different ways, but a corrective is for two or more observers to visit the same place and observe independently. The one notable strength of observation is that actual behavior can be observed, hence values observed that are actually lived rather than just professed. But the notable weakness is that observation alone, without inquiry, may leave the observer uncertain as to why the behavior occurred -- hence uncertain as to the value being expressed.

Apart from its use in anthropological field work, observation can be used wherever there is some control over those being observed, as in military settings, prisons and reformatories, school settings, and certain work settings. Hartshorne and May (1928), in one of the earliest moral values studies, contrived to test school children's honesty by placing them in situations where dishonesty was possible and the child did not know his behavior was being observed.

Observation in research studies today often takes the form of film or videotape recordings. Before development of videotape technology motion picture film records were made and later analyzed. Videotape technology is much more flexible and less costly, so potentially may be used in many settings. As a specific example, Haan and her associates (1985) videotaped all of the group sessions, where four-year-olds, adolescents, and university students played moral games and discussed moral dilemmas, and later analyzed them (all participants were aware of the filming and invited to view the videotapes). Videotaping with children is especially useful because they do so much more "doing" than speaking in their interactions.

Essays

Respondents might be asked to write some manner of report on their values. This technique would be appropriate only for educated persons, and is best combined with other techniques that would help get the person ready to think and write on this elusive subject. Certainly we should not expect an unprepared person to sit down and write comprehensively of his values. We would be doing well to get from him only a few of the moral values. Preparation could take the form of group discussions (as in a college course), reading of case report material on values of others, taking of values questionnaires, being interviewed on values, and the like. Writing the essay should be an excellent final step in a sequence of several of the above techniques and give the person an opportunity to make a personal statement in depth about his unique pattern of values. Even with good preparation, it still might be desirable to structure the task somewhat, as by suggesting pertinent classes of values.

Gillespie and Allport (1955) made interesting use of the essay technique in their above-mentioned research on youth's outlook on the future. Since their concern was with the outlook on the future of these young people, it seemed appropriate to have their respondents in the different countries write an autobiography on "From now to 2000 A.D." A page of instructions were supplied (p. 41) explaining that respondents were to look ahead over the years of their lives until the end of the century and write on their expectations, plans, and aspirations. This structuring calls for thought on more than just values, but does provide an excellent opportunity for expression of certain values, especially those of the goals/ways to live type.

Content Analysis

This involves analysis of written material for values. Psychologists do not make much use of content analysis since their primary interest is in the behavior of the living, but historians, biographers and other who must make use of written material out of the past for their research use it regularly.

One psychologist who did use it was Rokeach (1973, 1979(a), p. 194). He was led by his *Value Survey* studies to hypothesize that there is some minimum number of values that suffice to describe fundamental differences in major political ideologies, and further analysis led him to propose just two -- *freedom* and *equality*. The question then confronting him was how to test the theory empirically, for use of members of existing political parties as subjects might produce equivocal results because the "platforms" of parties are composed of a variety of ideologies and contemporary expediences. So he decided to make the test by first identifying examples of the major ideologies in the form of documents written by Lenin, Hitler, Barry Goldwater, and several widely-known socialists. Then by the method of content analysis it was ascertained how often the values of *freedom* and *equality* were advocated in these writings, in comparison with their advocacy of all other values. The results of this study were reported above in Chapter 3 so need not be repeated here. It might be added though that those doing the content analysis had never heard of the two-value model and thus had no idea of the specific hypotheses being tested, so had no possibly-biasing preconceptions. Later, another content analysis was done on the same material by other readers, as a check on the reliability of the original, and produced good agreement. A desirable follow-up.

Other examples may be mentioned. In Chapter 4 we reported the DeCharms and Moeller (1962) and Lanham (1979) content analyses for value content of school books used in American and Japanese schools.

The analysis by Stewart and Healy (1986) of biographical and autobiographical material on the life of Vera Brittain, reviewed at end of Chapter 4, gives us a good example of content analysis of material on specific persons. Along the same line, it is usual when doing full personality studies of the sort that were done over a space of years at the Harvard Psychological Clinic (see Murray, 1938) and by R. W. White in *Lives in Progress* (1975) to solicit written material and analyze for attitudes and values.

R.K. White (1950) did content analyses of a somewhat different sort, employing material as found in dictionaries, autobiographies, interview records, children's stories and advertisements. His search was for "self-evident" values; that is, for the things that the people of the given culture automatically assume to be desirable. For example, if at the end of a play the hero and heroine are joined and the villain driven off, what is being valued? Perhaps bravery and faithfulness, and disvalued, treachery and cowardice. Or, in an advertisement a well-dressed couple are standing beside a new automobile with a fine house in the background. Again, what is being valued, or which values appealed to? Perhaps wealth, comfort, and prestige. White's analysis of American material uncovered a great many such self-evident values, but these could be grouped into 50 general values, yielding values such as health, achievement, beauty, ownership, modesty, and tolerance. Such analyses begin to give us a picture of the whole range of values of a nation or society, though they do not tell us how widely held in the society the given value is. Direct studies of individuals and groups are needed for this.

It will be evident from these several examples that content analysis is another useful method of studying values.

Combinations of Methods

It is of course possible to use a combination of methods in a single study. We have already mentioned that interviews and questionnaires can be combined to good advantage, the questionnaire supplying broad survey-type information on many respondents and interview providing in-depth information on a fraction of the larger group. Observation provides valuable additions to the other two.

Though studies combining methods are not often seen in the literature, one fine example is available. In preceding chapters the nature and results of the study by Haan, Aerts, and Cooper (1985) were presented; now the methods may be described. It was a study of the development and nature of moral values. For the main part of the study friendship groups of university students were recruited -- 15 groups in all, composed of eight students each, half of each sex.

Each student was interviewed individually at outset of the study and asked to react to four hypothetical moral dilemmas, as well as describe self and other members of the group. Later he/she joined the group in a series of five once-a-week group experiences lasting from 2 1/2 to 3 hours. Ten of the 15 groups played moral games that threw them in direct moral conflict with each other. And to provide contrast, the remaining five groups discussed hypothetical moral dilemmas for five sessions.

When the five group sessions were completed, each student was again interviewed individually and again responded to four moral dilemmas, and described his friends. Three to four months later each was again interviewed and again responded to hypothetical moral dilemmas. The purpose the second and third interviews was to record any increase in moral development as a result of the experiences, though it was recognized that no great amount of change could be expected in that short time period.

The group sessions were observed (one-way vision windows) and videotaped. In addition, two trained observers independently described the group activity (group dynamics) that occurred within each group at each session (15 group x 5 sessions) using the Q-sort technique. Besides all these more formal sources of information, the students themselves were asked to react to and evaluate the events of each session.

It will be evident that this was an entirely different type of study from those that most of us do, where we give a questionnaire or two to learn the values of a group or investigate some question. These researchers mention the difficulty of doing research on real moral behavior -- yet that is exactly what we need to understand better. Most moral problems that psychologists have devised for study in the laboratory have been trivial and the one exception, Milgram's (1974) study involving the administration of electric shocks (which weren't actually given), was widely criticized for its causing the subjects moral distress. So laboratory study of morality seems to be caught between two poles: if it is ethically conducted the moral problems are likely to be bland and artificial; if the problems are vivid and real the experimenter is likely to be unethical. In this study an attempt was made to involve the students in real moral interactions but a variety of things were done to confine it to the group sessions themselves. Most determinative were the moral games. Games were chosen as the best activity because people readily involve themselves in games and become serious, as happened here, yet at end of the game it is possible for them to disengage themselves and perceive it as "just a game." This last was facilitated at end of each session by the staff leader asking the group to discuss and evaluate the session's activity -- an excellent way to induce detachment in someone who had become thoroughly ego-involved. Where necessary the staff leader could lighten the atmosphere with a touch of humor, divert attention to other things and divert irritation to the project. Their being friendship groups also was invaluable for they could interact with each other as familiars, rather than strangers, and in argument continue to perceive each other with goodwill and at end fall back on feelings of friendship. Another important feature was the researcher's complete openness with the students. They were told at outset the purpose of the study and why friendship groups were needed, the video-cameras and one-way windows shown and purpose explained and invited to come on a later date, with parents if desired, and see reruns, in the individual interviews they were invited to comment on anything, and, as mentioned, they were asked to discuss what had happened at end of each session.

So the ethical requirement of the research appear to have been met while being able to study near-real moral behavior (no experimental study of values is completely real -- the fact of its being an experiment makes it unreal).

General Considerations in Value Assessment

Strength or Depth of Commitment and Its Nature

Surely the most important thing to try to learn when studying people's values is the strength or depth of conviction of any value held; but strength will differ depending upon the type of value. On a moral values questionnaire a person might give *honesty* a high rating or ranking but we may be left uncertain as to what it means. Is the person merely saying in an impersonal way that it is good to be honest, or is he saying with some feeling, "It is unthinkable for me to be other than honest!" There is a world of difference between the two expressions of importance. If possible, we must discover ways of learning depth.

Honesty belongs to the group of moral values and here depth of commitment is especially important for these are nothing if not strongly held. But each type of value needs to be examined with two questions in mind: (a) what is the nature of the valuing (belief, conviction)? and (b) what is the nature of strong acceptance? The moral values may be contrasted with the category "valued traits of others," here focusing on the specific traits of *friendly* and *affectionate*. Because this is behavior shown by others, rather than one's own, there is no possibility of a "with all my heart" personal commitment to behave the given way, no possibility of guilt at shortcomings. So strength of commitment or belief or conviction here has to have a detached, impersonal quality (possibly it might be assessed with a questionnaire item which asked which of the below list of traits in others (e.g., friendliness) would you consider essential in a a) neighbor, b) work associate, c) good friend, d) husband or wife.) Valued structurings of society (specific examples: *a world at peace* and *equality for all*), another class of value, involves still a different sort of favorable feeling-image, perhaps more impersonal or detached than the above traits of others and strength of commitment indicated in a different way (conceivably by asking what you would be willing to do in support -- a) sign a petition, b) give $100, c) join a protest organization, d) risk injury or life). So for each type of value the nature of strength or importance should be asked and the means of learning it be decided.

Strength should also be considered relative to the two broad types of values, evaluative and worth, for the evaluative have the connotation of good-bad, right-wrong, should-should not, so often will have an all-or-none quality -- either you value or you don't, with few degrees of variation in strength possible (but this needs empirical exploration). The worth values appear to be largely free of the all-or-none quality so do permit degrees of experienced worth or importance.

There is no standard procedure for determining personal importance. Likely sensitive interviewing is most effective, using some such questions as "If you had to choose one life goal which would it be?" "How much of a sacrifice would you be willing to make?" "Is there anything you would be willing to die for?" It is especially difficult to determine importance with questionnaires because it is hard to find response schemes that force the respondent to express depth of commitment (though likely more can be done than has been done heretofore). A standard response format is the one: very important/important/neither-neutral/unimportant/ very unimportant (other terms may be substituted for "important") but this "very important" may not reveal real degree of importance; for one person it is really very important, for another just "a good idea."

Another standard response format is *ranking* the list of value concepts, as is done with the Rokeach *Value Survey*, and this, too, poses difficult problems of interpretation. Does the value that is ranked at the head of the list represent the person's deepest, strongest value, or is it merely felt to be the most important in the list of eighteen values, none of which are personally very important? And what about a person's subjective spacing of the values, perhaps regarding his top two as clearly most important and the next six as lower and equal to each other -- the method has no way of revealing this. One is aware of this problem of interpretation of significance especially when analyzing Rokeach's research findings because he studied such socially significant topics that it became important to know exactly where his respondents stood, what their rankings meant.

A good example of a technique that has promise with respect to some types of values is the *self-anchoring scale*, devised by Cantril (1965; Kilpatrick and Cantril, 1960). He used it for the specific purpose of eliciting people's opinions as to best and worst possible lives and where they are now, and would have to be adapted to other value uses. It is actually an eleven-position rating scale (most, like the above "important" scale, use only five positions), but the manner of presenting it on the page or card converts it into another thing. It is presented vertically in the form of a ladder, with an actual ladder diagram with ten rungs printed on the page (See Appendix B for an example). The person is asked to decide where he stands on the ladder. Cantril and his associates first asked people of various countries "What really matters in your own life, what are your wishes and hopes for the future?" and thus learned each person's conception of the best possible life for him. Then each was asked an opposite question about fears and worries, to establish his conception of the worst possible life. Then the person is asked to assume that the top of the ladder represents the best possible life for him and the bottom the worst possible, and he is now to judge where he stands on the ladder, then where he was five years ago, and finally where he will be five years from now. Nearly everyone anywhere in the world is familiar with the concept of a ladder, so readily adapts to the task. As used in this way, following establishment of the person's best and worst possible life, it becomes an "absolute" scale with no need to relate the responses of the given person to those of others (norms) in order to interpret his response. Cantril referred to the specific hopes and aspirations elicited as "values." Most pertained to material well-being, but the researchers found that they had to use a total of 45 categories to classify all the goals. Here are a few goals pertaining to personal characteristics: emotional stability and maturity, self-development or improvement, acceptance by others, achieve a sense of my own personal worth, resolution of one's own religious, spiritual, or ethical problems.

In most places in the world this has to be used as an interview technique because the people cannot be expected to read and write well enough to complete it by themselves, but it should be possible to employ it elsewhere as a write-in (write-on) questionnaire and administer it to groups of people. (Incidentally, the interview technique of learning respondents best and worst possible life is a way of eliciting important values, apart from use of the ladder.)

Adaptation of the ladder for other value assessments would have to take the form of substitutions for the "best possible life" at the top and "worst possible life" at the bottom. The substitute question might be, "What is the most important thing in life for you -- it might be staying alive and healthy, or being a good husband or wife, or being respected by everyone (etc.)? "What is most precious to you?" As he/she replies, interviewer will say, "We will write this in at the top of the ladder." "Now think of what you would most dislike in life -- perhaps losing your life or health, losing family, being hated by friends, sent to prison (etc.)?" "What would you most hate to have happen?" "We will write this at the bottom." "Now I am going to mention a list of things and I want you to tell me where on your ladder of importance you would put them." At this point interviewer would mention the list one by one, such as world peace, friendship, honesty, faithfulness. (I prepared such an instruction sheet, with ladder diagram, and separate response form, and used it with a group of upper-division students in one of my classes to elicit reaction to the above-mentioned *Clarification of Values* questionnaire. It may be of some use to others and is reproduced in Appendix B, pg 243.)

I have had good reason to be concerned about assessment of strength because it has been a constant source of doubt and frustration to me. Always following my giving values questionnaires to a group there has been the gnawing worry that I have not elicited real values. To be sure, the questionnaire elicited plenty of responses of strong value, but I could not trust the responses. It became a question of the validity of the results -- did they indicate what they seemed to indicate? In some cases I had fairly obvious reason to be doubtful. My subjects have all been college students and in spite of all my emphasis in the printed instructions on giving strong ratings only to those named values that were felt to be personally very important, the students tended to react positively to many of the value choices, often marking the strongest category. A few moved through the questionnaire so rapidly that there was no time for the person to stop and reflect about a given choice, so I could not help suspecting an absence of real involvement. Again, in India, I found myself fearing that students there were being carried away by youthful idealism and not being really critical. (In retrospect, I realize that I should have been interviewing samples of the students in depth in order to test my doubts.)

This leads to the observation that perhaps some persons, such as immature college students, have never believed anything strongly, never felt a commitment to anything, so are using the nearest they ever get to it -- a sort of "yeah, that's a good idea" -- for the real thing. Undoubtedly many have never been led to think about values and never had the opportunity to clarify own convictions and commitments, so are just giving spur-of-the-moment reactions to what obviously appear to be good ways to live.

Technically, the instrument, the questionnaire, is at fault in its inability to reveal this lack of depth in the person, but given the limitations of questionnaires it may be impossible and may require supplemental procedures. I have tried several variations in the wording of the response categories in an effort to solve the problem, but with little success. A good example, and one that seemed so promising when first conceived, was the wording, "Mark the first column [of the answer form], headed "This is me!", if it is a way to live that allows you to say emphatically, "Yes, this is me!" That is, this is a way to live that you consider to be very important, either because it is a strong personal goal or a desirable way of living for everyone." In spite of this effort to induce a highly selective personal reaction, when used with upper-division students in my classes many marked a considerable number of the values as "This is me!" Specifically, in a random set of fifty answer forms, an average of 25 values out of 70 possible on the *Clarification of Values* questionnaire were marked "This is me!" (smallest number chosen was 9 and six persons chose more than 40). Not a very selective reaction! (Incidentally, all were asked to *rank* their strongest fifteen, from most important to least, as means of inducing some sense of relative importance.)

Though a number of students in another class showed the same lack of maturity and discrimination when the above self-anchoring "ladder" response method was used with the same questionnaire, I tend to feel that it is somewhat more sensitive than other methods tried and more revealing of the person's degree of value maturity (but this would need to be verified with systematic testing). In part, it may be a result of having the person identify his "most important thing in all the world" and use it as a concrete standard of comparison when judging the statements of the questionnaire; in part, the large number of rating categories -- eleven -- may produce more "fine-tuning" of response, especially in deciding which of the four positive ladder ratings to assign -- extremely important (9), very (8), quite (7), or slightly (6). Another virtue is that impressions of value maturity emerge as one reads through a number of the answer forms. In the nature of the instructions, one would expect few or none of the value statements to receive the rating of "10" ("most important thing in all the world" -- I had intended that none be so rated), so any number of 10s above, say, four or five suggests degrees of immaturity (or misinterpretation of instructions). And even where few 10s are assigned, the specific choices are revealing: 10s given to such statements as those describing security and safety, marriage and home life, healthful living and health, and avoidance of bodily harm have an obvious reasonableness as "most important." But if all the 10s have been assigned to some such statements as those describing solving society's problems, religiousness, adapting to nature, self-love, wisdom, and world peace, there would be reason to suspect that these are conventional or "borrowed" values rather than personally thought-out. All are "noble" choices, but as a group belong more properly somewhere below "10" on the ladder. To give specific results for this response method, forty-two students were had to take the 70-statement *Clarification of Values* questionnaire and respond using the "ladder." Nine assigned no 10s at all and twenty-three assigned no more than four 10s. Upward from four, one or two persons assigned five, six, seven, etc. up to sixteen, with five persons assigning beyond sixteen (all of these last five probably misunderstood or were grossly careless).

Learning Real Values

Closely related in importance to strength is the need to learn the real values of the person. This is an obvious enough need but a variety of things can interfere.

Possibly the most obvious of these interferences is the social desirability or undesirability of the given value. All of the positive forms of the moral values (e.g. honesty), the ideal self-traits (e.g. friendly), and many other values are perceived as desirable and lead many of us to profess them even if only weakly held or not at all. Similarly, all the negative moral values (disvaluing of dishonesty), opposites of the ideal-self traits (unfriendly), and many other negatives or opposites are perceived as undesirable and lead us to deny them, whatever one's actual attitude and behavior.

A person may be asked his values but he may never have had to put a value into words before, so though it is there it is not explicit and he needs time and reflection for its emergence. The inquiry into values may also be a value clarifying experience.

If a technique is used that has predetermined wording and categories, as is usually the case with questionnaires, it is possible that none of the statements really fit the person and he has no way to express real values. Along the same line, our questionnaires may be too wordy or difficult to comprehend, too tiring or boring, etc., and in consequence we lose the person, lose his interest and involvement and real feelings, even though he may complete the questionnaire.

If he is forced to participate he may be quite disinterested and give superficial answers. Or he may feel that his values are no snooping behavioral scientist's business and again distorts in some way. Finally, if he has reason to suspect that the knowledge will be used to his disadvantage then he may not cooperate fully.

The antidotes to most these are so obvious as to need no comment but the social desirability effect is difficult indeed to counteract and no specific antidote can be suggested. It is much more of a problem when using questionnaires than when interviewing; sensitive interviewing should be quite penetrating and effective.

Norms

Norms are tables of figures that permit comparison of a single person's or a group's value questionnaire results with those of other identified groups. Thus, one might want to know how a group of delinquents answered a moral values questionnaire as compared with a population of normal teenagers. The investigator may accumulate his own norms if he wishes or must, but if they already exist for the given questionnaire then there is an obvious saving of effort to use them.

Norms may not be needed; the results of one's own study may require no comparison with others.

If norms do exist, they should be relevant. (A PhD student in India wrote asking for a copy of the Rokeach *Value Survey* together with norms, explaining that she intended to use it in a study of delinquent boys there. I replied that American norms would be of little value, that she should develop norms on Indian teenage boys for the comparison.)

Sampling

If the investigator intends to generalize about some group (population), say, all students in a given university, all residents of Santa Clara County, all residents of Oregon, all adult Americans, etc., then a sampling design should be used, since it is impossible to reach everyone in any of these groups yet one will want to correctly represent the values of all. It is a remarkable fact that if a sample of the total is asked, assuming they are reasonably representative of the total, then their views (their percentages) will correctly represent the views of all of the population in question. The national public opinion polling organizations have found that a sample of about 1500 persons will correctly represent the opinions of the entire nation of hundreds of millions with but a small degree of error.

Sampling is especially important to the values researcher because often the very purpose of his research is to describe the values of some identified group but cannot reach all.

But it is a major undertaking to do a formal sampling of even a single university or a small city, and most researchers lack the financial resources and organizational structure to do it. One almost has to have a sizeable research grant and the services of a professional polling organization. Instead, of necessity, investigators take what is readily available in the way of a sample and just generalize from the findings in an informal way. So instead of being able to state outrightly that the students of Penn University hold such-and-such values (as shown by a systematic sampling), the investigator may state that 250 students at Penn were studied and such-and-such values were found. The investigator may unwittingly generalize beyond the 250 studied, perhaps suggesting that the findings apply to all Penn students, or even all university students. Too, the reader of the study may unwittingly do the same, since all of us have some tendency to generalize. The most used and over-used study groups are college students, especially college freshmen enrolled in introductory psychology courses, as these are readily available and often required to serve as subjects in psychologists' research (a questionable practice on several counts).

Granted that we must use what is available, a few things can be done to improve the situation. A first is to avoid generalizing at all and simply describe one's study outcome. Likely it will be interesting in its own right (am reminded of the study by Haan and associates on fifteen friendship groups of university students -- a very informative study with no generalizing beyond the study groups). Another is to select smaller, more-specific groups for study, such as business-school graduates rather than all graduates, 15-year-old teenagers, middle-aged women, black welfare mothers as compared with white, etc.. Another is to coordinate ones own research with that of others, either by self duplicating (replicating) other's studies, or requesting others to repeat your study elsewhere, in either case achieving a degree of generality of sampling. This also can be extended internationally by asking foreign colleagues to repeat one's study in their countries, as those comparisons often are useful. A last fairly obvious action is to informally sample some target group and offer whatever generalization seems warranted. Of course the problem with informal sampling of groups, and generalizing, is that we never can be sure that our findings correctly represent the values of the whole group. Another sampling may produce different results.

Stability or Reliability

How stable are the person's values?

"Reliability" is the psychologist's term for forms of stability or consistency.

Three forms of reliability are recognized. The first is the actual stability or consistency of the disposition in the person. The second is the consistency of the assessment method being used. The third is the correctness or consistency of the sampling, for if one sampling produces one set of results and another sampling of the same population produces a different set, we are left uncertain as to the actual values of the full population. The above topic on sampling mentioned this last form.

Of all psychological dispositions, values are among the most stable. But it is unreasonable to expect perfect consistency in any disposition because humans, as living systems, vary in mood, frame of reference, motivation, tiredness-freshness, as well as in physical well-being and metabolic function. Also, stability will be affected by extent to which the value has been clarified, its strength, and whether it is a part of the self-image. If low in clarification, relatively weak, and hardly a part of the self-image there will be some instability.

Turning to the second form of reliability, probably most value assessment devices do have a satisfactory degree of reliability but if the above person-unreliability is not separated from method-unreliability, as has often been the case in the past, the method gets blamed for all of it. (Personality questionnaires are said to be notoriously unreliable, but actually it is the respondent's behavior that is unreliable because humans are such variable creatures.) But what could be producing different results from time to time that truly would be the fault of the method? Possibilities are poorly-worded or vaguely-worded questionnaire statements that cause the respondent to perceive the statement differently at second reading. Another is use of very general terms that result in the reader's giving one meaning at one time, a different another (this could apply especially to value questionnaires because values are general in nature and need general description). Pressure to hurry or any source of threat or tension can alter thinking and judgement from one time to the next. Devices that are uninteresting can result in superficial reading and variability. This will include questionnaires that are boring, too long, or too difficult to understand. Situational factors such as noise and distraction may also reduce consistency.

Interviews have their own form of unreliability, for the interviewer as a "living instrument (questionnaire)" experiences the above personal daily variability, so from time to time may perceive differently what the interviewee is saying and any two interviewers may perceive differently the values of the respondent. It is not unusual in cases where there are two interviewers in disagreement (as in Haan et al., 1985) for the interviewers to consult each other in hope of increasing agreement.

Validity

Validity has to do with the correctness or accuracy of our techniques. In other words, does the questionnaire or other technique assess what it is supposed to assess? Though questions of validity are properly raised with respect to all assessment techniques, they arise especially in connection with psychological tests and questionnaires. This is a warranted concern, because the instrument itself often does not permit a common-sense judgement as to what it assesses and there is always uncertainty as to what will prove most predictive.

Validity usually is expressed numerically as degree of relationship between a score on the instrument and some criterion, such as proficiency in some activity in the case of the aptitude test (e.g. effectiveness as a computer programmer) and presence of a trait (e.g. timidity) in the case of the personality questionnaire. Rarely is a high degree of validity demonstrated.

If value questionnaires be divided into separate-domain versus single-domain types, the first tends to have implicit or face validity, whereas the second is like other personality questionnaires and its validity needs to be demonstrated, though here too content validity may be quite evident.

Separate-domain questionnaires present some number of value concepts, each of which is independent if all the others. In effect, it is a number of separate questionnaires. Any concept can be dropped off and others added without affecting the usefulness of each remaining concept. If the wording is brief and straightforward, the concept can be referring to only one thing (e.g. "freedom" can be perceived as referring only to freedom), so has obvious content or face validity. No effort at proving that it does evoke a concept of "freedom" in the mind of the respondent is likely to add to the obvious.

In the single-domain type of questionnaire all the statements, perhaps 10 to 20, are intended to pertain to a single value, and replies to all are added to derive a single score, which is meant to indicate strength of the value. In order to avoid obvious duplication and get at different facets of the value, statements of different wording are used. But this diversity of wording creates a question as to exactly what is being assessed, and means must be found to try to find out -- so the scores must be correlated with a criterion. But the criterion may be less than ideal (of uncertain validity) and have its own sources of unreliability, so it is not unusual to find oneself having to resort to doubtful evidence to try to prove validity.

Another problem with this type of questionnaire is giving meaning to the numerical scores for in and of themselves they are meaningless. As a minimum, norms are accumulated permitting relating the given score to scores of some group(s) but strength of the value cannot be known without inspecting the replies and/or interviewing the person.

Though the potential sensitivity of the interview suggests good validity, it is only as good as the person using it and it is always possible that a given interviewer will misunderstand, distort, or fail to listen to what is said, hence produce a very invalid report. Having two interviewers talk to the same person is a usual way of increasing interviewer validity as well as reliability.

Incidentally, all the above points presented under "reliability," "strength," and "learning real values" also apply to validity, for unreliable procedures, in their inconsistency, reduce validity of the procedures, and failure to correctly learn real values and their strength obviously reduces validity of findings.

Other Considerations

Purpose of the project. A fairly obvious consideration in choice of methods is the purpose of the project. If the purpose is to learn the values of a group of people toward some issue(s), and decisions rest on the findings, then accuracy of assessment of present values is the major consideration and the various specific determinants of accuracy mentioned above become important -- reliability, strength, validity, sampling, etc.. But if the purpose is to help members of a group to start thinking about values, clarify, and in general grow in value maturity, then accuracy is a secondary consideration and stimulation of thought the major one. Now such specific techniques as group discussion, comparing of value alternatives (as by the method of paired comparison), reacting to descriptions of ideal societies (ways to live), writing about own values, and responding to the same questionnaire a second or third time may be useful. Too, if the method has diagnostic qualities that permit the group leader to estimate where the person is in his value maturing, as was suggested for the above self-anchoring "ladder" technique, this enhances its worth.

Generality versus specificity. The investigator might wish to give thought to the choice between general and specific concepts when preparing questionnaires. Most values questionnaires contain broad general terms since values ordinarily are general in nature, as are these, taken from the Rokeach *Values Survey*: freedom, equality, salvation, self-development. But there is always the possibility that a person will express commitment to a general concept but in practice have so many exceptions as to negate the value or render it a mere unpracticed ideal. So perhaps a series of specific questions should be asked, all relating to the one general idea, and the broad value inferred from the specific replies. But against this is the possibility that no general value disposition is held; it may just be several specific attitudes and an inference of generality be unwarranted. Surely the ideal here would be a combination of general concepts and specific choices.

Since the Rokeach questionnaire serves to exemplify the general approach, the second best-known and oldest of all values questionnaires, the *Study of Values* (Allport, Vernon, Lindzey), nicely serves to exemplify the specific approach. It assumes the existence of six broad orientations toward the world with the holder of each orientation valuing his sorts of interests and experiences -- social, theoretic, religious, economic, political, and aesthetic. Below are typical questions (but not actual questions from the questionnaire) and it may be noted how specific they are, and a main criticism of the questionnaire has always been that it is an interest-attitude test, not a values questionnaire:

Part I

1.   The main object of scientific research should be the discovery of the
        laws of nature rather than its practical application.
        (a) Yes   (b) No

4.   Assuming that you have sufficient ability, would you prefer to be:
        (a) a artist?
        (b) a clergyman?

15.   At an exposition, do you chiefly like to go to the buildings where
        you can see?
        (a) new manufacturing products?
        (b) paintings and sculpture?

Part II (These are to be ranked from most to least preferred)

3.   If you could influence the educational policies of the public schools
        of some city, would you undertake
        _____ a. to promote the study and participation in civic affairs?
        _____ b. to stimulate the study of environmental problems?
        _____ c. to provide additional laboratory facilities?
        _____ d. to increase the spiritual value of courses?

7.   Assuming that you are a man with the necessary ability, and that the
        salary for each of the following occupations is the same, would you
        prefer to be a
        _____ a. musician?
        _____ b. scientist?
        _____ c. manufacturer?
        _____ d. writer?

Wording for evaluative and worth concepts. In Chapter 2 it was suggested
that values be divided into the rough categories of evaluative and worth types.
Since the evaluative do involve feelings of should-should not, good-bad, right-
wrong and comparable judgmental feelings, it is logical to include judgmental terms
in the wording of these value statements or in the general instructions. An example
might be: Helpfulness *should* be the main thing in life. The worth type of values
involve feelings of importance, usefulness, interest, and other non-judgmental
feelings, so logically should have such terms as these in the statement's wording,
as in this example: Attaining enlightenment is the most *important* thing in life. But
different wordings should be tried to discover the most satisfactory (I experimented
but came to no conclusion).

Positive and negative values. It makes for a better balanced questionnaire if
concepts are included that span the spectrum from potentially highly valued to
strongly disvalued. But is is easy to end up with one that is composed solely of

desirable possibilities, each one perhaps warranting acceptance, since of course all valued things are desirable. Such a questionnaire has the weakness of encouraging the agreeing tendency of some people and leads others to fall into a response set of giving favorable responses to everything. It also makes for an uninteresting, unchallenging questionnaire (which may be a good part of the explanation for the agreeing and the response set). But it is very difficult to think of unacceptable choices that are plausible and still invite consideration. Many implausibles can be found, such as asking the subject if he values killing people, beating children, staying drunk, or exploiting others, but the ridiculousness of the examples will be self-evident. I have managed to think of a few choices that were plausible and which I was quite sure would evoke negative reaction among American subjects, a good example being "letting oneself be used by others for their needs and growth." I got the idea for this while doing research in India, for this is a very old value in that part of the world. Most of my other negatives were suggested by the values of others cultures and I recommend this as a source to others (see the *Clarification of Values* questionnaire, Appendix A, pg. 237, for a few other examples). Incidentally, the above implausibles (killing people, etc.) are all negatively-valued behavior and do properly belong in a questionnaire that is presenting possible negatively-valued behaviors. Were one constructing such a scale the above reasoning should of course be followed by mixing in a number of choices that are likely to be positive but have plausibility as negatives (work on that for a while!). Questionnaires that are intended to study negative values are rare, but two exist, those of Rettig and Pasamanick (1959) and of Ewell (1954), both moral values questionnaires.

Special Checks

Certain of the personality questionnaires contain "lie" scales as a means of checking for deliberate lying. Other special scales may be used to check for comprehension or other problems. Similarly, someone who is using value questionnaires might wish to include certain value statements as checks on one problem or another. I know of no way to include an outright lie scale in a values questionnaire but probably it is possible to check for such things as disinterest, carelessness, and superficiality. This might be done by including pairs of statements that are opposite in meaning and noting how the person responded. If both were strongly approved or strongly disapproved there would be reason to assume something amiss. In one questionnaire prepared for use in India I included three pairs of opposite-meaning statements, and did so in the knowledge that some number of college students there were weak in English comprehension, though competent English speakers, and felt I should try to locate their answer forms and discard them. The pairs were separated and spread about in the questionnaire so their oppositeness was not obvious (though to the discerning reader of course it was).

The three pairs of statements included the following value concepts: (a) sociability vs. solitariness; (b) openness to change vs. preserve the traditional; (c) acceptance of things vs. solving of problems. The sociability-solitariness pair had exactly the same wording though in reverse. Hence a person could hardly value both or disvalue both. The other two pairs of opposites are opposite in general concept. The first pair was used for rejection purposes. The criterion was worded so as to eliminate answer forms where both were valued or disvalued, but to accept combinations of neutrality toward both or valuing or disvaluing one and neutrality toward the other. This criterion was intended primarily to eliminate the superficial and foolish but also the uncomprehending, confused, and obvious agree-ers. The other two pairs of opposites were used to derive a "favorability" index. Such an index was needed because in several previous studies of values Indian students were more favorable toward a number of ways to live than students of other nationalities (Morris, 1956; Kilby, 1963). By this means I hoped to determine whether the Indians were generally more favorable toward any way to live. If so, a favorability index might be computed for each nationality and any difference between indices of any two countries be used to reduce the averages on all ways to live of the larger by the amount of the difference, before comparing the two sets of results. The index was derived in this way. If the person responded to the pair exactly oppositely, as "logically" he should, then his two scores when added together would equal 8 (e.g., score of 1, for "very valued," on the "openness" way and 7, for "very disvalued," on the "traditional" way, or two scores of 4, for "neutral," if neither was valued). A total for the two of less than 8 indicates some degree of favorability toward both ways to live, and the difference between the actual total and 8 gives an index of favorability. Following the same reasoning, the averages for entire groups on these pairs can be added and the index derived that group. The Indians did indeed prove to have a greater favorability on the two pairs of statements than the Americans -- on the "openness" pair it was 2.60 and on the "acceptance" pair 1.56 as against 1.73 and 0.45 for the Americans (e.g., the Indian's group average for the "openness" pair was 5.40, and this subtracted from 8 shows a favorability to the extent of 2.60 score points). But in the end I decided against making the correction on the total of the Indian averages on the ways to live because I was not convinced that the Indian favorableness was uniform toward all ways -- note that it was not uniform toward the two index pairs, and they did strongly reject some ways to live. Nevertheless, this strategy of inserting statements of opposite meaning may have usefulness for certain purposes.

Appendix A

An Omnibus Values Questionnaire

As mentioned in Chapter 5 , the *Clarification of Values* questionnaire below was prepared primarily for teaching purposes and contains all the value concepts that could be formulated at the time, hence its omnibus nature. It would need to be refined in various ways before use for research purposes. It is reproduced in full here in hope that the individual statements will prove useful to teachers and researchers.

Clarification of Values

This project is intended to help you clarify some of your values. Below are listed a number of statements which describe possible personal goals and desirable ends of life. All are ways to live considered important or valuable to someone. You are to read and weigh and compare these ways to live with the object of deciding how you feel toward each, and of picking those ways that are most important to you. Take plenty of time to make up your mind about each.

Each statement consists of a key word or phrase, such as ACHIEVEMENT or ENJOYMENT, followed by a series of words and phrases which describe or clarify the idea.

Use the separate Response Form to indicate your feeling toward each way to live.

1. RELIGIOUSNESS -- having a faith, worship and seeking Divine guidance, prayer or meditation, acts of faith.

2. SOLVING SOCIETY'S PROBLEMS -- attacking the problems that face us (disease, malnutrition, flood, etc.) and working toward their solution, making the world a fit place in which to live, mastering nature and putting it to work for us, willingness to work in science and industry.

3. LEADERSHIP -- influencing others, carrying out my ideas, winning positions of responsibility, perhaps being in charge of groups of people or organizations.

4. SENSORY PLEASURE -- seeking and enjoying sensory impressions, foods, sounds, sights, feelings, odors, colors, forms, movement, music, poetry, sunshine, swimming, dancing, perfumes, flower scents, etc..

5. ADAPTING ONESELF TO THE PLAN OF NATURE -- giving up self-assertion in order to be able to sense the plan of the world, learning to adapt and yield to the flow of the stream of life, losing self-importance and becoming a part of the harmony of nature, feeling the joy of unity.

6. FRIENDSHIP AND AFFECTION -- concern for the feelings and welfare of others, having affectionate relationships with others, being appreciative

and helpful to others, giving something of oneself to others and being able to accept the affection offered by others.

7.	PROSPERITY -- each person's learning an occupation, employment and good income for everyone, industrious effort, and enjoyment of the fruits of the modern industrial society, such as comfortable homes, education and medical care, television and automobiles, vacation and travel.

8.	SELF-CONTROL -- learning to control and direct the emotions and appetites, using the emotions to enrich life, learning to keep calm and controlled amid the strains and tensions of community living, attaining an inner balance and serenity.

9.	BEAUTY -- surrounding ourselves with forms of beauty (such as gardens, planned cities, music, home decoration, design of buildings), artistic self-expression, encouragement of appreciation, having experiences of beauty.

10.	EQUALITY AND TOLERANCE -- treating everyone else as my equal, helping the backward classes to become equal with the rest of society, accepting others whose religion, race, or customs are different from my own, tolerating diversity.

11.	CULTIVATION OF INDIVIDUALITY -- helping each person become a distinct or unique individual, allowing each person to discover his own beliefs and values, recognizing each person as unique and valuable, protecting the rights and freedom of each person.

12.	COMMUNITY LIVING -- group living, working and playing together, making decisions as a group, with everyone obeying the group's rules, sharing with each other, cooperation and companionship.

13.	LETTING ONESELF BE USED -- letting ourselves be used by other persons for their needs or growth, self-denial and self-sacrifice, making oneself the willing instrument of gods or nature, devotion and service, waiting patiently for what life brings, grateful for its joys, tolerant of its pains.

14.	ENJOYMENT -- seeking excitement and pleasures, regarding life as a great festival to be enjoyed, letting oneself go (having fun), developing our powers of appreciation and delight.

15.	SECURITY AND SAFETY -- having a safe existence, having a dependable job or income, having the necessities of life, avoiding taking chances or risks that might endanger safety and security.

16.	ENLIGHTMENT -- gaining a sense of unity with the universe, escaping painful ego-involvement, compassion toward living things, attaining peace of mind.

17.	ADVANCEMENT IN A CAREER -- learning an occupation, becoming more capable, winning praise, recognition, and advancement, working industriously.

18. SIMPLE WHOLESOME ENJOYMENT -- such things as the pleasure of just existing, tasty food, comfortable surroundings, talking with friends, rest and relaxation.

19. CONFORMITY -- doing as others are doing, agreeing, changing your wishes and behavior so as to be like others, avoiding being different or causing dissention.

20. PHYSICAL ACTIVITY -- making things and doing things, using hands and body in vigorous activity, being in an active type of work, taking part in sports and recreations.

21. SELF-DEVELOPMENT -- development of each person's talents and interests, education and travel, broadening our horizons, living a life full of satisfying experiences -- from the arts, reading, discussion, recreation.

22. PRESERVATION OF THE TRADITIONAL WAYS -- preserving the tried and true (good) things of our community and society, making changes slowly so that what has been achieved is not lost, enjoying the traditional customs, blending the new into the old so that the total change is not great.

23. HELPFULNESS -- helping others, giving one's time, energy, or money to others, encouraging and sympathizing, compassion for others.

24. EFFICIENCY -- doing things the best way with the least effort, practicality, carefulness, avoiding waste motion, coordination.

25. AGGRESSIVENESS -- getting what you want, defining your rights, resisting interference, forcefully overcoming opposition, revenging injuries.

26. CLOSENESS TO NATURE -- being out-of-doors and close to nature much of the time, in garden or forest, in field or at seashore, in the mountains or on the sea, a life of closeness to the things of nature.

27. SELF-RELIANCE -- each person's being able to take responsibility for his own life and destiny, feeling independent as a person, being able to take care of oneself, being industrious.

28. INTELLECTUAL ACTIVITY (USE OF THE MIND) -- having the opportunity to think and reason and discover, contributing to the advancement of knowledge, learning new things and growing in knowledge.

29. SELF-UNDERSTANDING -- discovering what I want from life, resolving conflicts, understanding my feelings, finding peace of mind.

30. ACCEPTANCE OF THINGS AS THEY ARE -- being content with things as they are, liking what cannot be avoided, the belief that the gods or nature control the world and they alone will change it when they wish, man's helplessness to make any real change.

31. MATERIAL COMFORT -- having a comfortable home and modern conveniences, attractive clothing, enough money to get what you want, an automobile.

32. ESCAPING BOREDOM -- avoiding feeling tense and frustrated, avoiding the "at loose ends" feeling, avoiding the feeling of not knowing what to do with oneself.

33. ACHIEVEMENT -- accomplishing something in life, effort, striving to be outstanding in some way, gaining satisfaction with oneself from accomplishment.

34. DEVELOPING A PLEASING PERSONALITY -- making yourself attractive to others, causing others to like you, self-improvement, self-acceptance.

35. BEING FORCEFUL AND COMMANDING -- commanding respect, being obeyed, asserting yourself, making others follow your lead.

36. POSSESSIONS AND WEALTH -- earning money, owning property, saving and increasing one's wealth, the security that wealth brings.

37. AVOIDANCE OF PROBLEMS -- avoiding getting involved in issues and problems, keeping detached, avoiding risks, escaping inconvenience and trouble, taking the safe, easy path.

38. VIGOROUS ACTION -- getting things done, facing obstacles and working to overcome them, exerting oneself, a life of action.

39. HUMAN ASSOCIATION -- having much human interaction, having acquaintances or friends, joining groups, enjoying the company of others.

40. FAME (PROMINENCE, SUCCESS) -- making a name for oneself, leaving a mark behind, doing something notable in occupation or community, achieving recognition or fame.

41. OPENNESS TO CHANGE -- readiness to change, wanting to try new ways of doing things, openness to new experiences, pointing ahead toward the future rather than backward toward the past.

42. BEING A USEFUL CITIZEN -- involving oneself in community problems and issues, having a sense of public responsibility, taking part in public discussion and serving on committees, voting.

43. DEMOCRATIC LIVING -- equality, participation in community affairs, the right to vote, election of officials.

44. BEING LIKED AND ACCEPTED -- being liked and wanted and accepted, feeling secure in relationships with others.

45. PERSONAL INDEPENDENCE -- the right of each person to direct his own life, being free of domination by others, being free to work and move about as you wish ("be my own boss.")

46. MARRIAGE AND HOME LIFE -- companionship of a mate, shared activities, exchange of affection, family life.

47. DEFERENCE -- respecting superiors, cooperating, following our leaders, doing what superiors ask.

48. NON-CONFORMITY -- being different, challenging things as they are, self-assertion, rebelling.

49. HONESTY (TRUTHFULNESS) -- truthfulness, sincerity, keeping your word, openness.

50. FEELING INWARDLY FREE -- feeling uninhibited, contented, untroubled, free of tension, at peace.

51. COMMITMENT -- devoting your life to something outside yourself, being involved, finding meaning in some ideal or activity, having a purpose.

52. BEING PHYSICALLY ATTRACTIVE -- having beauty or handsomeness, charm, appeal, being admired.

53. PLAYING -- having fun, laughing and joking, being easy going, playful, gay.

54. HEALTHFUL LIVING AND GOOD HEALTH -- having a sound body and good physical functioning, zest, energy, caring for one's body, avoiding unhealthful activities.

55. CREATIVITY -- making new things, inventing, experimenting, creating something.

56. SELF-LOVE -- self-admiration, feeling superior, being admired and appreciated by others, putting self forward.

57. AVOIDANCE OF BODILY HARM -- avoiding pain and physical injury, escaping dangerous situations, being careful and vigilant for safety.

58. BEING ADMIRED -- making an impression, being seen and heard, entertaining and amusing, being dramatic and spectacular.

59. HAVING LEISURE -- having no duties, freedom, an easy life, no problems.

60. BEING PROTECTED (SUPPORTED) -- being supported, helped, guided, forgiven, loved.

61. TO BE UNDERSTANDING -- being sensitive to the feelings of others, tolerant, insightful, aware.

62. SELF-ACCEPTANCE -- being content with self, feeling worthy, respecting self, feeling capable.

63. PATRIOTISM -- love of country, and defense and protection of homeland.

64. ORDERLINESS -- being methodical, neat, keeping things organized, planning, carefulness.

65. PERSEVERANCE -- staying with a task, not giving up, fighting back against opposition.

66. HIGH ESTEEM -- being well-regarded, respected, looked up to, admired.

67. SENSE OF HUMOR -- being able to be amused and enjoy the humorous, to be able to laugh at oneself, to see the humor in life.

68. WISDOM -- understanding what is true, right, or lasting, good judgement, common sense.

69. NON-ATTACHMENT -- "action without attachment," ability to pursue goals without becoming deeply ego-involved, and to give up when goals become unattainable, freedom from enslaving ego-involvements, self-detachment.

70. WORLD PEACE -- freedom from threat of war and from conflict, a world at peace.

Appendix B

Alternative Instructions for
A Self-Anchoring Scale

As mentioned in Chapter 5, Cantril and his associates devised the *self-anchoring*, or "ladder," technique for international use in learning people's conceptions of the best and worst possible lives, and where they are now. But as now worded, it has limited usefulness for studying values generally and the instructions would need to be altered to give it wider applicability. Below is an example of such altered wording.

Since it is difficult for one person to let another know how really important something is to him, we have devised the ladder below, with each step of the ladder representing a different degree of importance, varying from greatest (10) to least (0).

To give you a means of deciding how important each way to live is to you, you are asked to do two things before beginning the questionnaire:

a. First think of the one thing in all the world that is most important, most valuable, most precious to you, and write the name of that something in the space at the top of the ladder, opposite step 10. It could be that staying alive and healthy is that most important thing. Or it might be being outstanding at something -- the greatest tennis player on earth, the most intelligent person, the greatest actress, the most admired person, the most beautiful woman. Or it could be the satisfaction of seeing everyone prosperous and content. Or it might be your attaining some sort of insight, enlightenment, or wisdom that would have great significance to you. It might be being free to do absolutely as you wished with no interference of any sort. Or it might be having deep friendships or love relationships. Use whatever you choose (and have written in the space) as the basis of comparison in deciding how important any one of the ways to live of the questionnaire is to you.

b. Next think of the one thing in all the world that is most disliked, most undesirable, most worthless to you and write its name at the bottom of the ladder, opposite step 0. Perhaps having to live in constant fear of being killed or dying is that worst possible thing. Or it might be being penniless, or being utterly incompetent to do anything, or ugly, or being without a single friend, or constantly insulted and ridiculed. Or it might be having to live in a place where people, including yourself, deceive and abuse and kill each other. Or it might be having to spend your life in prison. Use whatever you choose (and have written in the space) as the basis of comparison in deciding how disliked and undesirable any one of the ways to live of the questionnaire is to you.

Human Values

10	<u>Most important thing in all the world:</u>
9	Extremely important (only slightly less than "most important")
8	Very important, very desirable (stands out in significance)
7	Quite important (good to have)
6	Slightly important (feel somewhat positive toward it)
5	Feel <u>neutral</u> toward or have mixed feelings
4	Slightly reject (feel somewhat negative)
3	Quite strongly reject (strong negative feelings)
2	Very strongly reject (very strong negative feelings)
1	Extremely strongly reject (intense negative feelings)
0	<u>Worst possible thing in all the world:</u>

REFERENCES

Aberle, D. F. The psychosocial analysis of a Hopi life history. *Comparative Psychology Monographs*, 1951, 21, (1) 1-133.

Aberle, D. F. The psychosocial analysis of a Hopi life history, p. 79-138. In R. Hunt (Ed.) *Personalities and cultures*. Garden City, NY: The Natural History Press, 1967.

Aldag, R. J., & Brief, A. P. Some correlates of work values. *Journal of Applied Psychology*, 1975 (Dec.), 60 (6), 757-60.

Allport, G. W., & Odbert, H. S. Trait-names: a psycholexical study. *Psychological Monographs*, 1936, 47 (Whole No. 211).

Allport, G. W., Vernon, P., & Lindzey, G. *Study of Values*. Third edition. Boston: Houghton Mifflin, 1960, 1970.

Allport, G. W. *Pattern and growth in personality*. New York: Holt, Rinehart and Winston, 1961.

Alwin, D. F. *see* Childrearing goals. *ISR Newsletter* Spring/Summer 1987. Ann Arbor, MI: Institute for Social Research, The University of Michigan.

Anderson, N. H. Likableness ratings of 555 personality trait words. *Journal of Personality and Social Psychology*, 1968, 9, 272-279.

Angell, J. W., & Helm, R. M. *Meaning and value in western thought*, Vol. I. Washington, D. C.: University Press of America, 1981.

Arbuthnot, J. B., & Faust, D. *Teaching moral reasoning: Theory and practice*. New York: Harper & Row, 1981.

Armsby, R. E. A reexamination of the development of moral judgement in children. *Child Development*, 1971, 42, 1241-48.

Ball-Rokeach, S. J., Rokeach, M., & Grube, J. W. *The great American value test: Influencing behavior and belief through television*. New York: Free Press, 1984.

Bandura, A., & Walters, R. H. *Social learning and personality development*. New York: Holt, Rinehart & Winston, 1963.

Baumrind, D. Current patterns of parental authority. *Developmental Psychology Monographs*, 1971, 4 (1, pt. 2).

Baumrind, D. Child care practices anteceding three patterns of preschool behavior. *Genetic Psychology Monographs*, 1976, 75, 43-88.

Becker, W. Consequences of different kinds of parental discipline. In M. L. Hoffman & L. W. Hoffman (Eds.) *Review of child development research* (Vol. 1) New York: Russell Sage Foundation, 1964.

Bem, D. J. *Belief, attitudes and human affairs*. Belmont, CA: Brooks Cole, 1970.

Berelson, B., Lazarsfield, P., & McPhee, W. *Voting: A study of opinion formation in a presidential election*. Chicago: University of Chicago Press, 1954.

Berkowitz, M. W. The role of discussion in moral education. Ch. 8. In M. W. Berkowitz & F. Oser (Eds.) *Moral education: Theory and applications.* Hillsdale, NJ: Lawrence Erlbaum, 1985.

Berkowitz, M. W., & Oser, F. *Moral education: Theory and applications.* Hillsdale, NJ: Lawrence Erlbaum, 1985.

Berns, R. S., Bugental, D. E., & Berns, G. P. Research on student activism. *American Journal of Psychiatry*, 1972, 128, 1499-1504.

Bishop, A. With suffering and through time: Olive Schreiner, Vera Brittain and the Great War. In M. Van Wyk Smith & D. MacLennan (Eds.) *Olive Schreiner and After.* (pp. 80-92). Cape Town, South Africa: David Philips, 1983.

Blatt, M., & Kohlberg, L. The effect of classroom moral discussion upon children's level of moral judgement. *Journal of Moral Education*, 1975, 4, 129-161.

Block, J. H. *Lives through time.* Berkeley, CA: Bancroft Books, 1971.

Blood, M. R. Work values and job satisfaction. *Journal of Applied Psychology*, 1969, 53 (6), 456-59.

Borrelli, P. Environmental ethics - the oxymoron of our time. *The Amicus Journal*, 1989, Summer, 39-43.

Braithwaite, V. A., & Scott, W. A. Values. In J. P. Robinson, P. R. Shaver, & L. S. Wrightsman (Eds.) *Measures of personality and social psycological attitudes.* New York: Academic Press, Harcourt Brace Jovanovich, 1990.

Brittain, V. *Testament of Youth.* Originally published by Victor Gollancz Ltd., 1933; reprinted in Great Britain by Virago Ltd. 1978; published in U.S.A. by Seaview Books, 1980; published by Viking Penguin, 1989. (Copyright 1970 by Virago Press, London, and Paul Berry, Literary Executor of Vera Brittain.)

Brittain, V. *Chronicle of Youth: The war diary, 1913-1917.* (Alan Bishop, Ed.) New York: William Morrow, 1982.

Bruner, J. *Actual minds, possible worlds.* Cambridge: Harvard University Press, 1986.

Buss, A. H. *Psychopathology.* New York: Wiley, 1966.

Campbell, A., Gurin, G., & Miller, W. E. *The voter decides.* Evanston, Ill.: Row, Peterson, 1954.

Campbell, A., Converse, P. E., & Rodgers, W. L. *The quality of American life.* New York: Russell Sage Foundation, 1976.

Cantril, H. The intensity of an attitude. *Journal of Abnormal and Social Psychology*, 1946, 41, 129-135.

Cantril, H., & Free, L. A. Hopes and fears for self and country. *The American Behavioral Scientist*, 1962, 6 (supplement), (2) October.

Cantril, H. *The pattern of human concerns.* New Brunswick,NJ: Rutgers University Press, 1965.

Carson, R. C., Butcher, J. N., & Coleman, J. C. *Abnormal psychology and modern life.* Glenview, Ill.: Scott Foresman, 1988.

Carter, R. E. An experiment in value measurement. *American Sociological Review*, 1956, 21, 156-163.

Centers, R. Motivational aspects of occupational stratification. *Journal of Social Psychology*, 1948, 28, 187-217.

Colby, A., & Kohlberg, L. *The measurement of moral judgement*, Vol. I & II. New York: Cambridge University Press, 1987.

Coleman, J. C. *Abnormal pychology and modern life.* Glenview, Ill.: Scott, Foresman, 1964.

Coleman, J. C., Carson, R. C., & Butcher, J. N. *Abnormal psychology and modern life..* Glenview, Ill.: Scott Foresman, 1984.

Connell, W. F. Moral education: Aims and methods in China, the USSR, the U. S., and England. In D. Purpel & K. Ryan (Eds.) *Moral education.* Berkeley, CA: McCutchan Publishing, 1976.

Conroy, W. J., Katkin, E. S., & Barnette, L. W. Modification of smoking behavior by Rokeach's self-confrontation technique. Paper presented at the annual meeting of the Southeastern Psychological Association in New Orleans, April 7, 1973.

Danziger, E. Value differences among South African students. *Journal of Abnormal and Social Psychology*, 1958, 57, 340-346.

DeCharms, R., & Moeller, G. H. Values expressed in American children's readers: 1800-1950. *Journal of Abnormal and Social Psychology*, 1962, 64, 136-142.

Dembo, T. A theoretical and experimental inquiry into concrete values and value systems. In B. Kaplan & S. Wapner (Eds.) *Perspectives in psychological theory.* New York: International Universities Press, 1960.

Dempsey, P., & Dukes, W. F. Judging complex value stimuli: An examination and revision of Morris' Paths of Life, *Educational and Psychological Measurement*, 1966, 26 (4), 871-882.

Diagnostic and Statistical manual of Mental Disorders. Third edition, Revised. American Psychological Association.

Durant, W. *The story of philosophy.* New York: Garden City Publishing, 1927.

English, H. B., & English, A. E. *Dictionary of psychological and psychoanalytical terms.* New York: Longmans Green, 1958.

Erikson, E. *Youth: Change and challenge.* Garden City, NY: Anchor, 1965.

Erikson, E. *Identity: Youth and crisis.* New York: Norton, 1968.

Ewell, A. H., Jr. The relation between the rigidity of moral values and the severity of functional psychological illness: A study of war veterans of one religious group. Doctoral dissertation, New York University, 1954. (Copyright to the *Inventory of Values* held by University Microfilms, Ann Arbor; publication no. 8002.)

Flacks, R. The liberated generation: An exploration of the roots of student protest. *Journal of Social Issues*, 1967, 23 (3), 52-75.

Flacks, R. Social and cultural meanings of student revolt: Some informal comparative observations. *Social Problems*, 1970, 17, 340-357.

Fogelman, E., & Wiener, V. L. The few, the brave, and the noble. *Psychology Today*, 61-65, August, 1985.

Frankl, V. *Man's search for meaning.* New York: Simon & Schuster, 1962.

Freedman, M. B. *Impact of college.* Washington, D. C.: U. S. Department of Health, Education, and Welfare, Office of Education, 1960.

Freud, S. *New introductory lectures on psychoanalysis.* (trans. W. J. Sprott). New York: W. W. Norton, 1933.

Gandhi, M. K. *The message of the Gita.* Ahmedabad, India: Navijavan Press, 1959.

Garraty, J. A. & Gay, P. *The Columbia history of the world.* New York: Harper & Row Publishers, 1972.

Gibbs, J. C., & Schell, S. V. Moral development "versus" socialization. *American Psychologist*, 1985, 40, 1071-1108.

Gillespie, J. M., & Alport, G. W. *Youth's outlook on the future.* New York: Doubleday, 1955.

Gorham, D. *Vera Brittain and great war.* Unpublished manuscript, Carleton University, Canada, 1985.

Granzberg, G. Twin infanticide - a cross-cultural test of a materialistic explanation. *Ethos*, 1973, 1 (4), 405-412.

Greenacre, P. Conscience in the psychopath. *American Journal of Orthopsychiatry*, 1945, 15, 495-509.

Haan, N., Aerts, E., & Cooper, B. A. B. *On moral grounds.* New York: New York University Press, 1985.

Harris, L. *Inside America.* New York: Vintage Books, Random House, 1987.

Hartshorne, H., & May, M. A. *Studies in the nature of character*, vol. 1-3. New York: Macmillan, 1928-30.

Heaver, W. L. A study of forty male psychopathic personalities before, during, and after hospitalization. *American Journal of Psychiatry*, 1943, 100, 342-46.

Hoffman, M. L., & Saltzstein, H. D. Parent discipline and the child's moral development. *Journal of Personality and Social Psychology*, 1967, 5, 45-47.

Hoffman, M. L. Affective and cognitive processes in moral internalizaiton. In E. T. Higgins, D. N. Ruble, & W. W. Hartup (Eds.), *Social cognition and* social development: A sociocultural perspective (pp. 236-274). Cambridge, England: Cambridge University Press, 1983.

Holahan, C. K. Lifetime achievement patterns, retirement, and life satisfaction of gifted aged women. *Journal of Gerontology*, 1981, 36, 741-749.

Hollen, C. C. *Value change, perceived instrumentality, and attitude change.* Unpublished Ph.D. dissertation, Michigan State University Library, 1972.

Holloway, M. *Heavens on earth: Utopian communities in America, 1680-1880.* New York: Dover publications, 1966.

Horney, K. *The neurotic personality of our time.* New York: Norton, 1937.

Horney, K. *Our inner conflicts.* New York: Norton, 1945.

Hsu, F. L. K. *Psychological anthropology.* Homewood, Ill.: Dorsey Press, 1961.

Hsu, F. L. K. *Under the ancestor's shadow.* Garden City, NY: Doubleday Anchor Books, 1967.

Jansen, D., Winborn, B., & Martinson, W. Characteristics associated with campus social-political action leadership, *Journal of Counseling Psychology*, 1968, 15, 552-562.

Jennings, M., & Niemi, R. The transmission of political values from parent to child. *American Political Science Review*, 1968, 62, 169-184.

Kagan, J., & Snidman, N. Temperamental factors in human development. *American Psychologist*, 1991, 46, 38, 856-862.

Keniston, K. The source of student dissent. *Journal of Social Issues*, 1967, 23 (3), 108-37.

Keniston, K. *Young radicals: Notes on committed youth.* New York: Harcourt, Brace & World, 1968.

Kilby, R. W. Personal values of Indian and American university students. *Journal of Humanistic Psychology*, 1963, 3, 108-145.

Kilby, R. W. Personal goals of Indian and American university students. *Journal of Humanistic Psychology*, 1965, 5, 122-146.

Kilpatrick, F. P., & Cantril, H. Self-anchoring scaling, a measure of individuals' unique reality worlds. *Journal of Individual Psychology*, November, 1960, 16 (2).

Kluckhohn, C. Values and value-orientations in the theory of action: An exploration in definition and classification. Ch. 2, pt. 4 In T. Parsons & E. shils (Eds.) *Toward a general theory of action.* Cambridge, MA: Harvard University Press, 1954.

Kluckhohn, F. R., & Strodtbeck, F. L. *Variations in value orientations.* Evanston, Ill.: Row Peterson, 1961.

Kohlberg, L. Stage and sequence: The cognitive-developmental approach to socialization. In D. Goslin (Ed.) *Handbook of socialization theory and research.* Chicago: Rand McNally, 1969.

Kohlberg, L. The Cognitive-developmental approach to moral education. Chs. 12, 13. In D. Purpel & K. Ryan (Eds.) *Moral education*. Berkeley, CA: McKutchan Publishing, 1976.

Kohlberg, L. Moral stages and moralization: The cognitive-developmental approach. In T. Lickona (Ed.) *Moral development and behavior*. New York: Holt, Rinehart & Winston, 1976.

Kohlberg, L. *The philosophy of moral development*. San Francisco: Harper & Row, 1981.

Kohlberg, L., Levine, C., & Hewer, A. *Moral stages: A current formulation and a response to critics*. New York: Karger, 1983.

Kohlberg, L. *The psychology of moral development: Essays in moral development* (vol. 2). San Francisco: Harper and Row, 1984.

Kohlberg, L. The just community approach to moral education in theory and practice. In M. W. Berkowitz & F. Oser (Eds.) *Moral eduction: Theory and applications*. Hillsdale, NJ: Lawrence Erlbaum, 1985.

Kohn, M. L. Social class and parent-child relationships: An interpretation. *American Journal of Sociology*, 1963, 68, 471-80.

Krebs, R., & Kohlberg, L. Moral judgement and ego controls as determinants of resistance to cheating. In L. Kohlberg (Ed.) *Recent research in moral development*. New York: Holt, Rinehart & Winston, ----------.

Krech, D., Crutchfield, R., & Livson, N. *Elements of psychology*. New York: Alfred A. Knopf, 1974.

Lambert, R. D., & Bressler, M. *Indian students on an American campus*. Minneapolis, MN: University of Minnesota Press, 1956.

Lanham, B. B. Ethics and moral prescripts taught in schools of Japan and the United States. *Ethos*, 1979, 7 (1), 1-18.

Lazarsfeld, P. F., Berelson, B., & Gaudet, H. *The people's choice*. New York: Duell, Sloan, & Pierce, 1944.

Lepley, R. The identity of fact and value. *Philosophy of Science*, 1943, X, 124-131.

Lifton, R. J. Thought reform of Chinese intellectuals. *Journal of Social Issues*, 1957, 13, 5-20.

Lifton, R. J. Thought reform of Chinese intellectuals. In M. Jahoda & N. Warren (Eds.) *Attitudes*. Baltimore, MD: Penguin books, 1966.

Linder, H. Jack Rabbit: A study in character disturbance, p. 290-306. In A. Burton & R. E. Harris (Eds.) *Clinical studies of personality*. New York: Harper & Brothers, 1955.

Lockwood, A. The effect of value clarification and moral development curricula on school-age subjects: A critical review of recent research. *Review of Eductional Research*, 1978, 325-364.

Maccoby, E. E. The development of moral values and behavior in childhood. In J. Clausen (Ed.) *Socialization and Society*. Boston: Little Brown, 1968, pp. 227-269.

Maccoby, E. E., *Social development*. New York: Harcourt Brace Jovanovich, 1980.

Mannheim, K. *Essays in the sociology of knowledge*. London: Routledge & Kegan Paul, 1952.

Marcus, C. E. Status rivalry in a Polynesian steady-state society. *Ethos*, 1978, 6 (4), 242-268.

Maslow, A. H. (Ed.), *New knowledge in human values*. New York: Harper, 1959.

Maslow, A. H. A theory of meta-motivation: the biological rooting of the value life, p. 153-200. In A. J. Sutich & M. A. Vich (Eds.) *Readings in humanistic psychology*. New York: Free Press, 1969.

Maslow, A. H. *Motivation and personality*. New York: Harper & Row, 1970.

Maslow, A. H. *The farther reaches of human nature*. New York: Viking Press, 1971.

McCord, W. E., & McCord, J. *The psychopath: An essay on the criminal mind*. New York: Van Nostrand Reinhold, 1964.

Mellown, M. Reflections on feminism and pacifism in the novels of Vera Brittain. *Tulsa Studies in Women's Literature*, 1983a, 2, 215-228.

Milgram, S. *Obedience to authority*. New York: Harper & Row, 1974.

Morris, C. *Varieties of human value*. Chicago: University of Chicago Press, 1956.

Muller, H. J. *The uses of the past*. New York: Oxford University Press, 1954.

Murray, H. A. *Explorations in personality; a clinical and experimental study of fifty men of college age*. New York: Oxford University Press, 1938.

Newcomb, T. M. *Personality and social change: Attitude formation in a student community*. New York: Dryden Press, 1943.

Newcomb, T. M. Attitude development as funciton of reference groups. In E. E. Maccoby, T. M. Newcomb, & E. L. Hartley (Eds.) *Readings in Social Psychology*. New York: Henry Holt, 1958, pp. 265-275.

Newcomb, T. M., Koenig, L. E., Flacks, R,. & Warwick, D. P. *Persistence and change: Bennington College and its students after twenty-five years*. New York: Wiley, 1969.

Osgood, C. E., Suci, G. J., & Tannenbaum, P. H. *The measurement of meaning*. Urbana, Ill.: University of Illinois Press, 1957.

Osgood, C. E., Ware, E. E., & Morris, C. Analysis of the connotative meanings of a variety of human values as expressed by American college students. *Journal of Abnormal and Social Psychology*, 1961, 62 (1), 62-73.

Packer, M. *The structure of moral action: A hermeneutic study of moral conflict.* Basel: Karger, 1985.

Packer, M., Haan, N., Theodorov, P., & Yabrove, G. Moral actions of four-year-olds. In N. Haan, E. Aerts, & A. B. Cooper (Eds.) *On moral grounds.* New York: New York University Press, 1985.

Parikh, B. Development of moral judgement and its relation to family environmental factors in Indian and American families. *Child Development,* 1980, 51, 1030-1039.

Piaget, J. *The moral judgement of the child.* (Marjorie Gabain, trans.). New York: Free Press, 1965. (first published in English, 1932.)

Plant, W. T. *Personality changes associated with a college education.* San Jose, CA: San Jose State College, 1962.

Prothro, E. T. *Child rearing in Lebanon.* Cambridge, MA: Harvard University Press, 1961.

Prothro, E. T. Child rearing in Lebanon, P. 247-260. In I. al-Issa & W. Dennis (Eds.) *Cross-cultural studies of behavior.* New York: Holt, Rinehart, & Winston, 1970.

Purpel, D., & Ryan, K. Ch. 5. In D. Purpel & K. Ryan (Eds.) *Moral education.* Berkeley, CA: McCutchan Publishing, 1976.

Radke-Yarrow, M., Zahn-Waxler, C., & Chapman, M. Children's prosocial dispositions and behavior. In P. H. Mussen (Ed.) *Handbook of child psychology,* vol. IV, Socialization, Personality and Social Development, 4th Ed. New York: Wiley, 1983.

Raths, L., Harmin, M., & Simon, S. B. *Values and teaching: Working with values in the classroom.* Columbus, OH: Charles E. Merrill, 1966.

Rawls, J. *A theory of justice.* Cambridge, MA: Harvard University, 1971.

Redl, F., & Wineman, D. *Children who hate.* Glencoe, Ill.: The Free Press, 1951.

Redl, F., & Wineman, D. *Controls from within.* Glencoe, Ill.: The Free Press, 1952.

Rettig, S., & Pasamanick, B. Changes in moral values over three decades 1929-1958. *Social Problems,* 1959, 6, 320-328.

Robinson, D. N. *An intellectual history of psychology.* New York: Macmillan, 1976.

Rogers, C. R. Toward a modern approach to values: The valuing process in the mature person. *Journal of Abnormal and Social Psychology,* 1964, 68(2), 160-167.

Rokeach, M. *Value survey.* Sunnyvale, CA: Halgren Tests, 1967.

Rokeach, M. *Beliefs, attitudes, & values.* San Francisco: Jossey-Bass, 1968.

Rokeach, M. *The nature of human values.* New York: The Free Press, 1973.

Rokeach, M. *Understanding human values.* New York: The Free Press, 1979(a).

Rokeach, M. Some unresolved issues in theories of beliefs, attitudes, and values. In M. M. Page (Ed.) *Nebraska symposium on motivation*, 1979(b).

Rokeach, M., & Ball-Rokeach, S. J. Stability and change in American value priorities, 1968-1981. *American Psychologist*, 1989, 44 (5), 775-784.

Rosenberg, M. *Occupations and values*. Glencoe, Ill.: Free Press, 1957.

Ross, F. H. *The meaning of life in Hinduism and Buddhism*. Boston, MA: Beacon Press, 1953.

Sanford, N. (Ed.) *The American college*. New York: Wiley, 1962.

Scheibe, K. E. *Beliefs and values*. New York: Holt, Rinehart & Winston, 1970.

Schreiner, O. *Woman and labour*. New York: Frederick A. Stokes, 1911.

Sears, P. S., & Barbee, A. H. Career and life satisfaction among Terman's gifted women. In J. C. Stanley, W. D. George, & C. H. Solano (Eds.) *The gifted and the creative: A fifty year perspective*. Baltimore, MD: Johns Hopkins University Press, 1977.

Sears, R. R. Sources of life satisfactions of the Terman gifted men. *American Psychologist*, 1977, 32 (2), 119-128.

Shneidman, E. The Indian summer of life. *American Psychologist*, 1989, 44 (4), 684-694.

Silvern, L. E., & Nakamura, C. Y. An analysis of the relationship between students' political position and the extent to which they deviate from parent's position. *Journal of Social Issues*, 1973, 29 (4), 111-132.

Smith, M. B. Personal values as determinants of a political attitude. *Journal of Psychology*, 1949, 28, 477-486.

Smith, M. B. Personal values in the study of lives, Ch. 14. In R. W. White (Ed.) *The study of lives*. New York: Atherton Press, 1964.

Snider, J., & Osgood, C. E. *The semantic differential: A sourcebook*. Chicago: Aldine Press, 1968.

Spranger, E. *Types of men*. (Trans. P. Pigors) Halle: Max Niemeyer Verlag, 1928.

Stewart, A. J., & Healy, J. M. The role of personality development and experience in shaping political comitment: An illustrative case. *Journal of Social Issues*, 1986, 42 (2), 11-31.

Telford, C. W., & Plant, W. T. *The psychological impact of the public two-year college on certain non-intellectual functions*. San Jose, CA: San Jose State College, 1963.

Titus, H. H. *Living issues in philosophy* (fifth ed.). New York: Van Nostrand Reinhold, 1970.

Tolstoy, L. N. "How much land a man needs," *What Shall We Do Then?; Collected Articles, etc.,* (Leo Weiner, trans.). Boston: L. C. Page, 1904.

Tomlinson-Keasey, C., Warren, L. W., & Elliott, J. E.   Suicide among gifted women: A prospective study. *Journal of Abnormal Psychology*, 1986, 95, 123-130.

Vitz, P. C.   The use of stories in moral development. *American Psychologist*, 1990, 45, 709-720.

von Mering, O.   *A grammar of human values*.   Pittsburgh, PA: University of Pittsburgh Press, 1961.

Webster, H., Freedman, M. B., & Heist, P.   Personality changes in college students.   In N. Sanford (Ed.) *The American college*.   New York: Wiley, 1962.

Westerhoff, J. H.   *Values for tomorrow's children*.   Philadelphia: Pilgrim Press, 1970.

White, R. K.   Verbal data and self-evident values. *Personality: symposia on topical issues*.   Symposium No. 1, April, 1950, 35-44.   Grune & Stratton.

White, R. K.   Verbal data and "self-evident" values.   In W. Wolff (Ed.) *Values in personality research*.   New York: Grune and Stratton, 1950.

White, R. K.   *Value analysis: Nature and use of the method*.   Ann Arbor, Mich.: Society for the Study of Social Issues, 1951.

White, R. W.   *Lives in progress*, (third ed.).   New York: Holt, Rinehart & Winston, 1975.

White, R. W.   *The enterprise of livng*.   New York: Holt, Rinehart & Winston, 1976.

Williams, R. M.   The concept of values.   In E. Sills (Ed.) *International Encyclopedia of the Social Sciences*, vol. 16.   New York: Macmillan and The Free Press, 1968.

Williams, R. M.   Change and stability in values and value systems: A sociological perspective.   In M. Rokeach (Ed.) *Understanding human values*.   New York: The Free Press, 1979.

AUTHOR INDEX

Human Values

SUBJECT INDEX